Creating the Secret State

CREATING
THE SECRET STATE

The Origins of
the Central Intelligence Agency,
1943–1947

David F. Rudgers

University Press of Kansas

Published by the University Press of Kansas (Lawrence, Kansas 66049), which was organized by the Kansas Board of Regents and is operated and funded by Emporia State University, Fort Hays State University, Kansas State University, Pittsburg State University, the University of Kansas, and Wichita State University

Library of Congress Cataloging-in-Publication Data

Rudgers, David F., 1941–

Creating the secret state : the origins of the Central Intelligence Agency, 1943–1947 / David F. Rudgers.

p.   cm.

Includes bibliographical references and index.

ISBN 0-7006-1024-3 (cloth : alk. paper)

1. United States. Central Intelligence Agency—History.   I. Title.

JK468.I6 R83   2000

327.1273′09′044—dc21   99-089870

British Library Cataloguing in Publication Data is available.

Printed in the United States of America

10 9 8 7 6 5 4 3 2 1

The paper used in this publication meets the minimum requirements of the American National Standard for Permanence of Paper for Printed Library Materials Z39.48–1984.

For Bette
My Muse of History

The necessity of procuring good intelligence is apparent and need not be further urged—all that remains for me to add is, that you keep the whole matter as secret as possible. For upon Secrecy, Success depends in most enterprises of the kind, and for want of it, they are generally defeated, however well planned and promising a favorable issue.

  —George Washington to Colonel Elias Dayton, July 26, 1777

Don't trust spies: they are more trouble than they are worth.

  —Napoleon Bonaparte to Eugene Beauharnais, June 5, 1805

Contents

Introduction

United States participation in World War II profoundly influenced all aspects of American life, American government, and the very conceptual bases of American domestic and international conduct. American leadership of the victorious wartime coalition and enhanced global position acquired as a result generated initiatives to reorganize the system for managing the combination of diplomacy and military policy that has come to be called "national security affairs" and which culminated in the passage of the National Security Act of 1947. This trend continued into the postwar period as the international scene became increasingly troubled, as the Soviet Union emerged in the minds of American policy makers as a new "evil empire," replacing the one overthrown by force of arms in 1945, and as the meaning of "national security" was expanded to include broad political, economic, and scientific matters. As a result, the ongoing process of "national security" reorganization and "reform" inevitably was cast in terms of enabling the United States to meet a new and even more dangerous global challenge. Clark Clifford has appropriately noted in his memoirs: "It was no accident that government reorganization coincided with the development of the Truman Doctrine, the Marshall Plan, NATO, Point Four, and the policy of containment: these new policies required new machinery."[1]

Although the overall story of these developments has been told in considerable detail,[2] one key aspect has been largely neglected, the creation of a national intelligence organization—the Central Intelligence Agency (CIA). As an authoritative congressional study observed: "In establishing a peacetime central intelligence body after World War II, the United States as one of the great powers came late to defining the need for an intelligence institution as an arm of foreign policy. . . . The decision to create a separate agency implied recognition of the intelligence function as an integral part of the foreign and military process."[3] This neglect has been a serious scholarly oversight. The CIA not only has played a dynamic role in the conduct of American foreign policy but also is a unique organization. Unlike any other major intelligence organization, it was created by public legislation, and, while not the largest of the entities composing what is now called the "intelligence community," it is the most multifaceted, engaging in all forms of intelligence collection, covert operations, and intelligence analysis. Moreover, because of its clandestine nature and mission, it largely operated outside the American political process until the collapse of the cold war consensus in the 1970s: its budgets secret, its administrative and personnel procedures separate from the regular executive branch civil service, its relations with Congress personal rather than institutional, and its activities largely free from press and public scrutiny. Hence its characterization as "the secret state." The way in which the "central intelligence" idea developed within the U.S. government, and the way in which it culminated in the creation of the CIA in 1947 are the subjects of this study.

"Intelligence" has been defined as the "product resulting from the collection, evaluation, analysis, integration, and interpretation of all information concerning one or more aspects of foreign countries or areas, which is immediately or potentially significant to the development and execution of policies, plans, and operations."[4] In its "national security" context, intelligence encompasses "all military, economic, political, scientific, technological, and other aspects of foreign developments that pose actual or potential threats to U.S. national interests."[5] The field is divided by means of collection: from human sources ("human intelligence"), the interception of communications and noncommunications electronic signals ("communications" and "signals" intelligence, respectively— which together constitute "electronic" intelligence), or from the study of aerial photographs ("photographic" intelligence). "Intelligence collection" can be as arcane as breaking codes ("cryptography") or as mundane as the examination of such "open sources" as newspapers, magazines, and public broadcasts. The process by which raw data ("intelligence information") are systematically examined to identify significant facts and derive conclusions is known as "intelligence analysis," and the final product ("finished intelligence") is intended for use by government officials in making policy decisions. An elaborate theoretical methodology (the "intelligence cycle") has been conceptualized to explain how the system works.[6] That the CIA does all these things makes it unique among U.S. government agencies; that it long did so in hiding allows it to be called "the secret state."

It is the "founding myth" of the Central Intelligence Agency that the organization was the product of the unique genius of William J. Donovan in the face of unenlightened resistance from troglodytes. This myth is both accurately and wittily described by historian Bradley Smith: "Donovan's 1944–1945 battle for survival took on the aspects of a crusade. OSS and CIA spokesmen have presented it as a religious parable, with Donovan as a far-seeing prophet, the military and the Bureau of the Budget as a blind and hostile mob, a naive Harry Truman as Pontius Pilate, and the execution (Executive Order 9621) followed by redemption and resurrection through the creation of the CIA in 1947."[7] This book, however, seeks to demonstrate that the idea of a postwar central intelligence organization developed institutionally among U.S. government policy makers in response to a perceived need. By focusing on the dynamics of institutional change in response to changing events, it looks beyond Donovan's wartime activities and ideas. While Donovan did, indeed, strongly advocate a postwar central intelligence organization similar to his wartime OSS, his efforts were carried on within the context of a recognized institutional need. Other men had other ideas that had equal intellectual merit, and these ideas eventually came to dominate the policy-making process. Although Donovan appears as a key figure in the initial chapters of this book, the account here demonstrates that events moved beyond him and that the creation of the CIA was a product of many minds. Donovan can clearly be considered the "godfather" of the CIA, but, as a Republican when the organization came into being under a Democratic administration, he remained, like Moses, outside the promised land, allowed to look in but not to enter (at least officially). That the present CIA came to so closely resemble the OSS is due largely to the coalescence of outside events that enabled it to metamorphose from its original conception.

I am a retired career civil servant with a doctorate in history from the George Washington University in Washington, D.C. From 1976 to 1998 I was employed by the CIA, primarily as an editor and intelligence analyst. This book, however, is the product of independent and unofficial research. With the exception of some librarians (particularly the redoubtable Ms. Emma Sullivan, who presides over the CIA's Historical Intelligence Collection with formidable efficiency), the CIA had no role in its research, writing, or editing. All source material is drawn from the public record. Any views, expressed or implied, are mine and should not be construed as representing those of the CIA or any other component of the U.S. government.

1

The Dual Road to Central Intelligence

Intelligence activities have been an integral part of American history. Even prior to World War II, an embryonic "intelligence community" existed, albeit in a highly fragmented form.[1] In 1882 the Navy Department established an intelligence unit within its Bureau of Navigation to report on the ships and weapons of foreign navies and on foreign naval policies in general. A separate Office of Naval Intelligence (ONI) was created in 1899 and made part of the Office of the Chief of Naval Operations in 1915. In the War Department, an intelligence function was established in 1885 with the creation of the Division of Military Information, soon renamed the Military Intelligence Division (MID). After several reorganizations, in 1918 MID was placed within the General Staff, as G-2, a step ratified by law in 1920.[2]

The State Department, by the nature of its duties, could also be counted as an "intelligence" organization, since, with the creation of a generally high-caliber foreign service, its diplomats, consular officers, and special missions effectively gathered information on foreign countries for the use of policy makers.[3] Finally, there was the Federal Bureau of Investigation (FBI). Although the FBI was exclusively a domestic crime-fighting organization before World War II, police work, by its nature, requires intelligence through "human sources" (i.e., informers) or "technical means" (such as forensic laboratories). Moreover, the FBI's responsibility for enforcing espionage laws gave it an opening into the "foreign intelligence" field.[4]

This prewar system never functioned in a coordinated fashion, however. Under J. Edgar Hoover, the FBI devoted itself exclusively to domestic crime, and, although the State, War, and Navy Departments shared the same building in Washington—a massive turn-of-the-century edifice next to the White House—they operated in different spheres and had little contact. The State Department devoted itself to diplomatic dealings with foreign governments, while the Army and Navy Departments focused on providing basic facts for war-planning purposes. The upward flow of information to cabinet officials supervising the military agencies and on to the president was negligible, and what diplomatic reports the chief executive received came from the occasional interpretive assessment of a foreign service officer. There also was no mechanism for combining data from all sources into evaluative or interpretive estimates.[5] Indeed, as Thomas Troy laments, "In 1929 no U.S. agency conducted clandestine foreign operations abroad. In 1929 no U.S. agency had foreign intelligence as its primary interest or activity. . . . In 1929 there was no adequate machinery for liaison for the sharing of information collected in and about foreign countries. . . . In 1929 intelligence was neither a profession nor a career."[6] Troy, while technically correct, nevertheless overlooks the fact that, in 1929, none of these things were necessary. In 1929 the United States had no foreign enemies, no foreign alliances, and no security commitments outside the Western Hemisphere (with the exceptions of Hawaii, the Philippines, and some minor Pacific islands). Since Washington was at peace with the world, the simple system he decries adequately served the needs of U.S. policy makers.

The steady deterioration of the international scene in the 1930s, leading to the outbreak of war in 1939 and increasing U.S. belligerency afterward, altered the geopolitical thinking of U.S. policy makers.[7] The pressure of the world crisis, culminating in the fall of France in 1940, brought about the first halting steps toward intelligence cooperation among U.S. government agencies. As the nation began to mobilize, the issue of espionage by Germany and its Japanese and Italian allies became a matter of increasing concern. Because of the seemingly successful use of "fifth columnists" by the Germans (a "threat" widely and vividly played up in the press, motion pictures, and popular nonfiction), initial government efforts were in the direction of counterintelligence to foil spies and saboteurs. On June 26, 1939, after considerable bureaucratic bickering, President Roosevelt issued a confidential directive to the secretaries of state, war, navy, the Treasury, and commerce, as well as the postmaster general and attorney general, stating that all responsibilities for investigating espionage and sabotage, including all counterintelligence matters, would be under the joint purview of Army G-2, ONI, and the FBI, which would mutually coordinate their plans and activities. In accordance with this directive, the three agencies formed an Interdepartmental Intelligence Committee, which began to meet on a regular basis. Not to be excluded, the State Department attached its own representative, first Ambassador George Messersmith (an early advocate of such coordination) and, following his posting to Cuba in 1940, Assistant Secretary Adolph Berle. Berle, a veteran New Deal "brain truster," served "as the members' friendly link to FDR."[8]

The inclusion of FBI director Hoover was a major portent. For the first time, a senior civilian official became directly involved in "foreign intelligence" activities. Although Hoover had been reluctant to join the coordination efforts until directly ordered to do so by Roosevelt, he was quick to exploit his new mandate. On June 5, 1940, Army G-2, ONI, and the FBI drew up an agreement to coordinate and define their mutual responsibilities in accord with Roosevelt's 1939 directive.[9] Later in the same month, and again at Roosevelt's direction, Hoover established his own foreign intelligence arm, the Special Intelligence Service (SIS), to collect nonmilitary intelligence in the Western Hemisphere.[10] To avoid jurisdictional battles, Hoover and his army and navy counterparts, Brigadier General Sherman Miles and Captain Alan Kirk, signed a detailed memorandum of understanding on May 15, 1941, which spelled out the responsibilities of each organization in matters of espionage, counterespionage, sabotage, and "subversive activities." The document, transmitted to the White House on May 22, also emphasized a high degree of existing mutual cooperation.[11]

Hoover's collaboration with the armed services paid him rich dividends overseas. In a series of agreements eventually codified on February 25, 1942, the FBI's Special Intelligence Service was given intelligence collection responsibilities for all of Latin America except Panama (an army preserve) and was directed to obtain "primarily through undercover operations supplemented when necessary by open operations, economic, political, industrial, financial and subversive information" as well as information concerning "movements, organizations, and individuals whose activities are prejudicial to the interests of the United States." Under the agreement, the FBI promised to share the information it collected with the army and navy, and all agreed to cooperate in developing collection needs.[12] Eventually the SIS deployed about 360 agents in Latin America, concentrated in major countries such as Mexico, Argentina, and Brazil. It became both highly effective operationally and well connected politically to pro-American officials in the region.[13]

Hoover, Miles, and Kirk were well pleased with their intelligence triumvirate and put their feelings into a paper entitled "Report on the Coordination of the Three Intelligence Services," forwarded to the president on May 29, 1941. The report stressed that coordination between the armed services and the FBI was working satisfactorily and that "the difficulties inherent in the operations of dissimilar organizations have been progressively eliminated." It went on to say that future conflicts of authority would be "rare," since the three organizations had "responsibilities to their own Department which lie outside the scope of their coordinated activities." Therefore, the three saw no merit in the idea of appointing an intelligence "Coordinator" beyond "the almost non-existent cases in which there may be a conflict of authority or responsibility between the three Services." The report concluded: "It would be extremely difficult to delimit the Coordinator's function to exclude these component parts of the operation of the three Services: and yet, were they not excluded, the resultant super-Intelligence Agency would be far too cumbersome and complicated for effective service to the three Departments, especially in the increased tempo of war." Thus, the "appointment of a Coordinator of the three Intelligence Services is unnecessary and would entail great complications in, if not serious detriment to the National Service, while offering only negligible advantages." [14] Hoover and the service intelligence chiefs were not speculating. Their premise, decentralization, was their emerging institutional response to what they readily recognized was a new trend and a new threat: the emergence of William J. Donovan as the key figure in all subsequent matters concerning intelligence policy.

The figure of William J. Donovan has assumed virtually godlike proportions in the history of American intelligence. [15] Born in Buffalo, New York, in 1883, he early demonstrated his legendary energy and enterprise by working his way through Columbia University, graduating in 1905, as well as earning a law degree there two years later. (He and Roosevelt were classmates but probably were unacquainted.) He began his military career in the New York National Guard along the Mexican border in 1911, where he reputedly acquired the nickname "Wild Bill." Entering the Regular Army in 1917, he served with distinction in France, ultimately earning the Medal of Honor in 1923. Returning to his law practice after the war, he became a millionaire as the head of a New York City law firm and began playing a prominent role in his state's Republican Party. Although serving as a U.S. attorney and assistant attorney general in the Coolidge administration, President Hoover denied him a sought-after cabinet position. Resuming his New York law practice, he became a strong critic of the New Deal. Possessing great energy, ability, personal magnetism, and an unequaled capacity for self-promotion, Donovan was not a man to shun the limelight. His wealth, personal connections, and consuming interest in public affairs made him a recognized commentator on the international scene, enabled him to travel widely overseas at a time when foreign travel was far beyond the reach of most Americans, and gained him entrance with important political figures at home and abroad. Early in his career he learned the importance of cultivating the press, and, in the course of the 1936 presidential election, became a close friend of Frank Knox, the Republican vice presidential nominee and internationalist editor of the Chicago Daily News. [16]

An active interventionist by 1940, Donovan had his moment when Roosevelt—to strengthen his cabinet, promote bipartisan foreign policy, and vex his isolationist Republican foes—named Knox and fellow Republican Henry Stimson as his secretaries of navy and war. In July 1940 Roosevelt and his advisers, dissatisfied with the reporting from U.S. Ambassador Joseph Kennedy on Great Britain's chances of survival, decided upon an independent assessment. Thanks to his connection with Knox and Roosevelt's desire to recruit prominent Republicans, Donovan received the task and was warmly welcomed by the embattled British, who recognized that he had Roosevelt's ear. Given wide access to British officials and bases, he returned sanguine over British chances. Obviously pleased with Donovan's endeavors, Roosevelt sent him on a second, more wide-ranging fact-finding mission that took him to the British Isles, the Iberian peninsula, the Balkans, North Africa, and the Middle East between December and March 1941.[17]

It was during this time that Donovan's fascination with "secret warfare" began to germinate. While in England, Donovan, an activist by nature, was intrigued by the United Kingdom's venerable intelligence services and particularly impressed by British plans for clandestine operations—sabotage, propaganda, and armed resistance—inside German-occupied Europe. Describing the British system in a May 1940 letter to Knox, he boldly set forth his own views on what sort of future intelligence system the United States should have: "Intelligence operations should not be controlled by party exigencies. It is one of the most vital means of national defense. As such, it should be headed by some one appointed by the President [who is] directly responsible to him and no one else. It should have a fund solely for the purpose of foreign investigation and the expenditures under this fund should be secret and made absolutely at the discretion of the President." The functions of his proposed agency would be "to have sole charge of intelligence work abroad"; to "coordinate the activities of military and naval attaches and others in the collection of information abroad"; and "to classify and interpret all information from whatever source obtained to be available for the President and for such of the services as he would designate."[18] Although Donovan would modify these ideas for tactical purposes in later years, they would remain his basic tenets forever afterward.

In Roosevelt, Donovan also had found the ideal patron. As both an individual and a political leader, the president was a man of powerful intelligence and wide-ranging interests. Throughout his prewar political career, Roosevelt had scorned convention and was always receptive to new ideas and unorthodox ways of problem solving. Such personality traits also made him interested in meeting a wide variety of people beyond the range of his official entourage for lively exchanges of views, and his enormous self-confidence protected him from ever being intimidated by even the most assertive. Such activism was readily transferred to Roosevelt's approach to international affairs. Thus, when circumstances allowed Donovan to press for the realization of his own ambitions, he found Roosevelt, safely reelected in November 1940, receptive to his boldest initiatives for coping with the crisis in Europe.

Donovan had conferred with Roosevelt following both his trips to Europe, and, although no records of their conversations exist, in March 1941 Roosevelt appointed a committee composed of Stimson, Knox, and Attorney General Robert Jackson to study intelligence issues. When his views were requested, Donovan was ready with a memo outlining a centralized intelligence system that he sent to Knox on April 16 and another that went directly to Roosevelt on June 10. Roosevelt responded on July 11 with a directive establishing the office of Coordinator of Information (COI), with Donovan as its head. Donovan's dreams of empire were overtaken by events, however, as Japanese bombs at Pearl Harbor blasted the United States into a war that was now a global conflict. As the government reorganized for full-scale military endeavor, the newly established Joint Chiefs of Staff (JCS) flatly refused to countenance a civilian organization in war zones. Roosevelt accepted the views of his military chiefs and, using Donovan's bureaucratic conflicts over the control of overt war propaganda as a rationale, issued a second directive on June 13, 1942, that reconstituted the COI as the Office of Strategic Services, a military organization responsible to the JCS through the army chain of command. Donovan resumed his old army rank of colonel, and, by the end of the war, had risen to major general.[19]

The wartime activities of the OSS are beyond the scope of this study and have been described well elsewhere.[20] Nevertheless, something must be said of the precedent set by that remarkable organization. By any standards, particularly those of Washington's wartime bureaucracy, it was a unique enterprise, engaging in foreign espionage, sabotage, guerrilla warfare, and "black" propaganda (i.e., disinformation) operations, as well as analysis of intelligence information on a multidisciplinary basis (an innovation in those days). As one OSS veteran later observed, the organization "sheltered screwballs, crackpots, and adventurers along with professors from Ivy League universities, ex-diplomats, and ex-soldiers, and an unprecedented number of heirs to great fortunes. Every sort of specialized and esoteric skill was represented, from professors of Sanskrit to demolition experts, cryptologists, judo instructors, sharpshooters, and specialists in guerilla warfare. . . . No scheme was too wild to be considered."[21] Despite the hostility of the War and Navy Departments, the State Department, and FBI director Hoover, the OSS expanded its presence in wartime Washington into a collection of ugly "temporary" buildings (which survived the war by two decades), an abandoned brewery, and a vacant roller-skating rink. Although excluded from Latin America by the turf-conscious Hoover and from the Southwest Pacific Theater by the imperious General Douglas MacArthur, the OSS also established a substantial overseas presence in Europe, the Mediterranean, and China.[22] By the end of the war, it had approximately thirty-five hundred civilian employees, as well as eight thousand army personnel and 800 from the navy, marines, and Coast Guard attached to it.[23]

Needless to say, the personality of William J. Donovan was stamped indelibly on the OSS. William Langer, the eminent Harvard historian who headed the OSS analytical arm (the Research and Analysis Branch), noted afterward that "Donovan was a truly charismatic personality. He had an exceptional gift for arousing the interest and enthusiasm of others and of enlisting their loyalty and devotion."[24] Langer was seconded by another OSS veteran, economist Calvin Hoover, who commented: "All of us who were to work intimately with Donovan through the years came to feel warm affection and admiration for him. . . . A character like Donovan could not possibly be a good administrator by ordinary standards. . . . To set up an intelligence service from scratch *after* hostilities had broken out required a man of the audacity and imagination of Donovan. An orderly administrator would never have gotten an intelligence organization functioning before the war was over."[25]

It is thus hardly surprising that such a vigorous organization containing an abundance of talented people should consider the future a challenge. Almost from the inception of the OSS, its officers actively embraced the concept of becoming a permanent postwar organization, and during its first two years numerous papers were drafted on this subject by OSS leaders in Washington, New York, and London.[26] One of the earliest and most forceful advocates for the future was Donovan's deputy, General John Magruder. In a paper of August 25, 1942, entitled "Proposed Plan for Joint Intelligence Bureau," he enumerated and strongly criticized the shortcomings of the existing JCS Joint Intelligence Committee and called for a new, broad-based organization within the JCS structure.

Like Donovan, Magruder felt that the "coordination of our intelligence agencies is an imperative need. . . . No single existing agency is organized to evaluate, analyze and draw conclusions which are sufficiently authoritative for the needs of the President, the Joint Chiefs of Staff and the Joint Planners. As a result, vital decisions affecting the conduct of the war must be made without complete and digested intelligence being brought to bear on the problem." He therefore called for establishing a "superior joint intelligence agency" to collate and analyze the information "on which decisions should be made and plans formulated." According to Magruder, the

> results of work of such an agency should be accepted as the authoritative intelligence basis for decisions and plans. No individual can possibly be sufficiently informed to justify vital national decisions being based upon his personal knowledge of current complex situations. No individual department of the Government can have either the information or the full comprehension of current problems sufficient to justify committing the whole nation to a line of military action. Only a joint national intelligence service can lay bare all the facts and factors upon which a sound national decision can be based.[27]

In subsequent papers, Magruder continued his campaign for a centralized intelligence coordination and analytical organization. In a memo of July 30, 1943, to the JCS executive secretary, he raised a second issue of "certain intelligence activities which should be exercised exclusively on a level higher than that of any individual bureau," such as "the conduct of espionage and counterespionage outside of United States territory. Responsibility for the establishment of a national secret service has long been neglected." Cagily remembering his audience, he added: "In fact, a secret service under the Joint Chiefs of Staff already exists in its OSS component."[28] When not writing to the JCS, however, Magruder had few doubts about where the leadership of the postwar intelligence system was to come from. In a paper to Donovan the following September, he noted: "We have to use to advantage what we already have—and obviously that is where the existing Intelligence Service of the OSS is more nearly ready-made than that of any Agency." To secure the OSS role "as the recognized and authoritative body of the future superior strategic intelligence service," Magruder considered it "essential that you concede some coordinating control to the brass hats. In return for your concession to the deadening effect of bureaucratic respectability, the military should accept your inspiring leadership which, in all truth, involves an individualistic approach sometimes confusing to your subordinates—but, nevertheless furnishes a fertile soil for the flowering of civilian initiative and vigor."[29]

One of the most thoughtful visions of the future came from William Langer, a man of global vision who would play a major role in shaping the structure of postwar American intelligence. As one of America's foremost authorities on European political and diplomatic history, he was worldly at a time when most other academic institutions in the United States were still trying to develop international affairs programs. Virtually from the inception of the OSS, Langer had been active in recruiting some of the nation's foremost academics for Donovan's fledgling organization and had been directing OSS analytical efforts since September 1942. In addition to a commanding intellect, he had a strong sense of civic duty that called for enlisting scholarship into government service as the provider of unbiased knowledge for making national policy and promoting national ends.

Writing in July 1944, Langer observed that the "need for an effective *national* system of intelligence is a compelling one. . . . For the future, it will continue to be a matter of vital interest and national security that an adequate secret intelligence and counter-intelligence service be maintained. Such a service would supplement the reporting of traditional, official agencies. It would supply the needs of the Department of State, of the Armed Services and, if need be, of other Government agencies." Langer boldly concluded that there was

> no need for setting up a new secret intelligence and counterintelligence service for the post-hostilities period because there has already been established in the Office of Strategic Services . . . such an intelligence agency. . . . In short, the solution of the problem in the post-hostilities period is not to be found in further experimentation in the multiplication of agencies, but rather in the proper development, expansion and full exploitation of the facilities already available. The creation of a new agency would add nothing but confusion and jurisdictional conflict.[30]

In a more reserved fashion, the OSS disseminated such views within the government in its various serial publications, such as one issued by its Planning Group entitled "Suggested Statement of Policy Governing Future OSS Activities," dated September 12, 1944. It advocated that "approved programs" in the China-Burma-India and Southeast Asia theaters of operations "be intensified" by transferring surplus personnel and equipment from Europe and the Mediterranean, and that similar plans for the Pacific theater "should be completed at once." In liberated and occupied areas of Europe, OSS intelligence assets under the control of the organization's Washington headquarters would be needed to assist American military commanders and civilian agencies. While wartime bases in Algeria and London could be reduced or eliminated, new bases "will be established on the continent to serve the U.S. military commander in Washington." In neutral European countries, secret intelligence and counterespionage activities "will continue as long as American military participation continues on the continent. Steps will be taken immediately to supplement and ultimately replace these activities by undercover penetration directed from Washington."[31]

The men of OSS did not have the field of dreams entirely to themselves, however. Other men had other ideas. The exigencies of waging combined-arms operations on a global scale compelled the army and navy to work together in all areas, including intelligence activities. Late in 1941, the two services established the Joint Intelligence Committee (JIC) as a "defensive alliance" against Donovan, as Dean Acheson dryly put it at a later date.[32] The JIC held its first formal meeting on December 3, 1941, and, by the later days of the war, it included representatives of Army G-2, ONI, the assistant chief of staff for intelligence of the increasingly autonomous Army Air Forces, the State Department, OSS, and the Foreign Economic Administration (established in 1943 to consolidate foreign assistance and economic warfare efforts). Similarly, in some overseas theaters, the army and navy pooled their efforts in joint intelligence collection agencies. These steps, although imperfect, encouraged discussions between senior officers of both services concerning the importance of intelligence cooperation after the war and enabled the idea to be melded into the greater issue of postwar "national security" reorganization.[33]

By 1943 the grand alliance had gone over to the offensive, making final victory over the Axis "evil empire" a matter of time and hard fighting. As the United States emerged as the primary member of the wartime coalition, virtually every aspect of America's prospective international role, as well as the instruments needed to carry out that role, became subjects of searching official consideration in the executive and legislative branches, as well as topics of widespread public discussion. While the State and Treasury Departments concentrated on developing the international organizations deemed necessary to create a stable political and economic world order, debate within the military establishment focused on ways in which the government could manage what today has come to be called "national security policy." As the debate progressed, its basic tenets became the "unification" of the armed forces within a Department of National Defense; the statutory creation of the Joint Chiefs of Staff; the establishment of an independent air force; the creation of an interagency "council" to formulate coordinated national security policy; and the development of consolidated agencies for research and development, matériel procurement, industrial mobilization, and the coordination of intelligence collection and processing. The debate was colored by intense bureaucratic rivalries, perceived weaknesses in the military machine fighting the war, and the fresh and painful memories of the disaster at Pearl Harbor. Although the intelligence issue was far overshadowed by most of the others, particularly the explosive "unification" question, it too became a bone of contention within the government and a matter of public debate.[34]

It is unclear when discussions concerning a postwar "central intelligence" organization actually began within the military establishment. In his 1946 memoirs, Admiral Ellis M. Zacharias, a veteran naval intelligence officer, recounted how he and Captain Sidney Mashbir of Army G-2 drew up a plan for Chief of Naval Operations (CNO) Admiral Ernest J. King that would create the Joint Intelligence Board, establishing "for the first time in our history a highest-level intelligence organization fully capable of aiding the war effort with top-quality intelligence." Zacharias said King carefully reviewed the plan, renamed the proposed organization the Joint Intelligence Agency, and promised to act on its implementation. However, recorded Zacharias, "After being fully prepared, presented, and approved in at least one of the highest echelons, it was suddenly pigeonholed, filed-and-forgotten."[35] According to Thomas Troy, the first known use of the name Central Intelligence Agency appeared in a memo of March 24, 1942, from the U.S. Marine commandant to the chief of the U.S. Fleet (then separate from the CNO) suggesting that such an organization be established at Pearl Harbor to serve as a "clearinghouse" for information gathered by "joint intelligence centers," which he proposed setting up throughout the Pacific.[36]

In their discussions concerning mutual intelligence cooperation, both services consistently favored a traditional "confederal" approach between independent agencies and, compelled by a deep distrust of Donovan's empire-building ambitions, explicitly rejected the idea of "centralization." On May 21, 1941, following a conference between representatives of G-2, ONI, and the FBI in which the issue of an "intelligence coordinator" was discussed, General Miles informed Marshall that all had agreed that existing coordination was "working satisfactorily and there is no need for a coordinator"; further, unless such a coordinator "would be content to limit himself to the very infrequent role of referee in countersubversion cases in which the authority of FBI, ONI, and MID might conflict, his office would be a positive detriment to the swift and secretive action required in the Intelligence services." He further noted that there was "every reason to believe that a coordinator named by the President would attempt to operate in the entire field of intelligence. This would mean that he would to a large extent control the collection and evaluation of military and naval intelligence required by the two armed services, a highly undesirable state of affairs."[37]

The navy was equally categorical. In March 1945, Secretary of the Navy James Forrestal (who had replaced Knox upon the latter's death in 1944) asked CNO King for his views on proposals for a centralized intelligence collection organization. King responded that while the idea of a single agency to collect intelligence sounded logical, it contained dangerous elements. He felt that over a long period such an organization might acquire more power than intended, and, once acquired, such power would be hard to take away. He also doubted that such an agency would be consistent with traditional American ideas of government.[38]

Military views on the future of U.S. intelligence organization were codified and formalized in a policy paper presented to the JCS by the Joint Intelligence Staff entitled "Post-war Intelligence Policy of the United States," dated October 23, 1944. As its central thesis, the paper declared: "Intelligence operations of the United States, in war and peace, fail to meet fully the requirements of a nation with worldwide vital interests and responsibilities. . . . Intelligence is especially defective at the national policy level where military, political, economic, psychological, and scientific intelligence mingle." The study noted a number of past intelligence failures in evaluating German, Japanese, British, French, and Russian capabilities and intentions in the 1940–1941 period; it then listed major problems: lack of coordination, failure to develop various types of intelligence, heavy dependence on the British, lack of adequate intelligence on the Soviet Union and newly liberated or conquered areas of Europe, and the "lack of an adequate framework of established administrative principles governing the intelligence operations of the United States." In addition, the paper noted such defects as duplication, subjectivity, inadequacies of coverage, inadequate training of personnel, and unclear responsibility for the development of "national" intelligence.

As a solution, the paper proposed a centralized system for defining intelligence objectives, mobilizing intelligence resources, directing clandestine intelligence operations, and synthesizing collected data into "national" intelligence. Although "complete centralization" was deemed "unworkable," since most intelligence activity was "inextricably bound up with the action responsibilities" of different agencies, such responsibilities "should be coordinated by a central agency in light of national intelligence requirements," and undefined "national level" intelligence operations should be centrally performed. The paper therefore recommended that a Central Intelligence Agency be established under a director appointed by the president, who, in turn, would be responsible to a board comprising the secretaries of state, war, and navy. Although each intelligence agency in the executive branch would continue to be responsible for its own intelligence needs, the new CIA would be responsible for "national policy intelligence," interdepartmental coordination, secret intelligence collection, the assignment and review of intelligence responsibilities, and the evaluation and distribution of "finished intelligence" on the national level.[39]

This plan represented the culmination of the evolutionary process by which the armed services came to accept the concept of central intelligence. As such, its purpose was to bridge the gap between the institutional proprieties of individual government agencies and the perceived need for some degree of centralized direction. While the FBI was not officially involved in the plan's development, the proposal clearly reflected the military's wartime experience of working with Hoover. It also maintained a broader "political" focus by implicitly recognizing the responsibilities of the State Department. Most important, the ideas set forth in this plan were destined to play an important role in future debates over intelligence, since they stood in direct opposition to revolutionary ideas developed by William J. Donovan.

2

General Donovan Proposes . . .

No one could ever claim that William J. Donovan was not a visionary. Virtually all the other men of affairs who came to Washington to administer the temporary agencies created to carry out the American war effort saw the future in terms of doing the job at hand and returning to private life at the first opportunity. Donovan, however, although he too headed a "temporary" agency, saw an important postwar role for his organization. The scope of his ambitions, in fact, was readily discernible to his critics at an early date. On April 8, 1941, acting army intelligence chief Miles wrote sourly to Marshall:

> In great confidence ONI tells me that there is considerable reason to believe that there is a movement on foot, fostered by Col. Donovan, to establish a super agency controlling all intelligence. This would mean that such an agency, no doubt under Col. Donovan, would collect, collate, and possibly even evaluate all military intelligence which we now gather from foreign countries. From the point of view of the War Department, such a move would be disadvantagous, if not calamitous.[1]

Donovan tipped his hand on May 1, 1943, in a presentation on the OSS given to a group of army officers. When asked "What is the present policy or trend of thought as to continuation of this work [of the OSS] in the future? Is there any though[t] of continuing it after the war?" Donovan replied, "I'd like to know that myself but we are concentrating on this war and if we do act intelligently and it can be integrated into the whole operation, I think we will have sense enough as a people to continue it."[2]

The following September, Donovan found an opportunity to set forth some initial ideas about postwar intelligence organization. While observing the Salerno landings with General Walter Bedell Smith, chief of staff to Mediterranean theater commander Eisenhower, Donovan raised the issue and elicited from Smith a request for a statement of his views.[3] On September 17 he submitted a paper with the unwieldy title "The Need in the United States on a Permanent Basis as an Integral Part of Our Military Establishment of a Long-Range Strategic Intelligence Organization with Attendant 'Subversion' and 'Deception of the Enemy' Functions." His report emphasized that national policy "is formulated in the light of information concerning the policies and activities of other nations," and each country, "in defense of its institutions and its people, must have an independent intelligence service to guide its policy in peace as well as in war."

In Donovan's view, a future U.S. intelligence service should be able to collect secret intelligence, perform analysis and evaluation, and have the responsibility for counterintelligence, psychological operations, and physical subversion. Organizationally, it should have a separate budget, unvouchered funds, independent communications by pouch or code, passport privileges, a civilian director, and a largely civilian staff. Donovan pointed out that these objectives had largely been realized in the OSS, which "today is a living organism which can be adapted to a permanent plan or as a design for a new but similar agency." He visualized this organization as a new coequal "Fourth Arm" of the "Fighting Services" responsible to the JCS, since to "place it directly under the control of the President, and responsible to him alone, would run the danger of distracting political consequences for both the Presidential incumbent and for 'Strategic Services.'"[4] Cooly received, the proposal went nowhere.

Donovan also sought to cultivate his official superior, Army Chief of Staff Marshall. On August 4, 1944, he sent Marshall a memo concerning "the carrying on of intelligence activities in Europe during the period following the cessation of hostilities." To meet postwar problems, Donovan felt that it would be necessary for the United States "to have an understanding of the security interests in the peace settlements as well as of the conditions that may exist in the period immediately following the fighting." Since the emphasis of postwar intelligence "will of necessity be on the political, economic, and social," he supplied Marshall with an OSS analysis of "American security interests in the European settlement" and requested "guidance on the statement of doctrine in order to meet the new requirements of national policy."

A staff officer, identified only as "BB," who was tasked with drafting a response, was quick to note that Donovan's request "would tacitly acknowledge a postwar mission for OSS" and urged Marshall to make a "non-committal and innocuous" reply. Marshall agreed. On August 10 he thanked Donovan for his report but pointed out that making foreign policy statements was not the responsibility of the War Department; he could not give unilateral instructions to an organization (i.e., the OSS) responsible to the JCS, and so he was referring Donovan's request to that body for consideration.[5] And there matters rested.

The identity of "BB" is unknown, but his judgment was on the mark. By the end of 1944, however, it was probably clear to Donovan that the military establishment was not a promising venue for realizing his ambitions. Particularly after the JCS developed a plan of its own for a postwar intelligence organization in October 1944, he likely recognized that the realization of his scheme for a postwar OSS depended on one man—Franklin Roosevelt. Recalling the president's fascination with unorthodox methods of warfare, he sought to exploit Roosevelt's past patronage, at one point flattering him by writing that "under your authority and with your support there has been established for the first time in our history an independent American Intelligence Service which has already won the respect of similar services in other countries." [6]

After considerable discussions with senior OSS officials, at the beginning of October 1944 Donovan began folding various proposals for a postwar foreign intelligence organization built upon existing OSS assets into his own general plan, "The Basis for a Permanent U.S. Foreign Intelligence Service." Actual drafting was done by two of Donovan's senior analysts, former professors Everett Gleason and William McGovern. Donovan also appointed an OSS staff officer, Major Joseph Rosenbaum, to lobby officials who had the president's ear. Donovan's initiatives were successful enough to elicit a request from Roosevelt on October 31 for a statement of his views on postwar intelligence organization. It was a critical moment for the OSS chief, and he made the most of it. His formal reply of November 18 was to be his magnum opus, which went not only to Roosevelt himself but also to eleven senior officials in the State, War, and Navy Departments, with emphasis given to the plan as a response to a presidential request. [7]

Donovan's plan set forth two primary requirements: that "intelligence control be returned to the supervision of the President" and that "a central authority" be established reporting directly to the president "with the responsibility to frame intelligence objectives and to collect and coordinate the intelligence material required by the Executive Branch in planning and carrying out national policy and strategy." Although considering his proposals "long-range," Donovan nonetheless observed in his covering letter to Roosevelt that there were "common-sense reasons why you may desire to lay the keel of the ship at once." In his judgment, immediate reform would effect economies and expedite prosecution of the war, more efficiently utilize and coordinate existing intelligence information, prevent the dispersal of trained intelligence personnel, and promote "informed decisions" by government leaders as the United States passed through its "period of transition" from war to "the tumult of reconstruction" in peacetime.

Apparently hoping for a bold stroke, such as those that created the COI and OSS, Donovan attached a draft directive that would create a centralized intelligence organization within the Executive Office of the President under a presidentially appointed director. The responsibilities of the organization would be establishing and coordinating all plans and functions of government intelligence agencies for an integrated national intelligence effort; collecting foreign intelligence either directly or through existing agencies; final evaluation, synthesis, and distribution of intelligence within the government for national security planning; the recruitment, training, and supervision of intelligence personnel; "subversive activities abroad"; and other duties assigned by the president in the intelligence field.

Under Donovan's directive, the agency would have an independent budget, and its director would be responsible for its internal organization and management. It would have "no police or law-enforcement functions either at home or abroad." In time of war or unlimited national emergency, all of its programs in areas of actual or potential combat would require the approval of the JCS and would be carried out under the supervision of the theater commander. Other federal agencies that were currently gathering intelligence for their own assigned duties would continue to do so, but the proposed director of intelligence would be authorized to use their personnel and receive their intelligence input. Within the new agency there would be an advisory board comprising the secretaries of state, war, and navy (as well as any others desired by the president) to assist the director in formulating basic policy and plans.[8]

Unlike in 1941 or 1942, however, Roosevelt did not deliver a beau geste on Donovan's behalf. On November 22 he passed Donovan's proposal to Admiral William D. Leahy, his personal military adviser and presiding officer of the JCS, who, in turn, forwarded it to the secretary of the JCS on November 25. Once received, it was issued as an internal paper (JCS 1181) and referred to the JIC for consideration.[9] Donovan's conception did not fare well at JIC hands. In a series of papers issued on December 9, it was subjected to sweeping criticisms. The first paper, entitled "Proposed Establishment of a Central Intelligence Service," called the plan "unsound and dangerous" because the proposed agency would have "the power of coordination and control over all intelligence agencies of the government, without responsibility to the heads of the departments concerned, as well as the unlimited authority to engage in intelligence operations of its own."

As an alternative, the JIC paper proposed that future intelligence coordination should be vested in a joint committee of the secretaries of state, war, and navy. This committee would be assisted by the Federal Intelligence Directorate, with powers of "inspection, coordination, and planning, but with no administrative or operating functions," which would be under a civilian director (to be appointed by the secretary of state) and two assistant directors (a general and an admiral). There would also be a Joint Intelligence Service (JIS) to "carry on operations of common concerns to the Departments" and a Joint Intelligence Committee to prepare joint intelligence estimates for the JCS. An attached draft letter to the president emphasized that "national security intelligence" (later known as "strategic intelligence") was a special and separate requirement, that the integrity of the military chain of command had to be respected in order that an individual with command responsibility had intelligence responsibility, that a single intelligence service was undesirable, and that coordination of intelligence collection efforts should be carried out by an agency not itself engaged in collection activities lest it emphasize its own operations at the expense of others.[10]

A second paper added further objections. While agreeing that improvements in the national intelligence effort would be of value during and after the war, it was felt that intelligence collection "except by clandestine methods" should be done by existing agencies. It also declared categorically: "Subversive operations abroad does not appear to be an appropriate function of a central intelligence service." Among the appended documents was a counterplan for an agency similar to that proposed by Donovan but responsible to a committee of the three cabinet secretaries.[11] A third paper suggested decentralized collection but a high degree of coordination in planning to avoid "confusion, unwarranted duplication, dangerous omissions and inefficiency."[12]

On December 22 the full JIC met to consider the issue of a central intelligence organization. Present were ONI director Rear Admiral Hewlett Thebaud, Army G-2 chief Major General Clayton Bissell, Assistant Chief of the Air Staff for Intelligence Major General John Hodges, Brigadier General John Magruder representing the OSS, and Fletcher Warren and John Fleming from the State Department and Foreign Economic Administration, respectively. As expected, Magruder earnestly defended Donovan's plan:

> The concept of this central intelligence agency is not an agency apart from the rest of the government but one operated by and for all of them. . . . Also we feel that secret intelligence should not be operated apart from this central agency because it would be a target at all times for the public, for legislation, and for the enemy. Whereas, if secret intelligence were incorporated in the body of a larger central agency, we feel that it would have excellent cover in being obscured by the overall operation. As part of this same concept, departmental intelligence agencies are in no sense

affected. It is recognized that they are just as essential to the operations of the various departments and bureaus as before.

As discussions went on, General Bissell proved to be the most outspoken challenger to Donovan's idea for a centralized intelligence empire. While admitting that some form of central direction for common intelligence operations was necessary after the war to prevent confusion and rivalry, he felt that Donovan's plan established "an intelligence director with too great power. He has his own money. He has a direct pipeline to the President. He has no responsibility to the Secretaries, because . . . the powers given him completely eliminate that. . . . Therefore I feel that this would be an extremely dangerous thing in a democracy." When questioned about the ability of the three secretaries to work together, he responded curtly: "The three Secretaries are not able to handle a Director who can give them the run-around to the President." He was also concerned that the director could slant the information which he controlled and believed that it was "a rather dangerous venture" to permit an independent intelligence budget. Since agreement could not be reached, the question was referred back to the JIS for further consideration. Bissell perhaps summed up the entire meeting: "I would feel that a problem of as far-reaching moment as this shouldn't be disposed of after a single session of two and a half hours." [13]

As the JCS debated, Donovan seethed. In a message to Roosevelt on December 26, he complained vocally about the various proposals for a decentralized system that had the director of the central intelligence organization reporting to a "board" comprising the secretaries of state, war, and navy. While he was willing to go along with proposals for such a board, even one including the service chiefs, he insisted that, "whatever the composition of the Board, the Director be free administratively to run his job, responsible as is a general manager to a Board of Directors." He concluded: "In discussing this matter with responsible officers in the intelligence field I have been surprised at their lack of understanding of the necessity for a sound intelligence organization, an organization comprising a central service in which career officers and civilian experts working together synthesize all available intelligence on the policy level and estimate before the event, political and military developments." [14]

At the end of the month Donovan departed Washington for an overseas inspection trip. His absence proved fatal to his ambitions, since the JCS proceeded to act without him to formulate its own postwar intelligence plan. In a position paper submitted on January 1, 1945, the JIC opposed adopting the Donovan plan and presented a "constructive counterproposal" of its own to the JCS. A draft letter to the president faulted Donovan's proposal for appearing "to grant to the proposed agency power to control the operations of departmental intelligence agencies without responsibility to the heads of the departments concerned, thus violating the integrity of the chain of command."

The proposed alternative reflected often-expressed JCS views and made major modifications in what Donovan had initially put forward. For purposes of overall planning, coordination, development, and inspection of all federal intelligence activities, there was to be a National Intelligence Authority (NIA), comprising the secretaries of state, war, and navy and a representative of the JCS. Attached to the NIA would be an advisory board composed of representatives from the principal civil and military intelligence organizations. Subordinate to it would be the Central Intelligence Agency (CIA), under a director who would be chosen by the president upon the recommendation of the NIA and who would sit on the NIA as a nonvoting representative of the CIA. Under NIA control and direction, the CIA would be responsible for analyzing, synthesizing, and distributing national intelligence; planning and recommending overall national intelligence policies and objectives; and performing "such other functions and duties related to intelligence" as the NIA directed. The CIA would have no police or law enforcement functions. Existing intelligence agencies would continue to collect and analyze intelligence relative to their responsibilities but, under NIA direction, would make such intelligence available to the CIA and would be subject to its inspection. The NIA would have an independent budget, which would also fund the CIA and any other designated intelligence activities. The CIA director would receive control over personnel and internal management, and could, with NIA approval, call upon other federal agencies for additional personnel.[15] This plan was eventually incorporated into a basic policy paper (JCS 1181/1) on February 20. Attached to this document was a study by the Joint Strategic Survey Committee, which recommended, among other things, that the FBI be excluded from the NIA because of its law enforcement responsibilities and that language be incorporated in future drafts of the proposal that specifically charged the NIA and CIA with responsibility for protecting "sources and methods" of intelligence.[16]

The JCS action highlighted the impasse that had clearly developed between Donovan and his nominal superiors. Events, however, outraced both Donovan and his opponents, breaking the bureaucratic logjam in a way none of the protagonists expected. On February 9, 1945, the *Washington Times-Herald* and the *Chicago Tribune* published a story by reporter Walter Trohan entitled "Donovan Proposes Super Spy System for Postwar New Deal," which included the entire text of Donovan's November 1944 proposal to Roosevelt. Trohan's animosity toward the

Roosevelt administration and its works was well known and deeply held, and the two papers carrying the story (along with the *New York Daily News*) had been bitter critics for so long that not even war or concepts of "national unity" had mellowed them. The result was a lurid, highly colored, and supercharged account.[17]

Trohan wrote: "Creation of an all-powerful intelligence service to spy on the postwar world and to pry into the lives of citizens at home is under consideration." Quoting from Donovan's proposal, he added that the apparent purpose of the "super-intelligence unit" would be "to spy on good neighbors throughout the world for the purpose of formulating a foreign policy and developing strategy. . . . Under the draft order the director of the new super-spy unit would have tremendous power in being charged with gathering and sifting intelligence for the White House and all Federal agencies. . . . The spy director could employ the facilities of such agencies and enjoin them from reporting to their superiors." Trohan also saw fit to take a gratuitous shot at a favorite target of Roosevelt's enemies. "In high circles where the memorandum and draft order are circulating, the proposed unit is known as 'Frankfurter's Gestapo' because the sister of Supreme Court Justice Frankfurter is said to hold a confidential post in OSS. It is assumed she would pick key personnel, at the suggestion of her brother, for Donovan when . . . he would be named spy chief." The article then went on to say that the independent budget would permit secret funds for spying and "luxury living described in the novels of E. Phillips Oppenheim." It concluded by warning that the chief of the new organization could "determine American foreign policy by weeding out, withholding or coloring" the information gathered and asserting that the power to coordinate intelligence efforts "would permit spying at home and employment of police powers of existing agencies whenever needed."[18]

In a second article published the following day, Trohan, with apparent glee, reported the hostile comments of congressional figures, mostly anti-Roosevelt Republicans and conservative Democrats. Senator Edwin Johnston, Democrat of Colorado, rumbled, "I don't want any Democratic Gestapo. I can't go along with a proposal for a domestic spy system." Senatorial Republicans, however, were less restrained. Harlan Bushfield of South Dakota was sarcastic: "What is it they call that Russian spy system—the Ogpu? It would certainly be nice to have one of those in our own country." To E. H. Moore of Oklahoma, it was "just another concentration in the President following the pattern of the collectivist states." Homer Capehart of Indiana declared himself opposed to "any new superduper Gestapo" and expressed confidence in the ability of the military services and the FBI to handle intelligence matters. Kenneth Wherry of Nebraska was against "any other Federal bureau to absorb anything," as well as "any superduper agency to pry into the lives of American citizens." Less apocalyptic was Chapman Rever-comb of West Virginia, who noted, "It sounds like a far-reaching and perhaps very dangerous proposal to place such power in the hands of one organization." House Republicans were no less vocal. Representative Paul Shafer of Michigan called the proposal "another indication that the New Deal will not halt in its quest for power. Like Simon Legree it wants to own us body and soul." Several others added that it would create a "Gestapo." [19]

A third, relatively brief, article reproduced the alternative JCS plan of December 1944 in full. In his commentary, Trohan wrote that a "pitched battle" was being waged between Donovan and "the high command of the Army and Navy" over control of "the super-intelligence agency the New Deal is projecting to spy on the postwar world and the postwar homefront." He said that the military had "no quarrel with the objectives of the Donovan plan" but "vigorously dispute its control." [20]

Newspapers friendlier to the Roosevelt administration sought to present a different, and far less sinister, interpretation of the proposals. The *New York Herald Tribune* emphasized on February 10 that Donovan's proposed organization was for information gathering, because "the President is determined that the United States in the future shall not be ignorant of threats to its own and to world security." The lack of internal police power was stressed, and, to refute the "New Deal Gestapo" charge, the newspaper commented: "The planning for the proposed agency was not in New Deal hands but in the hands exclusively of General Donovan, who . . . was a nationally known Republican when President Roosevelt appointed him to a key war post." [21]

A brief descriptive article appeared on an inside page of the *New York Times* on February 10, but it was followed on February 13 by a much longer one that gave the appearance of being based on a confidential interview with either Donovan or one of his close associates. Citing "informed circles" who refuted the "American Gestapo" charge, the article said that such misrepresentation could "only create an impression of glaring national weakness in respect to dealings with enemy countries." The proposed agency, the article observed, would be concerned with intelligence analysis, have no internal police powers, and be of vital importance when, after the war, the United States "would be virtually making its debut in intelligent participation in world affairs." Opposition to the plan was attributed to rival intelligence organizations. The article concluded: "Failure to support the proposal, it is said, would lay open the country to grave dangers from without." [22]

An even more vigorous debunking effort was made on February 16 by syndicated columnist Frank Kent in the *Washington Star*: "The folly of narrow nationalism has been put behind us and we are at last prepared to assume our international responsibilities. . . . To this end, it would seem particularly desirable that we be at least as well informed as our Allies and colleagues." He regarded Donovan's proposal as "a common sense plan" that was "free of sound objections," and one that would give the United States a needed system for the orderly evaluation of intelligence and for the coordination of intelligence work. Criticizing the opposition for misrepresentation and distortion, he felt that resistance came mostly "from the heads of certain services which want to be left alone, who fear they may lose their jobs, or may be overshadowed by the new director." He rejected the "Gestapo" charge by referring to the agency's lack of police power and congressional control of the budget. He concluded: "If we are going into this international co-operation business . . . we ought not to go in blindfolded. If we are going to be a sap, we at least should have our eyes open."[23]

For its part, the *Washington Post* registered its views in a long editorial on February 16. In its judgment, much of the unfavorable reaction came from hasty "headline reading," rather than consideration of the plan as a whole, and on the basis of intelligence needs and shortcomings. It continued: "For the basic assurance of our national security in time to come is the absorption of the lessons of the last few years. And the greatest lesson is that national security depends upon knowledge of what is going on in the world . . . synthesized by brains at the elbow of policy-makers. . . . Brains make intelligence, not snooping."[24]

Regardless of the public commentary, behind his security wall Donovan was outraged by Trohan's articles. In a harsh memorandum to the JCS on February 15, he cited internal evidence in the articles to prove that the leak had come from within the JCS organization itself. "Such public disclosure of a secret JCS paper strikes at the heart of military security. . . . Further, thousands in government service who would see such a violation occur with impunity might well feel no need of discretion in their own activities." He considered it a "serious offense" to "disclose to our enemies official expressions of the inadequacies of our intelligence services and the conflicts engendered by an attempt to remedy these deficiencies." He believed that the falsehoods he saw in the articles (such as the reference to Frankfurter, the "Gestapo" charge, and the term "'super-spy' scheme"), as well as the immediate canvassing of unfriendly congressional opinion, led to the conclusion that the news leak was "a deliberate plan to sabotage any reorganization of the intelligence services" through the "excitement of suspicion and antagonism" in order to prevent the establishment of any new system, particularly a centralized one. "The past history of the newspapers concerned may explain their readiness to make a political attack on the President by any means," commented Donovan. He added that the person who released the documents, "in willful disregard of the consequences to the nation, at so critical a moment in the war and in the planning of peace," was "guilty of something in the nature of a treasonable utterance." He concluded by calling for a special judicial commission, possibly outside the JCS, to investigate the disclosure of the documents.[25] The service chiefs, however, did not need Donovan to tell them how to do their duty. An investigation was undertaken, within military channels, but the documents had been so widely distributed (in some cases by Donovan himself) that the culprit was never located.[26]

The uproar generated by Trohan's articles nevertheless served to justify dropping consideration of all postwar intelligence organization planning.[27] When the story broke on February 9, Roosevelt telephoned Donovan with instructions to "shove the entire thing under the rug for as long as the shock waves reverberate."[28] The military chiefs also recognized the merits of a strategic retreat. Writing to his colleagues with soldierly directness on February 22, General Marshall noted that

> JCS 1181/1 processed normally would have had merit for establishing at this time a central intelligence agency. The honest differences of opinion, adverse publicity, critical opposition and ridicule, the injection of political issues, charges of "Gestapo" and "super spy agency" make it inexpedient and undesirable to take action now. If approved, Congressional investigation will be inevitable as the central intelligence agency is to have a separate budget requiring Congressional action. Advantage to be gained for overall intelligence would be more than offset by the hazard to our best sources of intelligence incident to Congressional investigation. It would be unwise for the Chiefs of Staff to become involved in this controversial issue particularly since improvement from centralization probably would not occur rapidly enough to have appreciable bearing on the conduct of military operations in this war. Placing the President in an embarrassing position by the Chiefs of Staff's action on this proposal must also be considered.

Marshall therefore advised his colleagues that the JCS should recommend to the president "that further consideration of and action on this proposal be deferred."[29] The chiefs agreed and, on February 28, informed Donovan that, due to the ongoing investigation, his plan could not be considered.[30] Marshall's views were incorporated into a formal policy paper on March 2.[31]

As he watched his ambitions collapse, Donovan was slow to cool. On February 23 he wrote Roosevelt, blaming the JCS for the leak and declaring that a "reading of these articles makes it clear that the disclosure was no mere leak but a deliberate plan to sabotage any attempt at reorganization of this government's intelligence services. . . . The entire situation is most disturbing because it looks like 'an inside job' or at least abetted by someone on the inside." Referring to the proposed JCS counterplan, he added, "You will note that the strong effort in the revised plan is to avoid the direct reporting of the Director of the Intelligence Agency to you."[32] On March 9 he sent the president a copy of a portion of Great Britain's iron-toothed Official Secrets Act, which imposed harsh penalties on persons leaking or receiving security classified material, suggesting it could serve "as a model for action at a later time."[33] Roosevelt offered him no support or solace, however, and, in two press conferences on March 2 and 16, avoided detailed responses to questions about Donovan's proposal.[34]

Speculation about the identity of the phantom leaker is a feature in intelligence literature. It is the conventional wisdom among many veteran intelligence officers that the guilty party was Donovan's old nemesis, J. Edgar Hoover.[35] Veteran Washington insider Clark Clifford accepts this view, even though he was not in the city when the leak took place.[36] Donovan's most capable biographer, Richard Dunlop, records that, following the leak, the OSS chief sent his executive officer, Otto Doering, out to investigate. Dunlop does not record how Doering conducted his investigation but quotes him as saying, "I told the General that J. Edgar Hoover had personally handed the memorandum to Trohan. Donovan never said a word."[37] The authors of the best of the numerous biographies of J. Edgar Hoover note that, while he did leak a copy of Donovan's plan to the press, it was to reporter Willard Edwards of the *Chicago Tribune*.[38]

Trohan himself was silent on the entire issue in his memoirs. Years later, however, in response to a magazine query, he said: "Roosevelt was afraid that Wild Bill Donovan . . . was getting too big for his britches. So he had [White House press secretary] Steve Early leak the memo to me and we ran with it. . . . Hoover was very helpful to me when I ran the [*Chicago Tribune*] bureau in Washington, but not on that one."[39] Trohan's assertion has been disquieting to Donovan's chroniclers. Richard Dunlop has written, "This could hardly have been the case, for FDR was not the sort of politician who willingly handed a political enemy a knife to drive into his back."[40] Trohan gave the same account to Thomas Troy, claiming that Early had said "FDR wants the story out." Troy said that he "was not ready for the revelation" and apparently had some difficulty in accepting it.[41] Nevertheless, in a 1987 interview with a scholar researching a biography of General Hoyt

Vandenberg, Walter Pforzheimer, a veteran senior official in both the OSS and the CIA, supported Trohan's claim.[42] Although conclusive evidence is lacking, Trohan probably should be taken at his word. It is quite possible that Roosevelt — whose deviousness even his greatest admirers acknowledge — had become weary and disenchanted with the flamboyant, ambitious Donovan and sought to derail his imperial aims with an act of artful political cunning.

The controversy over the leak abated relatively quickly, however, easily eclipsed by the titanic events of the last months of World War II. With animosities cooled, Roosevelt decided to mollify Donovan by giving him another opportunity to present his plan. On April 5 he wrote to Donovan, "I should appreciate your calling together the chiefs of the foreign intelligence and internal security units in the various executive agencies, so that a consensus of opinion can be secured." He suggested that, in addition to the views of the executive departments, those of the FEA and FCC be solicited as well, since all had "a direct interest in the proposed venture" and should be asked "to contribute their suggestions to the proposed centralized intelligence service." Accordingly, on the following day, Donovan circularized the appropriate agency heads, enclosing an outline of his earlier plan and requesting a response by April 25 so that the meeting suggested by the president could be organized. With this accomplished, Donovan departed Washington for an inspection trip to Europe.[43]

Although most of the agencies consulted showed little interest, the key cabinet offices (state, war, navy, and justice) acted quickly. On April 12 Attorney General Francis Biddle convoked a meeting on Donovan's proposal in the State-War-Navy Building next door to the White House with Under Secretary of War Robert Patterson (representing Secretary Stimson), Secretary of the Navy Forrestal, and Secretary of State Stettinius. The four recognized the need for some sort of consolidated organization to collect and evaluate foreign intelligence and agreed that it should be separate from the FBI. They were also willing to consider a continued intelligence role for Donovan. Nevertheless, they decided to defer consideration of the centralized intelligence plan until after the war because, as Biddle later wrote, "it was generally felt that since the new organization would work on a highly secret plane it should start from scratch and be on its own from the beginning."[44]

Shortly after 5:00 P.M., with the meeting still in progress, Stettinius received a telephone call from press secretary Early, summoning him to the White House immediately. There, he was taken to Mrs. Roosevelt, who informed him that the president had died a few minutes earlier. After arranging for a cabinet meeting and expressing his condolences, Stettinius hurried back to inform his colleagues. Needless to say, discussion on Donovan's plan ended. The news reached Donovan in Paris. Calling OSS headquarters, he received confirmation from aide Ned Buxton. When Buxton asked what would happen to the OSS, Donovan replied: "I'm afraid it's the end." [45]

3

. . . And Harry Truman Disposes

The new president, Harry Truman, was a marked contrast to his predecessor. Although devoid of Roosevelt's charisma and not well known in the country at large, he had been well regarded in the Senate for his competence and integrity. Self-educated and self-made, he learned by doing and, most unlike Roosevelt, had a strong sense of administrative order. He came to the presidency with a substantial knowledge of governmental (and particularly military) organization and management issues from his service on the Senate Appropriations Committee and the chairmanship of his own Special Committee to Investigate the National Defense Program, which oversaw the war effort. While he had considerable respect for the military leaders who had successfully prosecuted World War II, he was skeptical of its overall management and was sympathetic to proposals for "reforming" the "national security" apparatus. With a strong sense of public responsibility, he was more concerned with effectively transacting the affairs of state than in formulating global abstractions and contingencies. Modest and unpretentious personally, he honestly recognized his limited foreign policy experience and readily (but never uncritically) deferred to professional expertise. While he favored a formal policy-making process involving the regular participation of officials from the State, War, and Navy Departments, he never doubted his own ultimate responsibility for making decisions, and he rarely agonized over any of them.

In 1945 Truman brought to office a mind-set that represented an overwhelming national mood. With Germany and Japan crushed and the Soviet Union still regarded as an ally and a potential associate in maintaining postwar world peace, there was no longer any sense of pressing international threat. Few Americans had any great interest in or desire for an expanded international role for the United States beyond participation in the United Nations and the other multinational instrumentalities created during the war. The public at large viewed the sacrifices of war as a temporary emergency and trusted to the United Nations to keep the peace. After the ravages of the Great Depression, most Americans hoped to resume normal lives and enjoy the prosperity generated by massive wartime spending. It was generally assumed by the American people (and certainly by their representatives in Congress) that the wartime "emergency" agencies would disappear, wartime controls and regulations would lapse, and both taxes and government spending would be reduced.[1]

Although this perception of the postwar global order would shift relatively quickly as relations between the United States and the Soviet Union deteriorated, this change was not immediate. Thus, as the war ended, Donovan's ambitions for his "temporary" agency became vulnerable, since he had lost his primary patron with the death of Roosevelt, faced enemies in other executive departments, and had failed to develop either a congressional or a public constituency. Careful observers of the Washington political scene recognized Donovan's dilemma. In his "Washington Merry-Go-Round" column, champion keyhole peeper Drew Pearson commented astutely:

> Gen. "Wild Bill" Donovan of the Office of Strategic Services, sometimes called the "Cloak and Dagger Club" or "Oh So Social," will miss Roosevelt terribly. Donovan ran the giant espionage outfit which tried to find out what was going on behind enemy lines; and he had accumulated the most bizarre assortment of female spies, social register blue-bloods and anti-Roosevelt haters ever seen in Washington. As an old personal friend, Roosevelt gave him free rein, including grandiose plans for a postwar espionage service. Truman does not like peacetime espionage and will not be so lenient.[2]

Less colorfully, but no less keenly, the British embassy's political officer reported on May 21:

> His opponents say that General Donovan's position has been weakened by the death of Mr. Roosevelt. Whereas Donovan's Irish qualities and passionate interest in the international political underworld, as well as his Republican affiliation and influence, were assets with the late President Roosevelt, who liked to attract influential Republicans to his side, President Truman is a stricter party man and somewhat shy of international ramifications. . . . There is some nervousness within the Office of Strategic Services as to the future of that vast and omnivorous organization under the new regime.[3]

Truman was not long in office when he first encountered the unresolved issue of postwar intelligence organization. He had developed a certain understanding of the problem from his senatorial career and proved a quick study on the subject. As he later recalled, he had been disturbed that witnesses appearing before Senate committees from different executive agencies had different and conflicting facts on similar subjects; as a result, he concluded that a better-coordinated system was necessary. As president, noting the frequently conflicting nature of intelligence reports that he received, he asked Admiral Leahy whether improvements were being considered. Leahy then described the controversy between Donovan and the military on the subject. The deputy director of ONI, Rear Admiral Sidney Souers, also presented him with the JCS counterplan. Truman further discussed the question with his newly appointed secretary of state, James Byrnes, who believed that his department should have primary responsibility in the field of foreign intelligence, a view that the War and Navy Departments found objectionable.[4]

As the world changed around him, Donovan nevertheless continued to cling to his visions of postwar permanence and influence and would not easily yield his life's ambition. Shortly after Truman took office, Donovan renewed his lobbying campaign. On April 30 he forwarded a copy of his November 1944 proposal to Truman; on August 25 he wrote the president directly on the intelligence issue. To Donovan, the formulation of national policy was "influenced and determined by the knowledge of the aims, capabilities, intentions and policies of other nations"; he deplored the dangerous situation he saw arising from the lack of a centralized American intelligence organization. He observed: "What is needed is an organization which will obtain the necessary information, both by overt and covert methods, and will at the same time determine national intelligence objectives, provide procurement direction, and correlate for strategic purposes the intelligence material collected by all Government agencies."

In Donovan's view, such an organization would be responsible for the centralized collection, analysis, synthesis, and distribution of intelligence from all sources for the making of national political and strategic decisions. It would have no domestic or foreign "police function" and no authority to conduct "clandestine activities" within the United States. It would be supervised by a presidentially appointed director and overseen by a policy board comprising the secretaries of state, war, navy, and the Treasury. Its programs would be supervised by the military in time of war or national emergency, and it would not encroach upon the intelligence responsibilities of existing agencies. His proposed organization would be independent in budgetary, personnel, and communications matters and would discharge "only such services as espionage, counterespionage, and those special operations (including morale and physical) designed to anticipate and counter the attempted penetration of national security by enemy action." [5]

Although as articulate on paper as a lawyer could be, Donovan fared less well with Truman on a face-to-face basis. There is only one recorded meeting between the two men—for fifteen minutes on May 14—and, beyond a brief notation that Donovan "came in to tell how important the Secret Service is and how much he could do to run the Government on an even basis," there is no official account of what was said. [6] In any event, Truman never again saw fit to personally consult with Donovan on the intelligence issue, despite Donovan's clear desire to discuss the matter further after the demise of the OSS. [7]

Truman's relations with Donovan were probably motivated by personal dislike. Presidential intimate Clark Clifford later noted: "For reasons I never really understood, Truman never liked Donovan. Perhaps he regarded Donovan as a self-promoter." [8] Clifford, however, as a young lawyer in the 1930s, had met Donovan while involved in some antitrust cases; he described him in an interview with Thomas Troy as "big, breezy, with a tendency to roll over people" and speculated that Donovan, a Wall Street lawyer and Republican, was not the sort of person with whom Truman would be comfortable. [9]

Various OSS veterans offered their own theories. Thomas Braden reflected: "I always thought Truman abolished OSS because the Joint Chiefs of Staff said 'Let's get rid of this guy Donovan. He's a pain in the ass. He's all over the place.' That must also have been buttressed by the end of the war and the feeling of 'Let's get rid of it all. Let's get back to the peace.' " A colleague, James Murphy, noted: "Truman and Donovan never got along. They had no regard for each other. Truman was in World War I as a captain; Donovan came out as a colonel. Donovan got all the decorations. Donovan was a Catholic Republican. Truman was a Democratic Baptist. They never saw eye to eye on anything." In William Colby's view, "Truman considered him an empire-builder. And let's face it. Truman was a Democrat and Donovan was a Republican. And you know, if Donovan came home with a brilliant record, he could become a real candidate. So I think the worry was in Truman's mind that he could become a political threat." [10]

The views of the former OSS intelligence officers, while not without merit, nevertheless one-sidedly misrepresent Truman. In order to explain Truman's ill feelings toward Donovan, it is necessary to look at his overall personality and career. Despite his personal modesty, Truman possessed a strong sense of self-worth and was always fully conscious of the paramouncy of the office he held. As a result, he was far less tolerant of individuals whose posturings and assertions of their own importance seemed challenging to his own authority than was the insouciant Roosevelt, who could wrap himself in the mantle of aristocratic pretension. Nor is it correct to imply that Truman's hostile feelings derived from some sort of resentment over Donovan's public notoriety. Because Truman had such a strong character, he neither resented nor feared the eminence of others. For that reason, Truman could work with, and frequently defer to, such figures as the urbane and aristocratic Dean Acheson or the internationally renowned George Marshall (both of whom were far more eminent in 1945 than was Donovan, or even Truman himself).

Further, it does not follow that Truman disliked Donovan because of his Republicanism. Although a ferocious partisan on the domestic hustings, Truman truly believed that politics stopped at the water's edge. Where international security issues were concerned, he not only retained Republicans such as Forrestal appointed by Roosevelt in his administration but also named others in the course of his own tenure. In addition, Truman demonstrated nothing but the greatest respect and admiration for elder statesman Henry Stimson, the most eminent Republican of his day. For their part, all these individuals could readily work with an "up-by-his-bootstraps" politician from rural Missouri because they, unlike Donovan, always remembered who was in charge. In the last analysis, therefore, Clifford is probably correct. Truman simply did not like self-promoters.

Donovan's old enemies were quick to exploit the president's antipathy. Officers in Army G-2 made sure that Truman obtained a copy of a report by Colonel Richard Park that detailed reputed OSS excesses and shortcomings.[11] Critics also leaked unfavorable information, including Park's report, to Trohan, who used them as the basis for a series of highly critical articles on the OSS in May 1945. But it was FBI director Hoover who pressed the most ruthless attack on Donovan. He lobbied Attorney General Biddle, as well as his successor, Tom Clark, to oppose Donovan's postwar intelligence ideas, and worked to poison Truman's mind against the OSS chief. He not only opposed Donovan's organizational proposals but also leaked stories regarding the lavish use of unvouchered funds by the OSS and accounts of highly placed Communists in the organization. He also used Brigadier General Harry Vaughan, Truman's military aide, as a conduit to pass on information about an alleged extramarital affair by Donovan, believing that family man Truman would be deeply offended.[12]

With the end of hostilities, however, the fate of the OSS passed into other hands—those of the Bureau of the Budget and its director, Harold Smith. In 1945, before the proliferation of White House staffs, the Budget Bureau served as a presidential "secretariat" for monitoring the activities of the entire executive establishment. Its control over budgets gave it power that Smith, a highly competent civil servant, was quick to use. Originally from Kansas and an engineer by training, he had served as Michigan state budget director under Governor Frank Murphy and had followed Murphy to Washington in 1939, where Roosevelt, impressed with his work at the state level, named him Budget Bureau director. His incumbency was a fateful one for Donovan. During the war, the two had sparred repeatedly over psychological warfare and propaganda issues, and Smith had soon come to distrust Donovan's ambitions.[13]

Smith and his agency also were familiar with intelligence issues. In 1942 the Budget Bureau had conducted a detailed examination of Army G-2, and in 1944 it had participated in a second. In 1943 it had carried out studies of ONI and, in addition, had examined not only the OSS but also the intelligence functions of the State Department, Federal Communications Commission, Office of War Information, and Foreign Economic Administration, and the intelligence services of various foreign governments. As a result of this activity, Smith believed that his bureau should be consulted on the planning of any postwar intelligence system; on March 2, 1944, he wrote Roosevelt in this vein.[14]

On September 18, 1944, Smith got his mandate for involvement from Roosevelt. In a formal directive, Smith was instructed as follows:

> Upon the termination of hostilities, we must proceed with equal vigor to liquidate the war agencies and reconvert the Government to peace. . . . In order that I may most effectively fulfill my responsibilities as Chief Executive in the demobilization period . . . , I am asking you to reexamine the programs, organization, and staffing of Government agencies and submit to me at the earliest possible date recommendations for adjusting the Executive Branch of the Government from the needs of war to the needs of peace.[15]

In accordance with Roosevelt's directive, Smith, on September 23, 1944, contacted Donovan to request that, within thirty days, the OSS chief furnish him with his plans for such reductions in personnel and programs that he could initiate prior to the termination of hostilities. Donovan acknowledged the message on September 27 and promised full cooperation with Budget Bureau objectives.[16] As the war ended, Donovan was quick to recognize Smith's importance for the future of his ambitions. On August 25, 1945 — in response to a request two days earlier from Smith for information regarding the termination of the OSS — Donovan supplied the budget director with a strong statement of his views. After discussing the steps he had taken to phase out his organization by early 1946, he warned: "In our Government today there is no permanent agency to take over the functions which OSS will have ceased to perform. These functions . . . are in reality essential in the effective discharge by this nation of its responsibilities in the organization and maintenance of the peace." He discussed his past efforts to establish a postwar secret intelligence organization and appended a lengthy "statement of principles" for organizing an independent, centralized foreign intelligence system that closely followed the views of his earlier message to Truman.[17]

Smith's hand was greatly strengthened by his close rapport with Truman. As a senator, Truman had dealt with Smith on appropriation matters, held him in high regard, and probably felt comfortable dealing with another "son of the middle border." Truman met with him as president for the first time on April 18 and requested that he stay on as budget director. Until he finally stepped down in June 1946, Smith remained a key presidential adviser. In their discussions, they quickly agreed on the importance of prompt postwar retrenchment and reconversion.[18] In line with this thinking, shortly after the surrender of Japan, Truman appointed a Reconversion Committee comprising Smith, John Snyder (director of the Office of War Mobilization and Reconversion), and presidential counsel Samuel Rosenman to make recommendations for the disposition of the various war agencies. Truman followed the committee's advice by issuing a series of executive orders terminating many of the agencies, redistributing such of their functions as were to be continued, and closing down their operations.[19]

Smith also was quick to address the postwar intelligence issue with the new president. Writing to Truman on April 20, he emphasized that "much stronger and more effective intelligence facilities" would be needed after the war, warned against "premature" action by advocates of both the Donovan and JCS proposals, and stated that his own agency was preparing a plan of its own, based on its wartime work. He concluded: "Facilities currently available for the production of intelligence are extensive and not well coordinated. . . . In my judgment, well-considered and objective action is badly needed from this time forward. . . . It is my hope that you may utilize the Bureau's experience and Government-wide viewpoint to help you evaluate such proposals as may be made to you."[20]

In a meeting with Truman on April 26, Smith returned to the question. After describing his agency's ongoing reconversion work, he observed that it was a problem when "someone dashes into the President's office with an ex parte presentation" because that "causes a good deal of trouble . . . and upsets our efforts." Truman stated "emphatically" that no such end runs would be permitted. He affirmed that anything within the purview of the Budget Bureau would be referred to it, and he would not sign any executive order without its "careful clearance."

Smith then noted that "there was something of a tug of war going on" among the various agencies on the issue of intelligence organization. He considered it "very important for this country in its postwar relationships with other countries to have a sound, well-organized intelligence system, whether it be the counselor [sic] service or what not; that probably will require new concepts and better trained personnel."[21]

By his own admission, Truman had no clear ideas of his own at this time, except, as he later put it, "one thing was certain—this country wanted no Gestapo under any guise or for any reason."[22] While this view may now seem ironic, considering the stresses on civil liberties that accompanied the onset of the cold war during the Truman administration, it was sincere enough in 1945, when peace and international cooperation still seemed the wave of the future. As one historian of intelligence noted, "Truman's concern about the possible development of an American police state was the single most important factor in causing him to block early central intelligence agency proposals."[23] Indeed, in a meeting with Smith on May 4, 1945, Truman instructed him not to enlarge that part of the presidential contingency fund used for foreign intelligence work and said "with considerable vigor that he was 'very much against building up a gestapo.' "[24]

Armed with full presidential support, the Budget Bureau was ready to act on proposals that had been germinating among its analysts for months. In a memo to Smith on August 27, Assistant Director Donald Stone recommended that the personnel of the OSS's Research and Analysis Branch and Presentation Branch be transferred to the State Department; these units had "performed very creditably" during the war and had already "done a considerable amount of work for State, . . . and many informal relationships now exist." In addition, there was "the advantage also of obtaining for State a going concern which can continue its work with a minimum of interruption and confusion" in order to enhance that department's postwar intelligence role. He then commented that the remaining OSS activities, "with a few exceptions are of a nature that will not be needed in peacetime" and should therefore be assigned to the War Department "for salvage and liquidation."[25]

With this proposal in hand, Smith, Snyder, and Rosenman accordingly met with Donovan, Under Secretary of State Dean Acheson, Assistant Secretary of War John McCloy, Captain Lewis Strauss of the Office of the Secretary of the Navy, and General Andrew McFarland of the JCS to devise their own plan for an intelligence system conducted primarily within existing agencies rather than by a new, centralized organization. Under it, the State Department would have primary responsibility for foreign intelligence analysis; would receive the funds, personnel, and records of the OSS devoted to that purpose; and would be in charge of an interdepartmental committee intended to provide central coordination and direction. The War Department would receive OSS "operational" assets. The Navy Department and JCS raised no objections.[26]

Donovan, of course, was appalled and, with extinction now clearly close at hand, launched the kind of "end run" that Smith had warned against. Taking advantage of the termination of wartime censorship, the journalists in OSS ranks (such as Stewart Alsop and Thomas Braden), and his own well-developed press connections, Donovan put aside his past umbrage over the "treasonable" leak to Trohan earlier that year and initiated a clandestine public relations campaign to extol the OSS and, by extension, promote a similar postwar organization. Shortly after V-J Day, Donovan directed an aide, John Shaheen, a navy commander, to delay his return to civilian life in order to organize the campaign. After obtaining a list of OSS officers in the Washington headquarters who were writers, Shaheen and his assistants searched OSS files for appropriate material, hurriedly declassified the records, and passed the documents to favored journalists. Donovan and his aides also stepped up the wartime practice of giving background briefings designed to promote the OSS and Donovan's intelligence ideas to selected friendly newsmen and publishers.[27]

These accounts usually emphasized the colorful clandestine operational side of the OSS (ignoring the more prosaic matter of intelligence collection and analysis); as a result, "a series of sensational stories dominated the newspapers and magazines hailing the exploits of the OSS's secret war." By such means, Allen Dulles (OSS station chief in Switzerland during the war) was able to publish a lengthy account of his successful efforts to negotiate the surrender of German forces in Italy in the *Saturday Evening Post* in August. Other results included a five-part series in the *Chicago Daily News* by OSS officer Wallace Deuel and stories replete with names and details of adventures in the Associated Press, the *Washington Post*, and the *New York Times*. On September 12 Donovan released to the *Washington Star* the names of twenty-seven OSS officers whom he had decorated for valor. Donovan's gambit, however, backfired. Truman, already ill disposed toward the OSS chief, viewed the press campaign as an effort at self-aggrandizement by Donovan designed to further his political ambitions. In the end, it merely hardened Truman's resolve to terminate the OSS and return its chief to private life.[28]

Not content with propagandizing, Donovan directly lobbied newly appointed Secretary of State James Byrnes, the Bureau of the Budget, the JCS, and even the White House itself. In a strongly worded memo to Rosenman on September 4 he declared:

I understand that there has been talk of attempting to allocate different segments of the organization to different departments. This would be an absurd and unsatisfactory thing to do. The organization was set up as an entity, every function supporting and supplementing the other. It's time for us to grow up Sam, and realize that the new responsibilities we have assumed require an adequate intelligence system. Increasingly the President will see the need and I hope a new agency will be set up to take over a very useful legacy.[29]

He also appealed directly to Truman on September 13, asking him that "in the national interest as well as in your own interest as Chief Executive" he not allow the dissolution of the OSS. "Whatever agency has the duty of intelligence should have it as a complete whole. To do otherwise would be to add chaos to existing confusion in the intelligence field. The various functions that have been integrated are essential functions in intelligence. One is dependent on the other."[30]

But Truman, like Pharaoh, had hardened his heart, and once again Donovan's gambit failed. Meeting with Truman on September 13, Smith noted that Donovan "was storming about our proposal to divide his intelligence service." Truman replied that Donovan had been in touch with him as well and commented that he had his own ideas about "a broad intelligence service attached to the President's office." He then told Smith that "we should recommend the dissolution of Donovan's outfit, even if Donovan did not like it."[31] That same day, two representatives of the Budget Bureau called on Donovan to lay out the dissolution plan for the OSS. An angry Donovan demanded to know if the JCS had been consulted on the matter. He was told (erroneously) that they had not.[32] The OSS chief lost no time in complaining to his superiors on the matter, but to no avail. The service chiefs had reviewed the proposed executive order drafted by the Bureau of the Budget and had concurred in its contents with only minor suggested changes. Their response to Donovan was the September 15 approval of a paper (originally drafted on August 28) formally authorizing the rapid withdrawal of all military personnel serving with the OSS and directing that ongoing programs requiring such personnel be transferred to the War and Navy Departments.[33]

As things fell apart, Donovan also made a last-ditch attempt to help his deputy, Major General John Magruder. Upon learning that Magruder would revert to his lower peacetime rank of brigadier, he wrote directly to Marshall on September 18, declaring that "by direct and personal observation in the work of this Agency I know that he has made in the intelligence field an important and valuable contribution to this war. . . . In the event that recognition should be given to the need of an intelligence service which would enable us to meet our new national responsibilities, General Magruder would be of the greatest value in its establishment and operations." Marshall's deputy, General Thomas Handy, responded rather stiffly on September 23, promising that Magruder's "special qualifications will be kept in mind when he is due for reassignment"; nevertheless, "It is a matter of regret that General Magruder, along with many others, must with the end of the fighting, return to his normal status and rank, but I am sure that you are aware of the necessity for doing this." [34]

The final death sentence for the OSS came on September 20, when Smith presented Truman with the executive order officially dissolving the organization and transferring its functions. Smith recorded: "I told him that this was the best disposition we could make of the matter and that General Donovan . . . would not like it. . . . The President glanced over the documents and signed the Order. He commented, as he has done before, that he has in mind a different kind of intelligence service from what this country has had in the past." [35] The two then discussed the best way to inform Donovan. Smith suggested that Truman do so, but the president, not wishing to confront Donovan again, directed Smith to deliver the order. Smith had little enthusiasm for the assignment; upon returning to his office, he ordered his deputy, Donald Stone, to carry the news. Stone did his unpleasant duty, later remarking, "When I delivered the document, Donovan took it with a kind of stoic grace. He knew it was coming, but gave no outward indication of the personal hurt he felt by the manner in which he was informed." [36]

Executive Order 9621, which dissolved the OSS as of October 1, was the culmination of the Budget Bureau's thinking. Under its provisions, the Research and Analysis Branch and the Presentation Branch of the OSS (exclusive of those portions in the U.S. occupation zones in Germany and Austria) were transferred to the State Department as the Interim Research and Intelligence Service (IRIS) on a temporary basis, pending reorganization by the secretary of state in 1946. Remaining responsibilities were transferred to the War Department on a caretaker basis: "The Secretary of War shall, whenever he deems it compatible with the national interest, discontinue any activity transferred . . . and wind up all affairs relating thereto." [37] Along with the executive order, Truman issued an official letter of commendation to Donovan for his wartime services that concluded: "Great additional reward for your efforts should lie in the knowledge that the peacetime intelligence services of the Government are being erected on the foundation of the facilities and resources mobilized through the Office of Strategic Services during the war." [38]

A simultaneous official letter went to Secretary of State Byrnes, informing him of the executive order and instructing him to "take the lead in developing a comprehensive and coordinated foreign intelligence program" for all federal agencies concerned. Byrnes was to create an interdepartmental group, chaired by his department, to formulate intelligence plans for presidential approval. Such a procedure "will permit the planning of complete coverage of the foreign intelligence field and the assigning and controlling of operations in such a manner that the needs of both the individual agencies and the Government as a whole will be met with maximum efficiency."[39]

Only loose ends now remained. On September 24 Donovan and his senior staff met with Budget Bureau representatives to lay out procedures for liquidating the OSS. It was an unhappy meeting, marked by misunderstandings over the impact and implications of Executive Order 9621. One participant noted afterward that Donovan made it "abundantly clear that, in his opinion, the order was a mistake and that the Director . . . has made a decision without full knowledge of the facts involved."[40] Donovan, on September 28, bade an emotional and eloquent farewell to about two thousand OSS personnel crowded into the abandoned roller-skating rink that had served as office space, telling them, "You can go with the assurance that you have made a beginning in showing the people of America that only by the decisions of national policy based on accurate information can we have a peace that will endure." At the end of the ceremony, each member of the audience filed past him to shake hands. Donovan acknowledged each person by name, made jokes, and thanked all for their services.[41] On September 30 the JCS notified all overseas theater commanders that the OSS had been terminated and its operational functions assumed by the War Department.[42] *Time* magazine provided a mocking epitaph to the once-powerful agency: "By an executive order last week the fabled Office of Strategic Services lost its identity but not its life. . . . Wild Bill Donovan wanted the salvageable parts of this machine to get independent status under the President. Last week he could settle for its peacetime placement beneath Jimmy Byrnes' wing."[43]

Good soldier and loyal subordinate to the end, General Magruder, on October 1, contacted General Bissell at Army G-2, acting ONI director Admiral Thomas Inglis, and Alfred McCormack, the new special assistant for research and intelligence to Secretary Byrnes to suggest establishing an interim liaison committee to carry out the provisions of the executive order. The responses came on October 4. Inglis was friendly, welcoming the initiative and designating his deputy, Admiral Sidney Souers, as ONI's representative. Bissell's testy reply accepted the proposal "in principle" but called for a direct meeting beforehand

in order that we may all be informed of decisions taken to date with reference to the disposition of the Office of Strategic Services under the Executive Order and at which time all of us would be informed of the former OSS activities that have been demobilized, the plan for further demobilization and the activities that will be continued in operation with considerable detail on their size, scope, and mission. Unless these matters are clarified, either liaison officers or a liaison committee would be ineffective.

McCormack was even more unfriendly. While agreeing to eventually appoint a liaison officer, he felt that Magruder's proposal "does not seem to me to be in order," since Truman's directive to Byrnes mandated that the secretary of state take the lead in developing an intelligence program. He saw "no reason" for a liaison committee, since "most of the problems between the respective heirs of the former OSS are administrative and of no interest to the military intelligence units of the services. Unless you have something in mind that does not appear from your letter, my preference is to conduct liaison directly with G-2, MIS, and DNI."[44] Thus did the proposal die.

The last loose end was Donovan himself. On Admiral King's initiative, the JCS proposed presenting Donovan with a formal letter of appreciation for the work performed by the OSS. A draft was prepared and forwarded to Admiral Leahy for approval on October 8. Leahy, however, vetoed the idea with an acerbic comment: "It does not appear to me to be appropriate for the JCS to select any one of its subordinate agencies for a letter of commendation." Instead, the army approved awarding Donovan a Distinguished Service Medal.[45] As a further consolation, Truman appointed Donovan to the American prosecution team at the Nuremberg war crimes trials. Donovan, however, fell into a dispute over procedures with Supreme Court Justice Robert Jackson, the chief U.S. prosecutor, and resigned. Other than a brief tour as ambassador to Thailand in 1953–1954, he never again held public office.[46]

The successor agencies promptly claimed their legacy. On September 27 the secret intelligence assets of the OSS were transferred to the War Department as the Strategic Services Unit (SSU) responsible to the assistant secretary of war. Magruder remained as its head. With him came 9,028 personnel, including such veteran clandestine operators as Richard Helms, James Angleton, Harry Rositzke, and Lyman Kirkpatrick. Magruder was instructed to "continue the program of liquidation of those activities and personnel so transferred which are no longer necessary or desirable, and preserve as a unit such of these functions and facilities as are valuable for peacetime purposes, or which may be required by Theater Commanders or occupation authorities to assist in the discharge of their responsibilities."[47] Under Magruder, the OSS veterans fared relatively well in the SSU, despite inevitable postwar reductions, and a viable intelligence structure remained in place. The old OSS intelligence networks in Eastern Europe, the Balkans, and China were kept intact, and the development of liaison relationships with foreign intelligence services was begun. Thus, on January 15, 1946, Magruder could proclaim that "SSU today possessess the essential personnel, techniques and facilities for all the complex phases of clandestine peace-time intelligence procurement."[48]

Led by such figures as William Langer, Sherman Kent, and Ray Cline, 1,362 former OSS analytical personnel entered the State Department. In accordance with the executive order, the State Department issued two directives on October 26, formally establishing the Interim Research and Intelligence Service under a special assistant to the secretary for research and intelligence. His duties would be to carry out the order's mandate to develop a coordinated intelligence program for the department, devise a comprehensive program for all government agencies concerned with foreign intelligence, and direct any future departmental office resulting from the consolidation of all departmental intelligence functions that was to be accomplished by December 31.[49] Grafting the new intelligence presence onto the traditional State Department system in order to play the role called for by Truman's directive would prove a major challenge. McCormack admitted as much in a memo to Admiral Leahy on October 31, in which he felt "that this Department should formulate its own plans before going ahead with the interdepartmental group."[50] It is to this conflict within the State Department that consideration must now be given.

4

The State Department and Central Intelligence

American leadership in the global wartime coalition worked a sea change on the venerable State Department. A small and relatively homogeneous organization before the war, its personnel were content to carry out the traditional diplomatic functions of representation, observation and reporting, and negotiation. While the foreign service discharged its responsibilities with a high degree of competence, as an institution the State Department encountered culture shock when confronted with the challenge laid down by Truman's September 1945 directive to Byrnes. As Dean Acheson recalled of his wartime service, "With some brilliant exceptions, the bureaucracy was unequipped for appraisals of capability based on quantitative and technical judgments and of intentions by painstaking and exhaustive collection and correlation of intelligence."[1] In a witty presentation to Congress in 1945, he clearly described the State Department's predicament by pointing out that, prior to the war, its "techniques of gathering information differed only by reason of the typewriter and telegraph from the techniques which John Quincy Adams was using in St. Petersburg and Benjamin Franklin was using in Paris." Emphasizing the importance of intelligence analysis, he added that the State Department was not planning "to employ beautiful blonds who can worm secrets out of foreign officials" or "people who put on false whiskers and crawl out from under the bed."[2]

Acheson's strictures notwithstanding, the State Department had not ignored the question of creating some sort of consolidated intelligence organization during the latter part of World War II. On August 21, 1944, the under secretary's office forwarded a proposal to Secretary Stettinius for immediately establishing a Committee on Intelligence chaired by the State Department and containing representatives of the War and Navy Departments and the FBI to examine "joint intelligence activities in the several phases of planning, operations and the exchange of information. The statutory and legal aspects should be considered as well as the administrative and organizational." The proposal envisioned a planning board in Washington "to formulate policy and review and coordinate plans of the several operating agencies," while overseas operations would be coordinated by the local chief of mission or the local American military commander in occupied areas. According to the plan, the committee's members would exchange information and make recommendations to the secretaries of war and navy and the attorney general for approval and submission to the president.[3]

Although Stettinius did not formally adopt this proposal, it was in accord with his thinking. During discussions over Donovan's postwar intelligence ideas later that year, he wrote Roosevelt:

> I feel that it is of the utmost importance that there be established an interdepartmental board with responsibilities for coordinating foreign intelligence activities among the various departments and agencies. As I conceive it, this board would have the responsibility for seeing that the requirements of all federal departments and agencies were effectively met, and for formulating future policies and programs on foreign intelligence. I think that the State Department representative on this board should act as chairman inasmuch as we have primary responsibility for the conduct of foreign affairs.[4]

Because monitoring wartime international commerce had become a major State Department responsibility, the economists of its Division of World Trade Intelligence (WTI) took the initiative in pushing for an enhanced departmental postwar intelligence role. WTI had built up a substantial body of expertise and records concerning foreign economic intelligence, and its staff felt strongly (particularly when considering Donovan's schemes for postwar intelligence empire building) that such resources should be preserved within the State Department following the end of hostilities to assist in coping with the economic problems of Europe and the Far East. On May 24, 1944, WTI chief Francis Russell wrote his superior, Charles Taft, director of the Office of Wartime Economic Affairs, suggesting that "there is an urgent need for a well-organized general intelligence office in the Department." He proposed that it be organized around his own unit, observing, "Almost any well-run large newspaper has better organized informational files than the Department as a whole" because of bad organization and management. He added a cautionary note: "The Office of Strategic Services is actively considering a substantial enlargement of its foreign intelligence work for the post-war era, particularly in South America. . . . It is my belief that the handling of foreign intelligence should be centered in the Department. The Department should in peacetime be the center of all government agencies under strictly established and maintained goals." To serve this purpose, he suggested creating an "office of foreign intelligence" to "collect, analyze, and disseminate foreign political, economic, and biographical information."[5]

Russell was more apocalyptic in a follow-up memo on June 7:

> The necessity for an adequate handling of this work in the coming decade is no less clear. There will be numerous conferences at which decisions will be taken that will affect the history of the world for some time to come.... Of greater importance is the obvious fact that the coming decade will be one of unrest and readjustment. The elements in Germany which promoted the present program of German expansion will ... commence a new effort with new tactics immediately after the war. The emergence and spreading of a Fascist ideology from Argentina, backed by the remnants of Naziism in Germany, is certainly not out of the question. It will be of utmost importance to have as complete information as possible concerning the influence of Russia in various parts of the world. Our intelligence in the Far East is seriously deficient.... It should be unnecessary to labor the point that in the work of the Department knowledge is power and that knowledge can be obtained only as a result of a closely-knit organization having adequate authority and utilizing the most efficient procedures and systems available.[6]

Russell expanded upon his initial idea with a series of formal proposals to establish his Office of Foreign Intelligence. On October 5, 1944, he presented such a plan, based on a study done in cooperation with the Bureau of the Budget. Under it, the new office would report to the under secretary of state and be responsible for the collection, collation, analysis, and distribution of foreign political, economic, geographic, cultural, social, scientific, and technical intelligence; it also would determine foreign intelligence requirements and conduct intelligence liaison with other government agencies. The office would subsume the responsibilities of a number of scattered offices and focus on

> a broad area of intelligence which depends upon the assiduous development of all possible sources and the tedious chewing and relating of raw facts. The organizing of such information into valuable intelligence *can best be done in a central intelligence office*, staffed by competent researchers free from other pressures and responsibilities. ... Also, there is a large area of intelligence which cuts across the fields of several offices and divisions which can only be conducted in a central office. It would be essential to the success of the Office of Foreign Intelligence that it not engage in policy for-

mulation or functional activities. Its role would be to provide evaluated intelligence materials and research studies for the service of the whole Department.

The proposal concluded prophetically: "Since many of the geographical and functional offices presently attempt to carry on all of their own intelligence activities, an Office of Foreign Intelligence . . . probably will not be established without opposition. If the Office is to be successfully established, therefore, it will be essential that it receive the support of the Under Secretary and the Secretary."[7] Russell's plan, however, was far too sweeping for the cautious Stettinius, who left it languishing for the remainder of his secretaryship, despite appeals for action by Russell in order to head off Donovan.[8]

The intelligence issue nevertheless remained alive. On January 17, 1945, Roosevelt wrote Stettinius, directing him to discuss foreign intelligence organization with Donovan and the secretaries of war and navy: "At the end of this war there simply must be a consolidation of Foreign Intelligence between State and War and Navy and I think it should be limited to military and related subjects. This should not take in the commercial angle in the first place, though the organization should have the benefit of a commercial summary every month."[9] Discussion continued throughout Stettinius's tenure among the various assistant secretaries. Much of it emphasized the pressing need for the State Department to take the lead in developing a postwar intelligence system in order to preserve its leadership in foreign affairs and to prevent the establishment of a separate organization for the collection and analysis of intelligence information.[10] As a result of these discussions, State Department officials decided to create an intelligence office under a "special assistant" to the secretary with the equivalent rank of assistant secretary, in the belief that such a position would attract a highly qualified individual who would be solely responsible for directing the new office and would serve as the exclusive representative for interdepartmental liaison on intelligence matters.[11]

With the end of the war at hand, intelligence organization ceased to be an academic issue for the State Department and the incoming secretary, James Byrnes. With the termination of numerous temporary wartime agencies, the department inherited the residual responsibilities and personnel not only of the OSS but also of the Foreign Economic Administration, the Office of War Information, the Office of Inter-American Affairs, and the Office of the Foreign Liquidation Commissioner—a total of about four thousand people. It was hardly surprising, therefore, that Byrnes, at his July 3 swearing in, announced that he had requested the Budget Bureau to examine the State Department's structure and organization. For his own part, Byrnes was opposed to the transfer of so many new people from the defunct agencies. Thinking that the executive branch should be kept small and that the influx of newcomers would change the State Department from an advisory body into an independent policy-making agency, he was concerned over the personal backgrounds and political affiliations of some of the new personnel.[12]

Because Byrnes focused so much of his attention on the complicated and increasingly intractable problems of postwar Europe, he was frequently absent from the departmental conferences and thus left the issues of reorganization and restructuring to others. A primary player was Dean Acheson, who, as under secretary, administered the department while Byrnes was gone. Urbane and experienced in public affairs, Acheson was a man of commanding intellect and strong opinions who had little patience for the inertia of bureaucratic traditions; he felt that the talent inherited from the OSS was what the State Department seriously lacked and badly needed.[13] Actual responsibility for integrating the inherited wartime personnel, however, fell to Donald Russell, who became assistant secretary of state for administration in September 1945. Like Byrnes, Russell was a South Carolinian and a former law partner and government protégé of the secretary. Named as Russell's deputy in November was J. Anthony Panuch, a New York lawyer of Czech extraction who also had worked for Byrnes and had held a number of posts in the wartime government bureaucracy.[14]

In the specific area of intelligence, Acheson favored a centralized approach. Accordingly, on September 5, 1945, then-serving Assistant Secretary of State for Administration Frank McCarthy recommended that the "special assistant" be promptly appointed so that the incumbent could "proceed to build an organization as conceived by the Bureau of the Budget and, I believe, all others concerned."[15] Acheson agreed and, on September 12, cabled the secretary while he was in London for a foreign ministers' conference to request approval for establishing the post of special assistant for research and intelligence,

> whose office would be responsible for the collection, evaluation and dissemination of all information regarding foreign nations. These functions are now spread throughout the Department. To unite them in one organization, which would become the Department's encyclopedia, would free the operating offices of the intelligence function and thus relieve them of a very considerable burden. Intelligence would furnish the data upon which the operating offices would determine our policy and our ac-

tions. Sources of information would be our field installations and those of other departments as well as all Washington agencies and other domestic sources.

Acheson added:

We do not have even the nucleus of an Office of Intelligence in the Department at present. During the past few years we have depended heavily upon OSS for intelligence research and analysis. This agency has two highly effective branches around which we could build the Office. The personnel of these branches are experienced and they have done and are doing invaluable work for us. Their complete abolition would be disastrous and would impose a new and heavy load on the Department, one which we could bear only with great difficulty, if at all.

To head the new office, Acheson proposed Alfred McCormack, a colonel in Army G-2 and a prominent New York lawyer in civilian life. According to Acheson, "He is described as a brilliant organizer and intelligence man who could attract highest caliber personnel as he has done in the War Department. That Department considers his work most outstanding." [16]

Byrnes concurred on September 15, and, on September 27, the State Department announced McCormack's appointment. The announcement added that the absorption of the functions of the OSS and other agencies "constitutes the first steps in the reorganization of the Department to meet its expanding responsibilities." [17] McCormack, forty-four at the time of his appointment and a nominal Republican, did not lack for experience in intelligence matters. Recruited into the War Department by Stimson in 1942 and subsequently commissioned, he had been responsible for establishing a Special Branch in Army G-2 for exploiting the signals intelligence provided by ULTRA electronic interceptions and furnishing guidance to the Army Signal Corps in cryptography, traffic analysis, and similar matters. Field teams from his unit proved highly successful in supplying the intercepted intelligence to military units and had given welcome support to hard-pressed British cryptanalysts.[18] According to Sherman Kent, McCormack "made his mark with the high authorities, and the products of his labors . . . gained him enormous respect from the Chief of Staff . . . and Mr. Stimson himself. McCormack seemed to love intelligence work, and his work was one of the outstanding intelligence performances of the war." [19] In Kent's view, McCormack's decision to take the State Department post rather than return to his law practice was largely dictated by his belief that he would be named to head the new centralized intelligence organization that Truman, in his letter to Byrnes, had suggested would be established within the State Department.[20]

On October 1 Acheson presented McCormack with a memorandum outlining his responsibilities. He was to serve as the department's representative in all future interagency discussions concerning distribution of OSS functions, establish a board to determine what parts of the OSS transferred to the State Department would be retained after the beginning of 1946, survey all departmental components to determine which of their functions pertained to intelligence, and consolidate them under his control. Acheson concluded: "The steps which I have directed . . . will have the effect of uniting and consolidating the intelligence activities of this Department."[21] McCormack received a further grant of authority from Byrnes himself on October 23, designating him "the representative of the Secretary in all matters relating to communications intelligence activities, including the collection, analysis, decryption and translation of communications and the derivation of intelligence from those and related activities." In this capacity, he was to maintain liaison with other government agencies (particularly the War and Navy Departments) engaged in similar work, acquaint them with the relevant needs and resources of the State Department, oversee State Department involvement in foreign liaison activities concerning communications intelligence, and serve as the focal point for the receipt and dissemination of information derived from communications intelligence.[22] To complete the reorganization process, McCormack circularized a number of overseas missions (including London, Paris, Rome, and Chungking), informing them of the establishment of IRIS and its assumption of OSS analytical responsibilities, and adding: "It is desired that the work hitherto performed by the R and A staffs should be continued for the present and that State Department missions should aid and guide these staffs as far as possible."[23]

The new order of intelligence did not graft easily onto the traditional structure of the State Department, however. Primary opposition to the idea of a strong Office of Intelligence came from the department's regional geographic offices, led by traditional diplomats. These foreign service officers felt that the nature of their work made them "intelligence officers" who were capable of evaluating foreign events themselves. They therefore saw no need for an office that might second-guess their own judgment.[24] Sherman Kent, one of the most senior former OSS analysts entering the State Department, recalled that he was "keen" to integrate the analysts into the departmental organization "serving real policy-making offices with the kind of work which I knew our people could produce."[25] But, he continued:

When we moved to State, my colleagues and I had thought that we would be greeted with cheers of joy. What a good piece of luck for them to have inherited such a fine research and intelligence organization. But this was not the case at all. . . . We were usually given a polite reception, but there was always a certain chill in the air as we went into our description of what a fine group of people we represented and how State could derive such great benefit from calling on our services.[26]

Kent also reflected that the size of the OSS contingent, combined with those from the other defunct agencies, had a negative impact: "Perhaps with the hordes of new people, all with different expertise and background, coming into the Department, the matter of adding a whole separate intelligence arm was just too much."[27] Nor is it likely that McCormack's strong personality helped matters. According to Kent:

He was a man of little or no small talk and little or no jollying up to casual acquaintances. . . . Because of his resolute leadership and his unwillingness to back down in a dispute, he had a reputation of being a hard-boiled and successful administrator. It is my hunch that a good number of Foreign Service officers had no personal affection for McCormack and in their hearts feared the appearance of so strong, so tough and able a character on their turf. . . . It may be that some of the key officers had been personally offended by McCormack's abrasive manner and use of straight talk without considering the tender feelings of others.[28]

Others put an additional sinister spin on Kent's interpretation. Anthony Panuch believed that "for the most part" the new personnel had "little experience in foreign affairs" and had an ideology "far to the left" of Byrnes and Truman. To Panuch, these individuals aimed at "a socialized America in a world commonwealth of Communist and Socialist states," and their very presence was a result of a "massive infiltration" of "pro-Communists and personnel of subversive and revolutionary tendencies" who had originally entered the government as a result of the wartime expansion of the bureaucracy. In Panuch's view, these subversives aimed at nothing less than control of American foreign policy, and proposals for centralization of intelligence functions were means to that end.[29] Such views had resonance outside the State Department and focused on McCormack, despite (or perhaps because of) his impeccable "establishment" background. In an article published on September 30, Walter Trohan referred to McCormack as "a darling of leftists."[30] On January 20, 1946, conservative columnist Constantine Brown mocked McCormack's capacity and attributed his advancement in both the army and the State Department to his close ties to Assistant Secretary of War John McCloy, a former law partner.[31]

Nor did events go unnoticed by FBI director Hoover. In November 1945 he was informed about the State Department's centralized intelligence planning by Senator Styles Bridges, a conservative Republican from New Hampshire. Bridges also told Hoover about a letter to Truman from a former army intelligence officer who questioned the loyalty of McCormack's wartime associates and claimed that McCormack had tried to have information about their subversive backgrounds removed from FBI files. Thus alerted, Hoover and his congressional and military allies were able to organize opposition to McCormack's plans as they had against Donovan's.[32]

The contest over intelligence organization within the State Department began quietly. On October 11 McCormack requested that all departmental offices nominate representatives to an Intelligence Advisory Board, which met for the first time on October 19 and resolved that each office would cite its intelligence needs. Battle was joined in earnest, however, at a meeting in Acheson's office on October 27, when the under secretary presented the proposed procedural manual for a new centralized Office of Research and Intelligence. Present, in addition to Acheson, were McCormack, Russell, Willard Thorpe (representing Under Secretary for Economic Affairs Will Clayton), and four regional assistant secretaries — Spruille Braden for Latin America, H. Freeman Matthews for Europe, John Carter Vincent for the Far East, and Loy Henderson for the Near East.

Braden led the attack. A belligerent man, he fully lived up to Acheson's description of him as "a bull of a man physically and with the temperament and tactics of one, dealing with the objects of his prejudices by blind charges, preceded by pawing up a good deal of dust."[33] Believing, Braden himself wrote later, that Acheson had made a "take-it-or-leave-it" proposition, he launched a "real knock-down-drag-out fight" against the plan. Examining the portion dealing with Latin America, he declared: "I protest on this proposition because I have glanced through here and there is not one single item or function I can find on these pages which is not being fully and competently performed by the Office of American Republic Affairs. . . . There is no need for it. It is an extravagance, an inefficiency, and I protest." He was supported with less truculence by Henderson, who commented: "This is duplication. We are doing the work that is supposed to be done here. There is no rhyme or reason for it." Unsurprisingly, the meeting ended without agreement.[34]

McCormack also began encountering problems from a Congress intent on reducing the size of the wartime federal bureaucracy and cutting expenditures.

On October 23 the House passed and sent to the Senate a fiscal rescission bill concerning the reallocation of funds from defunct agencies, which included insufficient revenue for the operation of the OSS units transferred to the State Department. McCormack was compelled to go before the Senate Appropriations Committee to seek a supplementary budget request. Appearing on October 30, he requested that the State Department receive the full $11.5 million remaining for the OSS, rather than the $9.5 million allotted by the House. He explained that the extra money was needed to continue work in a number of programs, since the remainder had been committed elsewhere. Stressing the high quality of the personnel involved and the "need for carefully evaluated economic and political intelligence," he believed that "a specialized central organization in the State Department can do the job more thoroughly, more effectively, and more economically than it can be done by the operating policy-making divisions on a decentralized basis." Committee chairman Kenneth McKellar, a cantankerous conservative Tennessee Democrat, nevertheless showed scant interest and less consideration. He interrogated McCormack sharply, hectored him, and finally dismissed him cavalierly as a witness.[35] In the end, the House cuts were upheld.

Although Acheson later succeeded in securing a partial restoration, McCormack's troubles with Congress continued into 1946. Byrnes had submitted a request for $4.15 million on February 16 to specifically fund the departmental intelligence unit in 1947. On April 19 the House Appropriations Committee voted to deny the money, commenting: "If a separate unit is needed within the department to analyze and correlate the information received from missions abroad, such a unit may be created with the personnel that had been allowed generally for the department and field services."[36] Byrnes issued a statement deploring the committee's action as making it "impossible for the Department to undertake even a modest foreign intelligence program" while precluding effective cooperation with other agencies in intelligence work.[37]

McCormack encountered troubles of another kind on Capitol Hill as well. On March 14, 1946, the House Military Affairs Committee, chaired by Democrat Andrew May of Kentucky, charged that "pro-Soviet" individuals formerly in the War Department were involved in State Department intelligence work. The committee added that "representations" had been made to Byrnes to do something about it. Said a spokesman: "We named the names of the personnel involved and there are many of them." At a press conference the next day, Byrnes sought to smooth over the issue, saying that as long as departmental employees were "pro-American," their opinions of other countries did not concern him. After pointing out that screening of new employees was under way, he denied that any substantive approach had been made to him by the committee and suggested that any unresolved suspicions should be turned over to the FBI. McCormack was more combative, denying the charge on March 20 and calling the accusation "a tissue of lies, created by irresponsible and evil men with evil purposes." He sent a letter to the committee asking for a chance to rebut the charges, which he attributed to a former Army G-2 officer who was out to "get" him. Chairman May denied the request, announcing on March 25 that no further hearings were planned and that the investigation would proceed "along other lines." The next day, McCormack sent another letter to May, defending his subordinates and demanding that he either withdraw the charge or conduct a "proper investigation of the facts."[38]

The troubles McCormack encountered with Congress were soon matched by those he faced in the State Department itself, where the regional assistant secretaries had secured an important ally in Donald Russell. In a memo to Byrnes on November 3, Russell reviewed Budget Bureau proposals for a "decentralized" intelligence system with the analysts located at the "decision-making" level and concluded that this approach was the most appropriate for the State Department. He therefore argued: "The point of centralization, it would seem, would be the geographic desks, which should function, in my opinion, directly under the Secretary and Under Secretary. These desks represent the level of operations. They must take certainly the initial responsibility for suggesting decisions and actions to the Secretary and Under Secretary. . . . It accordingly follows that . . . intelligence should be attached to and made the 'handmaiden' of the geographic desks." In Russell's view, "The creation within the Department of a centralized over-all intelligence group . . . is as illogical as the centralization of governmental intelligence operations in a single agency." He therefore found McCormack's proposed organization "completely at variance" with the approach he favored, since it contemplated "a centralized intelligence unit, *not accountable to the operating levels.*" Such an approach was incompatible with his, and the Budget Bureau's, view of proper organization. He added in a postscript: "Intelligence is only as good as it is translated into action. Where is that? The geographic desks."[39]

On November 29 Russell appointed a seven-member working group to prepare a plan for the Intelligence Advisory Board. At issue were seven regional analysis divisions of the proposed Office of Research and Intelligence, with a total of 548 positions. The working group itself could not agree and, on December 12, submitted a centralized majority plan and a decentralized minority plan to the board. On December 19 the board met and voted 9 to 8 to approve a "centralized" ORI upon the termination of IRIS.[40] This was not what Russell wanted to hear, however, and, on December 29 he sent another memo to Byrnes and Acheson, recommending that, after the three months needed to secure office space and recruit and train personnel, the regional geographic and functional divisions of ORI be transferred to their counterpart departmental offices. He declared strongly:

> I believe that research at the geographic level must be under the immediate direction of those who use it. In my judgment, the divorce of research from policy action taken after the evaluation of information will lead inevitably to wasteful duplication and to compteing evaluations of information which will breed confusion and disorganize the operations of the Department. . . . No justification can possibly exist for different geographic breakdowns. It would place the Department in a ridiculously inconsistent position to approve a geographic division for a new Office in the Department wholly different from that established and approved for the traditional offices of the Department.[41]

Russell was backed by Braden, who wrote Acheson on December 31: "I am strongly of the opinion that the research and intelligence activities of the Department in order to be of real value and to avoid confusing duplication must be continued in, expanded, and integrated organizationally with the operations of the geographic Offices of the Department." Braden also secured important support from James Clement Dunn, the new assistant secretary responsible for Europe, who also wrote Acheson on December 31 to argue: "It would be disastrous to set up another organization within the State Department to duplicate the work which is now being done by the Foreign Service and State Department personnel. . . . I hope there will be no question of setting up a separate intelligence unit to cover the existing work of the Department, as the result would be nothing less than confusion and disorder."[42]

McCormack fought back with vigor. In a memo of his own to Byrnes on December 31, he stressed the importance of keeping ORI together, using language reminiscent of Donovan. "It is an integrated organization with common management, procedures, and files. It is flexible, in that personnel from one geographic unit can be shifted to meet peak demands in others. It does a *whole* job of processing information and collating it for everybody's needs." Such an office would be objective, he argued, because its mission of "fact-finding" was independent of policy making. He also believed that such independence would be "unthinkable" in the geographic offices and that decentralization "would end all possibility of organized State Department intelligence, and the President's idea of State Department leadership in government-wide intelligence could not be attained."

In his view, a centralized unit would serve the needs of offices throughout the State Department, not just individual divisions, and could "look at the national intelligence problem as a whole, coordinating the work of its component parts and gearing itself into other intelligence organizations of the government." He added: "The geographical desks have neither the time nor the training to engage in a systematic compilation of basic information for future intelligence purposes. Even if they had, they still could not do it, because different habits of thought and a different frame of mind are required for research work than for the daily operating job." He asserted that, in a decentralized system, "personnel who go to the geographic desks will have to find their futures in those divisions and the opportunities for promotion and advancement will come not in research, but in operating and policy jobs." Under centralization, those creating a departmental intelligence organization "will have control of their personnel and the opportunity to work out their relations with other departmental units within a definite framework of responsibility."[43]

Byrnes, however, facing the prospect of attending a United Nations conference in London, chose to temporize. On January 5, 1946, he instructed Russell to implement the centralized plan temporarily, pending a final decision around the beginning of March.[44] In the meantime, Russell prepared a lengthy paper on the subject for Byrnes to consider, dated February 25, in which he returned to his proposal for transferring the regional ORI research offices to the geographic divisions. ORI would be renamed the Office of Intelligence Coordination and Liaison, without basic analytical responsibilities beyond conducting "specialized research on economic or other technical subjects." Its responsibilities would be limited to establishing departmental intelligence standards, organizing special programs and projects among departmental components, conducting liaison with other governmental intelligence entities, and representing the State Department in interdepartmental meetings.[45]

Byrnes's continuing failure to act, however, allowed the issue to rankle and produce ugly exchanges between Russell and McCormack.[46] It was Russell who had the secretary's ear, however, and the sands were fast running out for McCormack. Byrnes had become increasingly unfriendly; by mid-April, he decided to resign rather than continue his battle with the regional assistant secretaries and their supporters. He had few supporters of his own; not even Acheson was willing to do battle on his behalf.[47] With victory in sight, Russell pressed his advantage, writing Byrnes on April 18 to urge the approval of his February 25 plan to end the impasse.[48] On April 20 he followed with a second memo that boldly asserted: "If the result is to be the administrative set-up I have recommended, why not issue my proposed order and end the Departmental bickering and indecision? Let's get the right result now and end the backbiting. . . . I believe the adoption of my proposal is the only way to tie the organization together. This is not a question of Intelligence—it is a question of sound Departmental organization."[49]

Byrnes at last agreed and, on April 22, issued orders putting Russell's plan into effect. For McCormack it was the end. Completely defeated, he submitted his resignation on April 23, effective immediately. In his letter to Acheson (Byrnes was again in Europe), he described Russell's ideas as "unworkable and unsound," asserting that instituting them not only precluded establishing "a real intelligence unit" within the State Department but also weakened its position "vis-a-vis the military components" of the intelligence establishment. Acheson accepted McCormack's resignation with regret. On April 29 the department announced the appointment of William Langer as McCormack's successor and subsequently issued a series of directives clarifying the responsibilities of his office along the lines set forth by Russell.[50] Langer, a "centralizer," had no significant influence on making intelligence policy. In July 1946 he "was anything but sorry" to resign in order to return to his old academic life at Harvard. As he later noted, "I did not flatter myself that a real solution had been found" to the State Department's intelligence dispute during his tenure.[51] He was replaced by Colonel William Eddy, a former OSS officer, the following month.

For their part, the "decentralizers" were jubilant. Several years later, Braden provided a postmortem that revealed his feelings: "An Office of Research and Intelligence was established, but on a very minor and insignificant scale in the Department."[52] In a memo to a colleague on May 20, 1946, Panuch commented: "What worries me is the utter failure on the part of Langer and people like Kent and Fahs [Charles Fahs, a senior analyst] to grasp what is involved in the business of setting up an organization. . . . If they do not force themselves into a state of mind where they are willing to accept integration with the State Department, the intelligence set-up will not work and the whole program will be hopelessly prejudiced."[53]

Probably unintentionally, Panuch had described exactly what came to pass. The bureaucratic battle had been hard on the former OSS analysts; as it went on, many departed, "either in disgust of one sort or another or in their desire to get back to their civilian jobs."[54] As Kent himself recalled:

I don't suppose there had ever been or could ever be a sadder or more tormented period of my life than that of the first half of 1946. It was bad enough being the object of the animus from the working policy officers of the State Department, but perhaps even worse was the kind of shabby treatment inflicted upon us by the administrative officers. Not convinced that we were going to be a permanent part of the workings of their Department, these administrators had done absolutely nothing about the regular recommended promotions or pay scale increases. Indeed, when our own appropriations which we had carried with us from OSS ran out, they did nothing about getting emergency funds to pay the salaries of the analysts. . . . Many of them had drawn on their savings and whatever else they had to keep themselves and their families going. . . . Nothing I did seemed to have the slightest effect. . . . I am sure that if I wasn't on the verge of a nervous breakdown, I was perilously close to it.[55]

Kent rescued himself by leaving the State Department to join the staff of the National War College in 1947 and then returning to his history professorship at Yale University.

The decentralizers had crowed too soon, however, because their victory proved reversible. By the beginning of 1947, both Byrnes's health and his relationship with Truman had badly deteriorated, and he submitted his resignation on January 7. Truman promptly nominated George Marshall to replace him, a choice confirmed without difficulty by the Senate. The organizational relationship between the regional offices and their newly acquired "research divisions" had not been settled at the time of his arrival,[56] and the organizer of America's global victory in World War II had scant tolerance for administrative disarray. Russell, probably recognizing that his own fortunes would suffer under the new order of things, resigned on January 20. On January 30 Eddy recommended to Acheson that, in order for his office to meet its responsibilities "for planning and implementing a positive foreign intelligence program," the geographic analysis divisions be returned to ORI.[57] The next day, Acting Assistant Secretary for Administration John Peurifoy forwarded a plan from Eddy incorporating this proposal to Acheson and Marshall. Acheson added his endorsement, and Marshall ended the battle with the note "O.K. G.C.M."[58] On February 5, 1947, a directive ordered the recentralization of departmental research and intelligence operations.[59]

Adjusting some personnel loose ends made the centralizers' victory complete. Panuch was fired, and Eddy stepped down voluntarily in September. By October, Braden's relations with Acheson having become intolerable, his resignation was sought over long-running policy differences concerning Argentina unrelated to the intelligence question.[60] Nevertheless, although the victory of the centralizers was complete, it was hollow, since, as Acheson later observed, it came "a year too late," and "in the meantime events had passed us by."[61] The new Central Intelligence Agency was well on its way toward creation. Acheson observed: "I had the gravest forebodings about this organization and warned the President that as set up neither he, the National Security Council nor anyone else would be in a position to know what it was doing or to control it."[62]

5

Designing a Postwar System

The demise of the OSS did not end the issue of intelligence organization. The dispositions made by Executive Order 9621 were explicitly provisional, and, because it filled a still-recognized institutional need, establishing some sort of centralized postwar intelligence system remained an objective for policy makers. Indeed, even in the waning days of their organization's existence, senior OSS officers could speculate on what its nature should be. On August 31, 1945, the head of OSS operations in Europe wrote to his division chief in Washington, stressing the importance of secret intelligence (which he defined as uncovering, by clandestine methods, information that its holder did not wish revealed). In his message, he cited what he considered the basic requirements for an effective secret intelligence organization: undercover agents in the field; a competent headquarters staff to manage them; "virtually complete independence" from public government controls over the identity of personnel, funding, and internal organization; all necessary support from other government agencies; the vesting of operational control "in professional personnel who are personally secure, completely dependable, free from political pressures, and totally divorced from the actual formulation" of government policy; and a large secret budget. So important did he consider secret intelligence that he believed the agency established to collect it "should be devoid of responsibility for and direct participation in the formulation of foreign policy and should be equally free from political control or that of any single or exclusive group of policy forming agencies."[1]

Even though the existence of a centralized intelligence structure was never a matter of dispute, its specific organization quickly became one. While the creation of the Central Intelligence Agency was only a small part of the postwar national security reorganization debate, and one obscured by the conflict over military "unification," it nevertheless led to fierce and protracted dispute within the Truman administration between September 1945 and January 1946. Former OSS officer and CIA ancient Lawrence Houston, who was deeply involved in this issue, later recalled: "I witnessed one of the toughest bureaucratic fights—

tougher than I'd seen before; as tough as anything I saw afterwards—about the future of the intelligence services."[2] In the midst of the dispute, Budget Director Smith was even more outspoken in a message to presidential counselor Samuel Rosenman: "I consider this whole subject of intelligence to be one of the most far-reaching problems of interdepartmental coordination that we currently face. My own gloomy opinion is that it will not be solved in an orderly fashion and that we will go through the usual two, three or more reorganization stages— God bless bureaucracy."[3]

In addressing the issue, Truman had asked Admiral Leahy to review various proposals for intelligence reorganization, but Leahy, preoccupied with broader armed service unification issues, turned responsibility for intelligence matters over to a handsome, crafty, and extremely capable young lawyer from St. Louis named Clark Clifford. Clifford, a successful and well-connected corporation lawyer, had become a naval reserve officer in the later days of the war and had come to Washington to work in the White House Map Room (Roosevelt's wartime operations center) as deputy to presidential naval aide Captain James Vardaman. Although Clifford was largely unacquainted with Truman beforehand, the president soon recognized, and came to value, his dexterity as a policy expediter. Initially concerned over his lack of intelligence expertise, however, Clifford turned for advice to Sidney Souers from ONI. Souers, born and educated in Ohio, had settled in St. Louis in 1930 and had pursued a successful career in merchandising and insurance. Like Donovan, he had held a reserve commission before the war (but in the navy) and had been assigned to intelligence work. Called to active duty, he rose to rear admiral in December 1943 and had become assistant director of ONI in July 1944. Unlike the flamboyant Donovan, Souers was a steady and sagacious man, skilled at getting people to work together. Although he was never a political crony of Truman's, his quiet competence soon made him a trusted adviser. These talents would clearly be necessary because, in the policy debates, it soon became apparent that the armed services were not prepared to give up an independent intelligence role and that the Departments of State and Justice, as well as the Budget Bureau, had ideas of their own on what should be the shape of future intelligence organization.[4]

The Joint Chiefs of Staff were first through the gate with a proposal for postwar intelligence organization that proved seminal in all subsequent discussions. On September 19, 1945, Admiral Leahy, as JCS representative, forwarded a "Memorandum to the President" (through the secretaries of war and navy) concerning "Establishment of a central intelligence service upon liquidation of OSS." Noting Donovan's 1944 proposals and his communications with Smith, the paper asserted: "The end of hostilities has tended to emphasize the importance of proceeding without further delay to set up a central intelligence system." In the Joint Chiefs' view, "Recent developments in the field of new weapons have advanced the question of an efficient intelligence service to a position of importance, vital to the security of the nation in a degree never attained and never contemplated in the past. It is now entirely possible that failure to provide such a system might bring national disaster."

The Joint Chiefs agreed with Donovan that such functions as "coordination of intelligence activities," activities of "common concern," and the "synthesis of departmental intelligence on the strategic and national policy level" could be "more effectively carried on in a common intelligence agency, provided that suitable conditions of responsibility to the departments primarily concerned with national security are maintained." They nevertheless felt that Donovan's specific proposals were "open to serious objection in that, without compensating advantages, they would over-centralize the national intelligence service and place it at such a high level that it would control the operations of departmental intelligence agencies without responsibility, either individually or collectively, to the heads of the departments concerned." The Joint Chiefs felt that the "success of the proposed organization will depend largely on the Director of the Central Intelligence Agency." Therefore,

> [H]e should have considerable permanence in office, and to that end should be either a specially qualified civilian or an Army or Navy officer who can be assigned for the requisite period of time. It is considered absolutely essential, particularly in the case of the first director, that he be in a position to exercise impartial judgment in the many difficult problems of organization and cooperation which must be solved before an effective working organization can be established.

Appended to the memo was a proposed directive for the new structure, which, the Joint Chiefs felt, "retains the merits of General Donovan's proposals, while obviating the objection thereto." This directive was fully in line with past JCS thinking. It called for a National Intelligence Authority (NIA) composed of the secretaries of state, war, and navy and a JCS representative that would be responsible for overall intelligence planning and policy development, "and such inspection and coordination of all intelligence activities as to assure the most effective accomplishment of the intelligence mission related to national security." The NIA, in turn, would establish a Central Intelligence Agency headed by a director appointed and removed on NIA recommendation. The director would be responsible to the NIA and sit as a nonvoting member. He also would be assisted by an Intelligence Advisory Board (IAB) comprising "the heads of the principal military and civilian intelligence agencies having functions related to the national security" as determined by the NIA. The first responsibility of the NIA, assisted by the CIA and the IAB, would be to prepare and submit to the president a basic organizational plan and draft enabling legislation.

Under the JCS plan, the CIA's responsibility would be to accomplish "the synthesis of departmental intelligence relating to the national security and the appropriate dissemination within the government of the resulting strategic and national policy intelligence"; plan for "the coordination of the activities of all intelligence agencies of the government having functions related to the national security and recommend to the National Intelligence Authority the establishment of such over-all policies and objectives as will assure the most effective accomplishment of the national intelligence mission"; perform, "for the benefit of departmental intelligence agencies, such services as the National Intelligence Authority determines can be more efficiently accomplished by a common agency, including the direct procurement of intelligence"; and to carry out "such other functions and duties related to intelligence as the National Intelligence Authority may from time to time direct." The proposal explicitly stated that the CIA would have "no police or law enforcement functions."

The draft directive also made clear that existing departmental intelligence agencies would be allowed to collect, evaluate, synthesize, and disseminate intelligence required to carry out their "proper functions," subject to NIA coordination. The NIA also could designate that such "departmental operating intelligence" be made available to the CIA for synthesis. In addition, the NIA could authorize the CIA to inspect the operations of departmental intelligence agencies "in connection with its planning functions." Both the NIA and the CIA would be responsible for "fully protecting" intelligence sources and methods. The NIA would draw its funding from the participating departments "in amount and proportions to be agreed upon" by its members. Within the limits of this funding, the director of the CIA could acquire the necessary personnel, supplies, facilities, and services to carry out his mission. With NIA approval, the director also was authorized to call upon the various government agencies and the military "to furnish such specialists as may be required for supervisory and functional positions."[5]

The JCS plan appeared at a time when the military services themselves were taking a close look at the subject of postwar intelligence. On October 11 Colonel R. Ammi Cutter, aide to Assistant Secretary of War John McCloy, sent a memorandum to the new secretary, Robert Patterson (who had replaced the venerable Stimson in September), discussing the army's postwar intelligence plans and proposing that a committee be established to formulate a War Department position on foreign intelligence activities. Patterson liked the idea and, on October 22, created the Committee to Study War Department Intelligence Activities under Assistant Secretary of War for Air Robert Lovett. The committee included representatives of the Operations and Plans Division (OPD), army and army air forces intelligence (G-2 and A-2), army ground and service forces (combat and support components), and the SSU. It was charged with considering all studies on foreign intelligence activities made by any government agency, examining the adequacy of the War Department's intelligence organization, and formulating a departmental position and a plan for future departmental activity in the foreign intelligence field by November 3.

The Lovett committee diligently addressed its task. On October 23 Lovett instructed representatives of army commands to furnish him with reports dealing with their respective wartime intelligence organizations and activities, their "frank appraisal" of relations with other intelligence agencies, and their wartime problems in the field. They were also instructed to submit their views on "the most desirable organization and program" for American postwar intelligence, in particular, "views with respect to the desirability of establishing a central foreign intelligence unit, the place or Department in the Federal Government where this unit should be located, and the broad functions, responsibilities, and composition of such a central unit."[6] The committee solicited the views of army officers, as well as those of a number of OSS and other secret intelligence officers in Europe, such as David Bruce and William H. Jackson. In addition, the committee requested those of State Department intelligence chief McCormack as well. ONI head Inglis and FBI director Hoover also were invited to submit their opinions, but both declined.[7]

SSU chief Magruder responded to the committee's queries on October 26. After reviewing the wartime history of the OSS and the status of the SSU, he noted that the shortcomings of the wartime agency were due to the lack of a "centrally controlled and comprehensive espionage system" when the war began, and "no experience in the development and direction" of one. Such being the case, it had been necessary to improvise, resulting in overly hasty recruitment, an uneven quality of personnel, organizational confusion, an overdependence on the British and French, and inadequate cooperation between OSS and the State, War, and Navy Departments for the gathering, interchange, and evaluation of intelligence. In Magruder's opinion, a centralized agency was needed and should be established, although existing agencies would continue their functional role. He saw this need as particularly important "in view of the implications of the pivotal position which the United States now occupies in foreign affairs and the inescapable consequences of the release of atomic energy." To Magruder, the new agency would have six main requirements: responsibility for the control and coordination of intelligence activities (but without policy-making functions), the capacity for comprehensive analysis and synthesis of foreign intelligence, sole responsibility for secret intelligence and counterintelligence operations, concentration on foreign intelligence (to limit "justifiable suspicion" and to prevent "internal political" use of the agency), denial of any domestic police powers, and an independent budget.[8] He elaborated on these views in a detailed report appended to the memo.[9]

OPD, as the War Department's "think tank," also had clear ideas about postwar intelligence. In its response of October 28, OPD claimed that "a well-organized and thoroughly integrated national intelligence system in peace would have considerably increased our capabilities to make sound and timely estimates in the years prior to this war and would have materially improved our wartime intelligence." Therefore, OPD asserted boldly, the "problems which now face the U.S. and will continue to face this country in the future dictate that the heads of the State, War, and Navy Departments have knowledge of intentions and capabilities, both political and military, of other countries. The Central Intelligence Agency should be charged with preparing the required estimates which should be made available to the State, War, and Navy Departments and to the JCS to guide them in their plans and preparations." OPD accepted the basic JCS proposals but urged that the "field of intelligence should be considered as a whole"; it held that, while "broad policies must be evolved on the committee basis for the Central Intelligence Agency, the administration and operations undertaken by this Agency should not be subject to the details, compromises and inefficiencies inherent in discussions by committees and subcommittees, but rather should be the responsibility of single heads of subdivisions responsible to the Director of the Agency." It called for "the development of a comprehensive intelligence plan," which set down "intelligence objectives" and then went on to devise "the scheme for collecting information" and "the way in which the various agencies undertaking intelligence operations will function in the over-all pattern."

In OPD's view, the proposed CIA, as part of its mission, should be responsible for making sure that all "raw intelligence" became available to every government component with an interest; for developing the proposed "plan and program" for "an adequate foreign secret intelligence program" through interagency coordination; and for coordinating the intelligence activities of government agencies to determine and correct "omissions and duplication." OPD accepted the idea of an NIA but commented that, because it would be "rather public in character," it "will be well to hide the activities of the Central Intelligence Agency. An obscure location and name in the State Department might be a satisfactory method of achieving this objective." Believing that the CIA "should have a talented analysis and evaluation section," OPD suggested that "the OSS personnel and organization now assigned to the State Department . . . be retained for use in the Central Intelligence Agency" to prepare studies "which assist the Director and the Authority in determining the current intelligence objectives and the mechanisms for obtaining them," as well as becoming "the nucleus in preparation of long range over-all intelligence estimates." Concerning operational matters, OPD maintained that "any secret intelligence networks" and their personnel controlled by the War Department "should be retained for review" by the CIA's director "to determine whether he desires to use any personnel or operating facilities directly under his agency, the remaining personnel to be absorbed in existing departmental agencies." [10]

One of the more perceptive responses to the Lovett committee came from Major General Wilton Pearsons, chief of the Legislative and Liasion Division, entitled "Congressional Representation on the Proposed National Intelligence Council." In it, Pearsons straightforwardly declared that "Congress and the American people have always looked upon any secret intelligence organization with suspicion." He believed that this "antipathy" was "one of the greatest obstacles" to the organization of a central intelligence authority. He felt that public opinion was "at present" in favor of such an organization, but that "within ten or fifteen years" such public support would decline and funds would become increasingly difficult to obtain. In his judgment, the problem would be even more serious if there was no congressional understanding of "the policies and aims" of such an organization; therefore, it was "a matter of primary importance" to keep Congress informed. To solve this problem, he proposed that the presiding officers of the House and Senate select members of the two chambers to sit as observers on the NIA. This, he felt, would permit congressional involvement to allay any suspicions, while avoiding congressional participation in what he considered to be executive branch business. He maintained that such an arrangement would greatly aid in establishing a close liaison between a national intelligence authority and Congress, would decrease congressional (and hence public) distrust and suspicion of such an organization, and would enhance the chances of adequate future appropriations. [11]

As instructed, the Lovett committee filed its report on November 3. After noting that "prior to the war there was no adequate foreign intelligence system and intelligence techniques were not properly understood," that intelligence co-ordination had been lacking, and that it was "vital that there be created an organi-zation and system . . . adapted to future growth which will retain competent per-sonnel," the committee "unanimously reached the conclusion" that "as promptly as possible" the government should establish an NIA and a CIA. The committee's report followed the JCS plan closely but suggested that the NIA include the sec-retary of air should an independent air force be established and that, to ensure continuity of policy, the CIA director should have a term of at least six years. The committee also proposed that, within the CIA, there would be an Intelligence Board chaired by the director and comprising the heads of all government intel-ligence agencies, who would provide advice on agency operations and resolve interagency disputes. In the event of a disagreement between the director and the board, the director's view would be controlling, subject to appeal to the NIA. He would also consult the board "before delivering any estimates and appreciations to the President or any member of the cabinet," and any differences of opinion "should accompany the Director's report."

The CIA director would sit as a nonvoting member of the NIA and, under its supervision, be "independent" and "be supported by an independent budget" secured by appropriations that "should be obtainable without public hearings." The responsibilities of the CIA set forth by the Lovett committee also closely fol-lowed those enumerated by the JCS plan. The report made clear, however, that the CIA "should not conduct espionage activities within the United States" and "should have no police or law enforcement functions" either at home or abroad. Both the CIA and the NIA were to be charged with the responsibility for "fully protecting" sources and methods of intelligence, "which, due to their nature, have a direct and highly important bearing on military operations and national security." Provisions for the conduct of intelligence activities by existing agencies and co-option of personnel by the CIA also closely followed those of the JCS.[12]

In the Navy Department, the question of intelligence organization became part of a master plan for reorganizing the "national security" structure concep-tualized by Secretary James Forrestal that shaped the postwar American govern-ment. Forrestal, born in upstate New York not far from the Roosevelt estate to a family of moderate means, was a man of powerful intelligence and driving ambition who rose by his own efforts to become a millionaire Wall Street in-vestment banker. Appointed under secretary of the navy in 1940, he was instru-mental in making the U.S. Navy into the most formidable maritime force in his-tory. A driven and humorless man, Forrestal was a hard-shell realist in public affairs who, as navy secretary in 1945, viewed the world in the context of un-alloyed power politics. Guided by a strong sense of duty, he was determined that the United States would be prepared to meet its postwar global challenges. His wartime experiences gave him great admiration for the British "war cabinet" sys-tem, with its cadre of professional civil servants who could effectively translate decisions into action; he thus favored a similar system.[13]

Less formally than in the War Department, Forrestal began surveying the views of his department. On September 19 Forrestal's special assistant, Mathias Correa, sent him a memo based on the JCS plan concerning central intelligence. While unwilling to make a final proposal before studying the matter further and consulting "people with experience in the field" such as FBI director Hoover, Correa did delineate several "basic" propositions: that a centralized collection point for intelligence gathered by different agencies was necessary; that co-ordination was needed, and should be the "primary function" of a centralized agency; and that the State Department had the primary role in directing national policy based on the collected intelligence, including determining "appropriate action" by government agencies.[14]

In sharp contrast to Correa's restrained note was a message from Vice Admi-ral Samuel Robinson, chief of the Office of Procurement and Materiel, on Octo-ber 4. In his advocacy of a centralized intelligence system, Robinson presented an apocalyptic vision of the postwar world. "As a result of the developments of this war, it is believed that the United States has lost completely its security." Since it was possible, he felt, for the country to have excellent armed forces but still be defeated by surprise, it was necessary to have an adequate scientific research effort and properly organized intelligence. He believed that the first requirement was in the process of being met; on the second, however, he saw "no moves or plans that in the slightest degree are adequate to handle this situation." He considered State Department efforts to be "completely inadequate" for military intelligence purposes. Therefore, he proposed an intelligence organization that reported directly to the president, that received direct appropriations free of nor-mal government accounting procedures, with employees who were not part of the regular civil service, and with a director who would have a free hand in inter-nal administration. Most of the career personnel would be assigned abroad and be stationed in "those countries which are able to make war against the United States or which may in the near future be able to make war against the United States and especially those whose motives are at the present time unknown." The "sole directive" of the organization would be "to obtain advance information as to what foreign countries are preparing to attack the United States."

His delineation of potentially hostile states was equally horrific, even xenophobic. He saw three countries as potentially hostile: the Soviet Union, China, and Argentina (which, although admittedly weak, could become powerful). His view of other regions was equally bleak: "If our forces are withdrawn from Germany in the near future, that country would undoubtedly have to be added to the list. It may be that in a few years France and Great Britain would be added to the list. I can conceive of conditions arising in Brazil which would make it necessary to establish agents there, and, of course, the situation in Japan will depend entirely upon how long we occupy it." He maintained that since other nations were strengthening their postwar intelligence organizations, it was necessary for the United States to do likewise, lest "we will be destroyed some day by a jealous neighbor and without the slightest warning." Calling again for an independent intelligence organization, he concluded that the "adequacy with which we provide this service will probably decide the life of this nation." [15]

Forrestal was enough taken by Robinson's blast to refer it to Admiral King on the following day. On October 9 the chief of naval operations (CNO) replied: "As you know, and as Admiral Robinson probably does not know, the Joint Chiefs of Staff have recognized the inadequacy of the present organizations in various Governmental departments and have submitted to the Secretaries of War and Navy their recommendations for the creation of a central coordinating authority for the operation of an intelligence service of the United States." After summarizing the JCS plan, King concluded that "the present unsettled question concerning the reorganization of intelligence activities . . . should be resolved at the earliest practicable date. I recommend that the Navy Department press for an early establishment of the central intelligence agency along the lines recommended by the Joint Chiefs of Staff." [16]

King elaborated upon his views in a follow-up message to Forrestal on October 12. He advocated an effective postwar ONI, elimination of all "unnecessary duplication" of intelligence functions, unification of intelligence activities "of common concern . . . in order to synthesize Departmental intelligence of the strategic and national policy level" and to improve the facilities for the acquisition of secret foreign intelligence. While he favored postwar continuation and expansion of the joint army-navy intelligence activities established during the war, in his view: "Complete merger of the intelligence services of the State, War, and Navy Departments is not considered feasible or desirable since each of these departments requires operating intelligence which is of no value or interest to the others and in the acquisition and processing of which peculiar abilities and background knowledge are indispensable." He again endorsed the JCS plan and concluded by recommending that the secretary of state "be urged to expedite the establishment of an interdepartmental group" as called for by Truman in order to put the plan into effect.[17]

On October 15 the regular meeting that Forrestal held with his top aides dealt primarily with intelligence matters, and ONI chief Inglis did most of the talking. Launching into a lengthy discussion of the topic, Inglis said that one of the lessons of the recent conflict was that the United States must always be informed of the war potentialities of foreign countries, as well as their political philosophies. He believed that the United States and its allies had an excellent intelligence establishment, and he was unconcerned over adverse publicity, since criticism "places foreign nations off their guard and opens up sources of intelligence which we wouldn't have enjoyed in case they were alerted to our successes." Discussion moved to the navy's wartime intelligence work; Forrestal talked about the value of communications intelligence,[18] while Inglis described the close cooperation that had existed between the navy and other agencies.

In discussing postwar centralized intelligence plans, Inglis mentioned Donovan's 1944 scheme and its leakage to the press. ("The newspapers don't know just how accurate their reports were.") When asked by Forrestal about a role for the FBI in Donovan's plan, Inglis replied that the matter had not come up, since the proposed organization would be operating abroad. Emphasizing the autonomy of the proposed centralized intelligence agency, Inglis added: "Another objection, which perhaps is a little bit tenuous—some people might call it far-fetched—is that this man [the director of the proposed agency] being so close to the President, might, if the agency got into the wrong hands and with the wrong kind of personality as President, oversee what might become sort of a local Gestapo."

Inglis expressed his preference for the JCS plan but believed, "in view of the current political situation," that some sort of centralized agency would be created, whether the Departments of State, War, and Navy "want it or not." Therefore, he thought it would be necessary for the navy to maneuver carefully in any bureaucratic controversy in order to make sure that the new agency would not be hostile to naval interests. Although the navy had received nothing from the dissolution of OSS, it was united internally on intelligence matters; in case of conflicts, "if we exploit our balance of power position, . . . we stand a good chance of coming up pretty well."

He concluded by describing what he felt were basic intelligence requirements. In his view, only a few people in any new agency should deal with combat intelligence; along with Forrestal and the others attending, he believed that the military should be in charge of communications intelligence. He and Forrestal also agreed that the navy should begin negotiations with the State Department, in accordance with Truman's directive, on postwar intelligence plans in order that departmental interests could be protected. In response to a question from Forrestal, Inglis answered that the head of the projected agency could be either a civilian or a military officer; to him, it was important that he be a man "of mature judgment, of great tact, and yet considerable force of character, because he will be dealing with a number of conflicting personalities, a number of conflicting interests." [19]

With the War and Navy Departments largely of the same mind on the issue of postwar intelligence organization, they lost no time in making common cause. On October 13 Forrestal wrote to Patterson, suggesting cooperation in developing postwar intelligence plans. Forrestal, praising the September JCS plan as "soundly conceived," proposed that, "if you agree, I think we should push it vigorously at the White House." [20] The decision to collaborate was ratified by the postwar military chiefs as well. On December 29, newly installed Army Chief of Staff Eisenhower, in response to a proposal for closer intelligence collaboration between services from his navy counterpart, Admiral Chester Nimitz (who had assumed the CNO post earlier that month) said the idea was "fundamentally sound and must be done," since the matter "grows increasingly important with the development of armored forces, air forces, guided missiles, as well as naval forces." He then added:

> There is also the important field of foreign secret intelligence . . . which we developed from practically nothing before the war to a system of vital significance during the war. It has been proposed that this activity be placed in the National Intelligence Authority, if or when one is established, for the purpose of eliminating duplication and centralizing direction of this activity toward the purposes which have the greatest significance from the viewpoint of national security and policy. I think this is a correct view of the matter because the slender resources we have in this field must be conserved and the complicated nature of the work to be performed must receive the closest control of coordination, covering devices, security of sources, and verification of reports. [21]

Although the armed services were united behind the JCS proposal, they did not have the field of postwar intelligence planning entirely to themselves. Three civilian agencies—the Budget Bureau and the Justice and State Departments—had ideas of their own about the structure of postwar intelligence. For its part, the Budget Bureau had been examining the intelligence issue throughout the war.

As early as 1941, it had prepared a plan for a Central Intelligence Service organized on both a regional and a functional basis within the executive office. This plan envisioned a research organization providing the president and other senior officials with "immediate and background" information "on questions in the field of foreign policy and national defense" and "[c]riticizing on the basis of fuller information proposals submitted by government departments." It would also be responsible for "preparing factual releases on questions concerning which more accurate information is essential in the formation of public opinion."[22]

In July 1943, at the request of the army's deputy chief of staff and the navy's vice chief of naval operations, the bureau initiated a study of military intelligence and internal security operations. It was expanded in April 1945 to cover the government as a whole because, as analyst George Schwarzwalder wrote to his colleague Arnold Miles,

> of the large number of agencies and diversity of programs contributing to, or justified on the basis of, the intelligence needs of the government; the considerable overlap of these programs; the necessity for the Bureau to view them from an over-all point of view; the importance of safeguarding against the unplanned liquidation and loss of facility or operation useful to post-war needs for intelligence; and the vital need to coordinate and integrate the various programs which will provide maximum result with the minimum of cost, confusion and waste of effort.[23]

Following a series of staff studies, the Budget Bureau presented its official views to Truman on October 31 in a report entitled "Intelligence and Security Activities of the Government." This report, dated September 20, emphasized the disorderly growth of wartime intelligence activities from the "equally unplanned" prewar situation. The greatest past weaknesses were inadequate and poorly organized departmental facilities, lack of coordination, an emphasis on counterintelligence (called "security intelligence" throughout the report), and lack of centralized facilities to serve the president. These problems, in turn, led to a failure to properly set intelligence requirements, recognize trends, and develop overall perspectives. Pearl Harbor was cited as illustrating "the inadequacy of our total intelligence operation." The report concluded that a more widespread understanding of intelligence doctrine was necessary, that counterintelligence and intelligence collection should be separate functions, and that a high degree of coordination and cooperation was needed in the intelligence field.

The report specifically rejected the establishment of a highly centralized organization such as the OSS because "the principal intelligence operations of the

Government must be organized at the point where the decision is made." The OSS had been an emergency wartime agency resulting from inadequate prewar departmental intelligence programs. Therefore, it was not deemed wise to "continue a complete structure superimposed on top of the normal structure of Government beyond the period when our war needs demand it." The report did, however, concede that some centralization was appropriate for the conduct of secret intelligence, communications intelligence and cryptology, the maintenance of intelligence files, "to secure and harmonize intelligence, to reconcile conflicting intelligence," and to ensure proper utilization of all intelligence resources. The report was firm, nonetheless, stating: "Central facilities should not be created . . . to engage in operations which can be performed at the departmental level." Any independent facilities should be organized on a small scale within the presidential office and do nothing that could be done on an interdepartmental, coordinated basis.

To deal with intelligence coordination matters, the report proposed an Interdepartmental Intelligence Coordinating Committee, comprising the assistant secretaries of state, war, navy, and commerce, to deal with foreign intelligence, and an Interdepartmental Security Coordinating Committee, comprising the assistant secretaries of state, war, and Treasury and the assistant attorney general, which would be responsible for internal security and counterintelligence. Each committee would have its own staff to formulate overall policy and prepare government-wide directives and plans. For basic intelligence work, each department or agency was to put together an independent, centralized organization for the collection, analysis, and distribution of intelligence material. The War and Navy Departments were to be called upon to adjust their postwar operations to broader interdepartmental needs of a "national" nature and to place less emphasis on operational intelligence and counterintelligence. The primary role in the postwar system, however, was envisioned for the State Department. It was to lead the interdepartmental committees, serve "as a staff agency to the President," and "provide the principal facilities for bringing to bear on any high level problem the total intelligence available anywhere in the Government." To this end, the report urged the creation of a centralized intelligence office within the State Department to meet a long-held need and "to provide the place where leadership of the Government-wide intelligence activities would be centered." [24]

Because the Budget Bureau derived its bureaucratic influence from refereeing the programs of other agencies, and, with its emphasis on the predominant role of the State Department, its own plan never had a chance against that of the military establishment without a more active role by Byrnes. This was recognized in a memorandum to Smith on November 28 by Leonard Hoelscher, assistant chief of the bureau's Administrative Management Division, which complained that "the proposals for working out a total intelligence system continue to be confused with, or be subordinated to, secret intelligence operations," and that "there needs to be reemphasis placed upon the position of the State Department as the leader in the interdepartmental efforts through which a satisfactory solution of the postwar intelligence program will necessarily have to be developed." At Hoelscher's suggestion, Smith sent Truman a statement of bureau views, coupled with a request for presidential support. He repeated Hoelscher's argument that proposals for "a coordinated government-wide system" of intelligence were being subordinated to "centralized secret operations" under the "War Department" (i.e., Donovan) and JCS plans. He expressed the hope that Truman would meet with Byrnes to develop independent intelligence collection machinery under State Department authority.[25]

As the war approached its end, the Justice Department looked to the wartime experience of the FBI in Latin America as a model for a postwar foreign intelligence system. On February 20, 1945, Hoover received a detailed staff study on the issue, which faulted the Donovan and JCS proposals for establishing a new organization. The study claimed that the new organization would be too independent of existing departmental authority, too costly, too cumbersome and unwieldy to be effective, too duplicative of other agency activities, and too large to maintain the security necessary for intelligence operations. Instead, it proposed expanding "the time-proved program in operation in the Western Hemisphere" to a worldwide basis. Under this proposal, in each country "except those which are active theatres of [military] operation," Army G-2, ONI, and the FBI would maintain attachés with clearly defined intelligence responsibilities and "a sufficient number of open personnel . . . to permit proper gathering, correlation and transmission of information." In addition, each would have "such undercover organization as is necessary to a proper discharge of defined responsibility under all the circumstances existing in a particular country. Undercover agents operating on special assignments will function either directly under the Attaches or direct from the Washington headquarters of the three intelligence agencies when the occasion justifies." This plan "would not call for any superstructure whatsoever but would continue to operate with the same committee as originally set up by the President, . . . with the addition of a representative of policy-making rank for the State Department."

As far as intelligence analysis was concerned, the report recommended that "the analysis and research functions incidental to the operations of any intelligence agency designated to operate throughout the world" should be in the State Department, since a separate agency "in presenting its independent analysis of the information gathered would in effect control 'national planning and security' of the regular government agencies, inasmuch as they would be dependent on the agency for basic policy making, and would not have access to the original information. The danger of bias and coloring of the information gathered and of the final analysis would be inherent." [26]

Attorney General Biddle took up the matter with Truman not long after the new president took office. In a memo of April 20, 1945, he wrote:

> Bill Donovan of OSS suggested to President Roosevelt a rather complicated overall intelligence service in the foreign field. I think the President was never particularly enthusiastic about it, but asked for comments from various Departments concerned. . . . Ultimately, a foreign intelligence service should undoubtedly be organized. . . . A practical approach would be to build up the system presently used in Latin America where each Embassy is attached a Military Attache, a Naval Attache, and a Legal Attache (FBI in disguise). This has worked well and there are funds in various departments available for expanding it. I am strongly opposed to any legislation, or asking Congress for an appropriation. An intelligence service must be built gradually and secretly, not with a brass band. [27]

Biddle soon resigned over a political disagreement with Truman, however, and on August 29 Hoover raised the intelligence issue with his successor, Tom Clark. Noting the activities of Donovan and the State Department, he observed that "time is of the very essence in reaching a decision as to the future of the SIS program. As I have told you previously, I am not seeking for the Federal Bureau of Investigation the responsibility for a world-wide intelligence system. I am firmly convinced, however, in light of our experiences during and even before the current world war that the future welfare of the United States necessitates and demands the operation of an efficient world-wide intelligence service." He stated that SIS operations in Latin America had been "completely successful" and had "produced results which were beyond our hope and expectations when we went into this field and these results were brought about without the slightest friction in the countries where we operated." Hoover felt, therefore, that, because of the need for a global intelligence system, it was "most logical that the system which has worked so successfully in the Western Hemisphere should be extended to a world-wide coverage." In his view, establishing such a system could be accomplished without legislation that would call attention to "the operation of an international espionage organization." He concluded by urging Clark to take the matter up with Secretary of State Byrnes without delay.[28]

The result of the Justice Department's thinking was a memorandum from Attorney General Clark to the Budget Bureau's director Smith and assistant director Appleby on September 21, entitled "A Plan for U.S. Secret World-Wide Intelligence Coverage," based on the FBI's Latin American experience. The memo strongly declared: "Intelligence coverage must be had immediately. There is no time for training and organizing a new corps. . . . It is proposed that the time-proved program in operation in the Western Hemisphere be extended on a world-wide basis with certain modifications." The plan proposed setting up, in every diplomatic mission, a committee composed of representatives of G-2, ONI, and the FBI. Each member would concentrate on his special area of competence, but the committee would confer daily with the ambassador, closely correlate its operations, and report through State Department channels. A board composed of the secretaries of state, war, and navy and the attorney general would make basic intelligence policy, and an "operational committee" would include an assistant secretary of state, the heads of G-2 and ONI, and the FBI director. Within the State Department, there would be an evaluation unit to receive intelligence data from the field. Boasting of how successful such an organization had been in Latin America and how rapidly it could be instituted worldwide, the memo emphasized: "Foreign and domestic intelligence are inseparable and constitute one field of operation. . . . In order to cope with the activities of various subversive agents in the United States with speed and dispatch, it is entirely evident that their activities must be followed throughout the various countries by one intelligence agency of the United States Government." It argued further that internal police work and foreign intelligence collection could thus be combined, and, although the charge of "Gestapo" could be raised, the highly successful system thus described had a record of protecting civil liberties that had been "highly praised even by the American Civil Liberties Union."[29]

The Justice Department's plan nevertheless did not prosper. Upon learning of McCormack's appointment, Hoover again wrote to Clark on September 27, commenting that the action "clearly indicates that the World-Wide Intelligence Service will be operated by and as a State Department project. I think, consequently, that it would be well . . . to bring to President Truman's attention in the immediate future our views to the most desirable way to establish the World-Wide Intelligence Service."[30] In accord with this view, Hoover sent his deputy, Morton Chiles, to the White House on October 2 to discuss the issue directly with Truman. While Truman was congenial, praised the work of the FBI, and agreed that it was difficult to separate foreign and domestic intelligence, he nevertheless indicated his view that the FBI's responsibilities should be domestic and observed that the Justice Department's plan would raise concerns over creating a "Gestapo." He told Chiles that he was considering plans for some sort of intelligence agency that would be directly responsible to the president. Chiles suggested that before he made a decision, Truman should consider conferring with Hoover on the subject.[31]

The Justice Department's plan met its end at the hands of the Budget Bureau. On October 26, in a memorandum coordinated with the State Department, Donald Stone, assistant director in charge of the bureau's Administrative Management Division, described the plan's shortcomings to Appleby. Although seeing some merit in overseas counterintelligence work, Stone thought that the FBI's experience in Latin America was not applicable to the "big league" because the intelligence effort had not been directed at those countries but rather toward third parties and had enjoyed official cooperation locally. He also questioned whether it had been as successful as advertised. In addition, the plan seemed to center all activity under the "legal attaché," neglected "basic intelligence," and distorted the local ambassador's "over-all view" by concentrating on counterintelligence. Considering the coordination proposals unsatisfactory, Stone concluded: "Coordination can only be achieved by central preparation of detailed operating plans. . . . The Justice proposal actually would permit the FBI to have all responsibility for secret intelligence under only the mildest kind of direction."[32]

Clark was informed that his plan had been rejected on October 31. In his memorandum, Appleby explained that the FBI's Latin American experience had been far too limited to be used worldwide and had concentrated too much on counterintelligence to meet the needs of "more fundamental and long-range matters" in a large number of other areas. Noting Truman's instructions to Byrnes on September 20, and the need for careful planning, he concluded: "I am informed that the State Department will soon be taking the initial steps to create the interdepartmental committees necessary to begin this long-range job."[33]

Appleby understated the case, since it was the State Department that mounted the most significant challenge to the JCS-originated plan favored by the military establishment. Byrnes, his mind usually on the ordering of postwar Europe, had few ideas of his own on intelligence matters. At a meeting with Patterson and Forrestal on October 16, he went along with the JCS idea of a single intelligence organization responsible to a cabinet committee comprising the secretaries of state, war, and navy, but usually gave little attention to details.[34] The State Department's advocate, therefore, became the dynamic and ambitious McCormack, who had strong views of his own on how a postwar intelligence organization should be structured, which he made clear to ONI chief Admiral Inglis in a conversation on October 31. While McCormack went along with an oversight committee made up of the three secretaries, he was strongly opposed to any sort of Central Intelligence Agency and maintained that each department should have its own "unfettered" intelligence service. Duplication did not bother him, since he felt that competition was "healthy."[35] In November, McCormack prepared a detailed staff paper in which he recommended that, although foreign espionage and counterespionage operations could be centrally conducted, analysis should be carried out on a decentralized basis, coordinated by two interdepartmental bodies — one responsible for foreign intelligence and the other for internal security and domestic counterintelligence. The production of "national intelligence estimates" (i.e., a complete overall assessment of a foreign situation relevant to the formulation of national security policy) would be the responsibility of his office within the State Department, in collaboration with representatives of other interested agencies.[36]

McCormack's strong views could not fail to generate contention with his War and Navy Department counterparts. At a meeting on November 19 with Lovett and General George Brownell from the former and Souers and Correa from the latter, matters quickly reached an impasse. McCormack argued that Truman's September 20 letter to Byrnes was a mandate for the State Department to take the lead not only in developing an interdepartmental intelligence program but also in putting it into operation, while the others felt that it meant only that the State Department should have a leading role in formulating plans for presidential approval. McCormack also felt that the head of the overall intelligence coordinating body ought to be chosen by the secretary of state, whereas the others argued that he should be appointed by the president upon the recommendation of the three secretaries and be responsible to them.[37]

On December 3 Byrnes sent a memo to the War and Navy Departments, as well as to the White House, setting down a State Department blueprint for a foreign intelligence organization, based on McCormack's thinking. Like the JCS plan, it accepted an NIA, but it would be chaired by the secretary of state and be authorized to call upon the resources of all federal agencies to develop a comprehensive, government-wide intelligence collection program. To avoid publicity and to "reduce competition and duplication between the central agency and the intelligence organizations of existing agencies," personnel would be drawn from all agencies, and there would be no "independent agency with a separate budget." Overall supervision of the intelligence program would be in the hands of an executive secretary from the State Department, appointed by the secretary of state with the concurrence of the secretaries of war and navy. Continuing, the memo observed: "In that manner the coordinating responsibility of the State Department for matters involving foreign affairs is recognized, but the executive is made a representative of the Authority as a whole and not merely of a single Department." The executive secretary would provide "planning mechanisms" that would vest responsibility for particular subjects, areas, or operations in a single existing agency or establish working groups from several agencies. While the plan conceded that such "clandestine activities" as foreign espionage and counterespionage could be conducted by a "central agency," it did not provide for one. Under the supervision of the executive secretary, the coordination of intelligence collection and analysis would be done through a series of interdepartmental committees, each chaired by a representative of the agency with the primary subject matter interest. In addition, there would be committees focusing on such "internal security" matters as travel control, personnel investigations, communications and information security, and censorship planning. Attached to the executive secretary's office would be interdepartmental advisory groups for intelligence and security, and administrative services would be provided by the State Department.[38]

McCormack himself expanded on Byrnes's memo in messages of his own to the secretaries of war and navy. Writing on December 15, he emphasized that the executive secretary would represent the NIA "as a whole" and could be removed by a majority decision. He also emphasized that the War and Navy Departments could appoint their intelligence chiefs to the advisory boards that would review all recommendations "for the intelligence program or for any operating plan designed to carry it out." Again conceding a centralized foreign espionage organization, he nevertheless felt that giving it an independent budget "should be avoided for security reasons" and that "a nondepartmental agency without an independent budget appears to be impossible." Therefore, an "interdepartmental type of organization" should be in the State Department "because of the responsibility of the Secretary of State for foreign affairs."[39]

The military establishment clearly recognized the challenge posed by the State Department plan to its own ideas. Writing to newly installed Chief of Staff Eisenhower on December 20, Secretary Patterson observed: "Efforts are being made, as you doubtless know, to organize a Central Intelligence Agency Government-wide but principally State, War, and Navy." Noting the ongoing discussions, he added that "there was no agreement on the central question which was whether the post of Director should be in an independent agency under the leadership of the three Secretaries or whether this post should be primarily under the Secretary of State."[40] Similarly, in the Navy Department, Admiral Nimitz, not long after being installed as CNO, wrote Forrestal to endorse the JCS plan and declare that the State Department alternative was "unsatisfactory in many respects." He felt that the strength of the JCS plan was in its creation of a CIA, since such an organization was "needed and when functioning properly should eliminate much unnecessary duplication through the pooling of personnel from the participating departments. It should provide the same intelligence estimates directly to the President and the three Secretaries to enable them to be uniformly informed. It should also supply the participating departments with intelligence of common interest which they require." He favored the idea that the president appoint the CIA director, upon nomination by the NIA, but recommended that the nominee be a military officer, since this would "assure a non-political administration of the intelligence effort and objective intelligence estimates." A military officer would also be "subject to military discipline" and could be "required to avoid publicity which is undesirable in the conduct of intelligence activity."[41]

On December 27 McCormack and his deputy, Ludwell Montague, met again with Souers and Correa from the Navy Department and General George Brownell and three other generals from the War Department. Disagreement soon became intractable. McCormack felt that, at least initially, the new CIA should not have operational functions. The war and navy representatives disagreed, feeling that operations should be included, along with planning and coordinating responsibilities, at the outset. The War Department representatives favored an independent intelligence agency but were willing to have it within the State Department as long as its chief had no departmental intelligence responsibilities. This McCormack found unacceptable. Although dubious about an independent budget, the navy representatives also favored an agency free of any connection with an existing department. McCormack again registered opposition and suggested that the question be resolved by the three secretaries and the president.[42]

Faced with McCormack's resistance, the military establishment sought to exploit its "Missouri connection" to lobby the White House. On December 27 Souers wrote presidential adviser Clark Clifford concerning the rival JCS and State Department plans. He complained that the State Department's proposal denied the armed services an adequate voice in intelligence activities, insisted that "every safeguard should be imposed to prevent one department from having the opportunity to interpret information in such a way as to make it seem to support previously accepted policies or preconceived opinions," and maintained that under the State Department plan, it would be "inevitable" that the new organizational setup "would be looked on in time as a State Department intelligence system and not an inter-governmental system." On the other hand, the JCS proposal "seems more likely to provide the President with unbiased intelligence derived from all available sources, and approved by all three departments of Government primarily concerned with foreign policy." He therefore recommended that any future intelligence directive be in accord with the JCS proposal because it established clear presidential authority, operated "on a level higher than any single department," effectively pooled many functions carried on by various agencies, provided for preparing intelligence summaries and estimates, and contemplated "a full partnership between the three departments, created and operated in a spirit of free consideration, and with a feeling of a full share of responsibility for its success."[43]

The line was finally drawn on January 6, 1946, when Forrestal and Acting Secretary of War Kenneth Royall presented Byrnes with a formal rejection of the State Department plan, finding it "inadequate" in two "essential" respects. First, it failed "to provide for a centralized executive organization responsible only to the National Intelligence Authority and actively assisted by the chief intelligence officials of the three departments." It also failed "to provide for centralized performance of two important operating functions, evaluation on a national level and direction of foreign secret intelligence and counterintelligence, with appropriate dissemination in each case." As concessions to the State Department, Royall and Forrestal suggested that the new centralized organization would be "in," but not "of," the State Department and that its director could be, or could become, a departmental official but would be appointed by the president and be responsible to the NIA. Administrative services would be performed by the State Department, and personnel seconded from other parts of the government would have no responsibilities to their home agencies. The director of the CIA also would have no such responsibilities, but they insisted that "national-level" intelligence evaluation and the direction of foreign intelligence and counterintelligence had to be centralized in the NIA.[44]

The combative McCormack did not give ground easily, however, and clung rigorously to his original plan. On January 7 he dismissed the compromise proposals from the War and Navy Departments to Byrnes as "unworkable"[45] and responded to the military's lobbying of the White House with a démarche of his own. On January 10 he forwarded a brilliantly written memo to Budget Bureau director Smith defending his plan, which Smith promptly passed on to presidential adviser Rosenman. McCormack's paper, representing as it does a major "road not taken," is one of the seminal documents in the intelligence debate. It offered an alternative to both the imperial vision of Donovan and the confederal approach of the JCS, and therefore must be considered at length.

McCormack began by discussing several "concepts" of a Central Intelligence Agency. The first was a Central Evaluating Agency involving "a single place into which every paper of possible intelligence value comes and is read, circulated to those interested and 'evaluated.' . . . Such an organization working in peace-time, covering the whole world and serving the needs of the whole government, would be so large in size as to be wholly impracticable, even if desirable." In describing his second concept, a "Coordinator of Information," McCormack observed that this had been

> the original concept of General Donovan — an agency that would receive the "processed" information and intelligence reports produced by all other agencies of government and would put them together, coming out with a finished product called "strategic intelligence." General Donovan found that it was almost impossible to fill such a role, partly because it was difficult to get the information from other agencies, partly because it was impossible to judge how good the information was without having a separate research organization to check it out and a field organization to verify it, and to get additional information.

This line of reasoning led McCormack to his third concept, which he called the "Coordinator of Information Plus." In his view, this had been "the role that the OSS attempted to fill during the war — a Coordinator of Information with his own intelligence collecting organization, plus a research staff to do the evaluating and produce the final studies." McCormack was equally critical of this concept.

> While the OSS accomplished a great deal during the war, it came nowhere near to filling the role that it desired, chiefly because of its remoteness from the operating units. Where, as with certain of the political divisions at the State Department, the OSS research organization found a good customer and got very close to operating problems, the results were excellent. When that condition did not prevail, the reports tended to be academic and unrelated to the real problems of the Government. Reports were frequently based on less than all the available information, not because the information was withheld but because OSS tried to cover so large a field of intelligence that it could not maintain adequate machinery for getting all the available information.

McCormack's final concept (and the one he favored) was that of an Inter-departmental Coordinating and Planning Mechanism, which was based on his view that government agencies had "vast resources for the collection of information and the production of intelligence" to be "harnessed and used" in a time of government retrenchment. The best way to do this, he felt, was "to distribute the intelligence function widely through the Government, giving to each specialized unit the job that it is best qualified to do, providing for cooperative undertakings on subjects of inter-departmental interest and setting up machinery that will insure the flow of intelligence to those who need to have it." He went on to develop this concept by arguing that, while "the importance of collecting more information is not under-estimated (including the importance of using unconventional methods where necessary), the critical process in intelligence is performed at the research desk. . . . Adequate performance of the research function requires the use of experts, and they are to be found in those departments and agencies which have the operating and policy responsibilities in a particular field." He thus felt that the "great need in Government today is not a super-intelligence agency but is the development of a Government-wide intelligence program that can be translated into specific operating plans, under which responsibilities will be clearly defined and allocated."

This conclusion led him to object to the "War Department plan" for "a new, separate and 'independent' agency (though their 'independent' director would be subject to so many controls by the military that his 'independence' would be nonexistent)." He felt that "a new, separate agency will have difficulty getting money from Congress, or by means of departmental contributions of funds; and it will be in competition with existing intelligence agencies for funds, personnel and assignments." In addition, if the United States was "going to do secret intelligence, we should not advertise the fact, nor should we set up an agency with pretentious titles. I think the term 'Central Intelligence Agency' is both misleading and dangerous. . . . To my mind, a sound program would attempt to build up the existing intelligence units to maximum efficiency and would allocate to the central agency only those functions which clearly can be performed by a central organization." He then described how various analytical roles could be accomplished by specific agencies (e.g., various types of economic and financial analysis by the Departments of Commerce, Treasury, and Labor, or the Federal Reserve) or on an interdepartmental basis (e.g., "weekly reporting of foreign events" or "geographical intelligence"). Responsibility for administering this program would be in the hands of a "central planning and programming organization."

He further objected to the idea of centralized conduct of "secret intelligence" and the preparation of "strategic" intelligence reports. He agreed that

"secret" intelligence, in the sense in which it is done by the British Secret Intelligence Service, should be done by a single agency. But in no Government, including the British Government, is there the kind of exclusive franchise that the War Department [sic] is talking about. In fact, the most important "secret" intelligence is done so secretly that nobody knows who does it. . . . The State Department has not opposed putting secret intelligence under a central agency, but it would oppose it if the central agency were under the President, because such operations might compromise the President.

As far as the preparation of "strategic intelligence" was concerned, McCormack felt that "apart from the strictly military aspects for which it is necessary to rely on the Armed Forces, 'strategic intelligence' is by definition a function of the Department of Government which is responsible for foreign affairs." In his view, if the State Department "is not now equipped to discharge the [intelligence] function," this weakness was "not a good reason for refusing to strengthen it by giving it its appropriate functions in foreign intelligence and the means with which to discharge them."

McCormack concluded by discussing the conduct of intelligence operations overseas. In such activities, "the chief coordinating responsibility is now vested in the representatives of the State Department abroad, who have administrative supervision of the Service Attaches and of the various civilian attaches. . . . The counter-espionage organization of OSS . . . operates outside the theaters [of military operations] under State Department cover. . . . The same is increasingly true of the SI [secret intelligence] personnel in countries not under military occupation." This led him to declare that such a coordinating role overseas "calls for somewhat the same type of coordination at the seat of Government."[46]

For all its vigor and lucidity, however, McCormack's paper represented no more than a brave last stand. His very intransigence on the issue was a manifestation of his isolation within the bureaucracy. Not only was he outmatched by the combined power of the War and Navy Departments, but by January 1946 he was isolated in his own department as well by the resistance of the regional assistant secretaries and the tepid support of an increasingly distracted Secretary Byrnes. In addition, his weak position was known in other government agencies.[47] For their parts, the unity and common purpose of the civilian and uniformed leaders of the military establishment gave them overwhelming influence when the White House decided to take a direct hand in resolving the intelligence issue.

On November 7, 1945, Truman had received an unsigned staff memo that noted: "It appears that the development of plans for a coordinated Foreign Intelligence Program for all Federal Agencies concerned is bogged down because the War and Navy Departments believe that the problem is being worked out by the Department of State in obedience to the President's letter to the Secretary of State dated 20 September 1945." The memo observed that the "only apparently promising prospect of getting useful action on this problem in the near future" would be for Truman himself "to call a conference with the Secretaries of State, War, and Navy and direct them to work together in preparation of a plan for the establishment of a Central Intelligence Service" that would be mutually acceptable by December 31. On the margin, Truman scribbled a note to his appointments secretary, Matthew Connelly: "Set this up."[48]

Under presidential goad, the three secretaries met to resolve their differences on November 14. Also present were Lovett and Colonel Charles McCarthy from the War Department, Correa, and Assistant Secretary of State H. Freeman Matthews. Patterson and Forrestal promptly embraced the JCS plan, and Byrnes implicitly abandoned that advanced by McCormack. The three secretaries also dismissed the Budget Bureau proposal. Byrnes felt that the plan was too elaborate and left collection in too many hands, and he objected to the heavy emphasis on research and analysis. Lovett, who added his opinion that the plan had "too many aspects of a town meeting," disliked the multiple collection approach within separate departments. All agreed that the FBI should not be included in the NIA, in order that police work and foreign intelligence remain separate. In Lovett's view, combining the two would lead to a "gestapo." All agreed, however, that the FBI should be included on any advisory board, because of its skill at preparing false documents and its excellent personality file. All also concurred with a suggestion by Byrnes to institute a working group to resolve further details, since an agreement had been reached for a centralized intelligence agency. Patterson concluded the meeting by asking for suggestions on the best man to head the new agency. Lovett replied that the only name he had heard was that of Allen Dulles, at that time a prominent New York attorney and wartime chief of the OSS station in Switzerland.[49]

Budget Bureau director Smith also had been pressing for a meeting, complaining to Truman on November 28 that the intelligence reorganization issue, "like too many other things now," was "getting royally bitched up." In raising the idea for a meeting including the president himself, he added that his own presence might be helpful. Truman responded, "Of course I would like to have you sit in. I will let you know when we have any such meeting."[50] Events moved in the direction Smith favored. Even as their subordinates bickered, the three secretaries had been working on a settlement, and it was clear from the results that McCormack's plan never had a chance. On January 7, 1946, Forrestal, Royall, and Byrnes presented Truman with a proposal for a consolidated foreign intelligence system that closely followed the JCS plan of September 1945. Concluded the secretaries: "It is believed to be desirable that the details of the organization should be worked out in the first instance by the officials who will be responsible for its performance."[51]

On January 9 Truman held his meeting on the intelligence issue. Also in attendance were Admiral Leahy, Truman's military aide, Brigadier General Harry Vaughn, naval aide Vardaman, counsel Rosenman, Smith, and several naval representatives. No one from the War Department was present. McCormack had gone out of town after preparing his lucubration to Smith; his absence was fatal, since the meeting sounded the death knell for the State Department's pretensions in the intelligence field. Smith recorded: "The implication of most of the statements made at the meeting was that intelligence could not be handled in the State Department because that department was too weak." In the discussions Smith pointed out that, during the war, the army and navy, as well as the FBI in Latin America, had "people falling all over themselves in the field of intelligence," and "while we might put up with this kind of situation during a war, we could not do so as a practical matter while carrying on a continuing basis a 25-billion-dollar budget during peacetime."

When Leahy commented that Smith was heavily focusing on the budget, Smith replied that the issue was one of organization. Leahy conceded that "intelligence had been handled in a disgraceful way, and he said that he could not get any intelligence out of the Army, the Navy, or the State Department during the war." In his presentation to Truman, Smith emphasized that the issue was an important one and that "when a subject is left to the departments to divide up among themselves, the worst possible compromise results, and that the President himself must decide how he wants intelligence activities organized." He continued that he had followed the subject closely because it had great bearing on the expanded American role in international affairs and had come to the conclusion that there did not seem to be a clear understanding of what kind of intelligence was being discussed and there was a need for some definition. He concluded: "I am not so sure that we are not approaching the subject of intelligence in the most unintelligent fashion." [52]

With no major alternatives presented, Truman readily accepted the well-developed state-war-navy intelligence plan.[53] Clifford drafted the appropriate presidential directive,[54] which was forwarded to Attorney General Clark for legal review. Clark returned his concurrence on January 19,[55] and, on January 22, 1946, Truman issued his Directive on Coordination of Foreign Intelligence Activities to the secretaries of state, war, and navy. The three, together with a "personal representative" of the president, were designated the National Intelligence Authority, in order that "all Federal foreign intelligence activities be planned, developed and coordinated so as to assure the most effective accomplishment of the intelligence mission related to the national security." Subordinate to the NIA, under a presidentially appointed director of central intelligence (DCI), was a Central Intelligence Group (CIG), which would draw its funds, facilities, and personnel from the three departments represented on the NIA. The DCI was responsible for the "correlation and evaluation" of intelligence information, its dissemination as "strategic and national policy intelligence" within the government, coordination and planning of intelligence work by the three departments of the NIA, the performance of such "services of common concern" as the NIA determined, and "such other functions and duties related to intelligence affecting the national security" as determined by the president and the NIA. The CIG was denied any "police, law enforcement, or internal security" functions. Although departmental intelligence agencies would continue to function, their operations and collected information would be open to inspection by the DCI. An Intelligence Advisory Board, comprising "the heads (or their representatives) of the principal military and civilian intelligence agencies of the Government having functions related to the national security," was established to advise the DCI.[56]

With the organization now in place, the next step was naming its leaders. On January 23 Truman chose Admiral Leahy as his "personal representative" on the NIA.[57] Naming the DCI became a matter of speculation as the directive had neared completion. On January 18, businessman and former senior OSS officer David Bruce wrote to Forrestal to suggest Allen Dulles. Although admitting that, since Dulles was a Republican, his appointment "might be politically impracticable," Bruce claimed that his view represented that of many who had worked with Dulles. Bruce added that he considered Dulles "a man of extraordinary ability in the foreign intelligence field. He would command the respect of all scholars associated with the enterprise, he served for many years, with great distinction in the State Department, he knows the political scene thoroughly, his technical knowledge of clandestine operations is unsurpassed, and his personal integrity and character would be a guarantee that funds placed under his control would be scrupulously expended."[58] If Forrestal passed this suggestion on to Truman, he paid it no mind. On January 23 he named the competent and reliable Souers as DCI.[59] Parallel letters informed Byrnes, Patterson, and Forrestal of the appointments.[60]

On the following day, Truman staged his own special induction ceremony for his new appointees. Lunching with Leahy, Souers, and members of the White House staff, Truman rose, asked the two to stand, and read a mock "directive" naming Leahy as "front end snooper" and Souers as "rear." Truman then called for "appropriate" uniforms, and naval aide Vardaman produced two black cloaks, two black hats "of the highwayman style," and two wooden daggers. Amid considerable laughter, Vardaman put a flowing black false mustache on Leahy. (Souers had a natural one already.) Commented assistant press secretary Eben Ayers: "The two admirals made an excellent pair of 'cloak & dagger' men."[61] At a press conference that day, Truman called the NIA "a practical program" and "a necessary arrangement" in order to "have all the information available for the people who need it in implementing foreign policy." He also denied that the NIA was a revival of the OSS.[62]

In such an informal fashion did America's peacetime central intelligence system come into being, and its birth did not pass entirely unnoticed. In a concise, accurate article, *Time* (then America's premier news magazine, exercising considerable influence on public opinion in those pre-television days) commented that the new system was "based on a modified proposal from the Joint Chiefs of Staff." It observed, in its own unique style, that "Bill Donovan, back in Manhattan practicing law, did not mourn too loudly the kicking around his original plan had got. Any kind of intelligence coordination agency, he argued, was a realistic step in a confused and dangerous world." Not missing the impact of Truman's action, the magazine noted that the United States "is going to join, after all these years, in the game of spying on the neighbors. Harry Truman did not say so, but that is the idea. Other great powers have always maintained espionage systems along with their armies and navies. The U.S., with a mixture of trust and indifference, never has. . . . That historical innocence, which ended with the fiasco at Pearl Harbor, is now gone."[63]

The *New York Times* (then the only really "national" newspaper in the United States) carried a brief descriptive article on Truman's action on January 23,[64] and it fell to the paper's renowned military analyst, Hanson Baldwin, to fully evaluate the importance of the event. In an article entitled "Defense Improvements," he hailed the creation of the NIA, along with the establishment of the new multi-service National War College, as "the two most important basic developments in the national defense picture since the end of the war." He observed: "In an age of atom bombs, of transoceanic rockets and of submarines that can cross the Atlantic at twenty-five knots submerged [a high speed in 1946] any effective military system is impossible without adequate intelligence of what is going on . . . in all parts of the world. Intelligence today is most emphatically the first line of defense." In reviewing the past development of U.S. intelligence, he faulted both the army and the navy in the prewar period for inadequately collecting and analyzing information about potential adversaries, noting tartly, "nor did the establishment of the virtually independent Office of Strategic Services make up for this." He believed that the OSS had been, at best, a "spotty" organization, "which did some brilliant work, and some almost unbelievably amateurish" because "intelligence organizations of OSS scope are not created in a hurry; they are a product of slow and painful growth." He concluded, therefore, that it was "high time" for the creation of the NIA, "which becomes, in a sense, the peacetime counterpart to the OSS." He regarded the new system as a "very considerable forward step" but felt its future effectiveness "will depend entirely upon the cooperation given it by Government departments, the support of the Administration and Congress, and the type of personnel Admiral Souers selects."[65] Souers, and his successor, would focus on those problems in the months ahead.

6

The Central Intelligence Debate

Because the Central Intelligence Agency was established by legislative enactment, its creation was preceded by a public debate on intelligence issues that was quite extensive, considering the clandestine nature of the topic. Although this issue, like most concerning national security matters, was far from the general public's attention, the question of a centralized intelligence organization, as a component of a comprehensive U.S. national security apparatus, was clearly defined in the public record. In these public discussions, several basic themes were repeatedly emphasized: the inadequacy of America's prewar intelligence system (which was held responsible in large part for the surprise at Pearl Harbor); that in the future (as a result of long-range bombers, guided missles, and atomic bombs) the oceans would no longer serve as a protective moat for the United States—thus making a "future Pearl Harbor" fatal; and, finally, that a centralized intelligence system was necessary not only to give warning of aggressive intent by a hostile foreign power but also to furnish the information necessary for the United States to meet its postwar responsibilities.

One of the boldest assertions of this new level of threat to the United States was made by General Henry "Hap" Arnold, chief of the army air forces, in a published "report" to the secretary of war, which asserted: "With present equipment, an enemy Air Power can, without warning, pass over all formerly visualized barriers or 'lines of defense' and can deliver devastating blows at our population centers and our industrial, economic, or governmental heart even before surface forces can be deployed. . . . War may descend upon us by thousands of robots passing unannounced across our shorelines—unless we act now to prevent them."[1]

This handsomely produced and lavishly illustrated booklet was obviously prepared for public consumption and did indeed receive journalistic attention. In November 1945 *Life* magazine carried Arnold's message to millions in a well-illustrated article entitled "The 36-Hour War," in which an unnamed aggressor launches an attack upon the United States with nuclear-armed intercontinental missiles. Although some of the missiles are detected by an American early warning system and destroyed by U.S. anti-missiles, the initial attack wipes out thirteen major cities and kills ten million people. The United States launches a retaliatory attack with its own missiles (housed in underground silos connected by tunnels to atomic bomb factories) and destroys the enemy country. Although the United States thus "wins the atomic war," forty million Americans have been killed, and every city with over fifty thousand inhabitants has been leveled.[2] This sort of horrific vision not only shaped the central intelligence debate but also became a fixture in American thought and culture for the next fifty years.

Perhaps the first government official to publicly discuss postwar intelligence reform was the ubiquitous Harold Smith. In a statement presented on May 18, 1944, to a select House committee on postwar military reform, he emphasized the need for organizing "a coordinated intelligence system" after the war, adding that "we need to adjust our intelligence system to the broad basic factors which move and control people and nations, and to conceive it on a global basis. Our intelligence needs to interpret these factors, aware of but not confused by their outward manifestations in governments."[3] Shortly after becoming secretary of state in 1945, James Byrnes put his name to an article on postwar military reorganization in a popular magazine that included a discussion of the intelligence issue. He cited the need for "coordination" by pointing out that the War, Navy, and State Departments—as well as the OSS—had performed intelligence functions. "There is no excuse for four or even two intelligence organizations. We need only one." He argued that until "all swords are actually beaten into plowshares," the United States required an intelligence service equal to any in the world. This would not be possible, however, "as long as our many intelligence officers are duplicating one another's work and operating without any central direction."[4]

Leaders of the armed services were particularly forthright in their concern for an adequate postwar national intelligence system. Testifying before the Senate Military Affairs Committee on October 18, 1945, Army Chief of Staff Marshall stated:

> [W]e should know as much as we possibly can of the possible intent and capacity of any other country in the world. . . . Prior to entering the war we had little more than what a military attache could learn at a dinner, more or less over coffee cups. . . . Today I think we see clearly we must know what the other fellow is planning to do, in our own defense. . . . The important point is that the necessity applies equally outside the armed forces.

It includes the State Department and other functions of Government and it should therefore be correlated on that level.[5]

In testimony following Marshall's, Secretary of War Patterson added: "There is no question in my mind as to the prime necessity of having the most adequate military intelligence we can possibly get. . . . Of course, it would have to go further than that, I believe, and would have to be integrated with the intelligence of the State Department."[6] In his "report," General Arnold could be more outspoken on the role of intelligence in meeting future national security needs: "Detailed moment-by-moment knowledge of all aspects of civilian and military activity within the territory of an enemy is essential to sound planning in times of peace or war. . . . There is a great need for a permanent national organization which not only deals with broad questions of policy but also collects, evaluates and disseminates a continuous stream of intelligence data."[7]

It was the Navy Department, however, under Forrestal's vigorous leadership, that ended up taking the lead in spelling out the nature and structure of a postwar central intelligence organization.[8] In May 1945 Senator David Walsh of Massachusetts, chairman of the Naval Affairs Committee, faced with various War Department proposals on the military "unification" issue, suggested to Forrestal that the Navy Department undertake a detailed study of postwar national security organization. Forrestal was amenable, and, with considerable canniness, he sought to enhance the project's credibility by giving it an air of "independence." Instead of entrusting it to a committee of admirals or the under secretary of the navy, in June he called upon his lifelong friend, New York banker and lawyer Ferdinand Eberstadt, to prepare the study. Assembling a largely civilian staff with strong navalist views, Eberstadt worked through the summer of 1945 and presented his report to Forrestal on September 25. Forrestal, in turn, submitted it to Walsh on October 18.[9] This so-called Eberstadt Report proved to be not only a milestone in the development of the postwar "national security establishment" but also the most comprehensive official public statement on intelligence organization yet to appear.

In discussing the importance of intelligence for national policy making, the report criticized the overly compartmentalized and uncoordinated prewar system in the United States but praised the well-organized, amply funded British intelligence organization. It noted wartime improvements but stated that too much duplication still remained, that too many trained and experienced individuals would soon return to civilian life, and that no provision had been made for "clandestine intelligence operations" abroad. Although a complete merger of the intelligence functions of the State, War, and Navy Departments was not considered practical due to the unique missions of each department, the report did favor increased coordination, a "synthesis of departmental intelligence on the strategic and national policy level," and an agency to handle common, government-wide intelligence problems. It also added grimly:

> Intelligence of scientific, technological, and ideological developments affecting the war-making potential of foreign countries cannot be obtained wholly by overt methods. . . . If the importance of an adequate peacetime intelligence service is not recognized and adequate provision made for the utilization of sufficiently trained personnel in the reduced military forces of the postwar era, retrogression to the situation which existed during the period following World War I is a likely result. . . . All of the considerations herein brought forth are, of course, heavily underscored by the pivotal position which the United States has come to occupy in world affairs. As the sphere of our responsibilities has widened, and our interrelationships with other nations have been extended, our need for accurate, comprehensive, and up-to-date information has become more acute.[10]

To provide for the intelligence needs of the American government, the report recommended establishing a Central Intelligence Agency subordinate to a National Security Council whose services would be available to government agencies concerned with national security matters. It was considered "imperative" to create such an organization so that "timely, full, and authoritative information on conditions and developments in the outside world that relate to, and should influence, our foreign and military policies" could be supplied, particularly in view of "the uncertainties of the postwar world" and new developments in weaponry. Although the report recommended that intelligence should continue to be gathered by several agencies and "private sources" (otherwise undefined), its "compilation, analysis, evaluation, and dissemination" were to be coordinated by the CIA, which "should be headed by an experienced and competent executive director supported by a thoroughly trained and adequate staff capable of proper evaluation of the techincial material at its disposal." In a separate section, the report also called for a closely related, high-level agency devoted to the collection and analysis of communications intelligence.[11]

Forrestal presented the Eberstadt Report as the official Navy Department position on all aspects of the military unification issue when he appeared before the Senate Military Affairs Committee later in 1945. On October 22 he endorsed the creation of a centralized intelligence organization "in order that those responsible for our national security policy may have complete, up-to-date and accurate intelligence, properly analyzed and made available in usable form." [12] In a second appearance on December 13, he observed, concerning a centralized strategic intelligence organization: "I would not recommend it be made statutory because intelligence by its very nature should not be advertised. The fact that we have had to reveal the breaking of the Japanese codes, to my mind, is very unfortunate." Senator Burnet Maybank, Democrat of South Carolina, wondered how intelligence matters could be kept confidential, since "things that work in war don't always work in peace." He asked Forrestal: "How can you keep the intelligence?" Forrestal replied: "I would hope that the lessons of the war—that out of them might come some benefits and the public might realize that the military must have certain latitude." Maybank agreed. [13]

The stillborn State Department plan was given to the public on December 22, 1945, on the National Broadcasting Company's *University of the Air*. Appearing with series director Sterling Fisher to discuss the topic "A National Intelligence Program" were intelligence chief McCormack and Assistant Secretary of State for Public Affairs William Benton. Since Benton generally confined his remarks to cultural and public information matters, McCormack did most of the talking. He emphasized the need for foreign intelligence to enable government officials to make proper decisions on matters of both war and peace. He added: "If we are threatened with war again, we are not likely to have two and one-half years preparation of essential intelligence. We may not have two and one-half months."

In public as in private, McCormack focused on overt collection of intelligence and played down espionage and secret operations: "Our hardest job is to overcome this romantic but false idea of what intelligence work is. The notion that it is all gun-running, espionage, and sabotage is still very prevalent. . . . We don't have to drop in a secret agent by parachute to get the business, trade, political, and most of the other information we need." He dismissed the idea of "one big intelligence agency" as "unrealistic" because "the subject-matter of intelligence is too varied and too complicated and because intelligence work must be done where the decisions are made, and by those who are specialists in each field." Later in the discussion, however, he did concede that some centralized operations would be necessary, citing the Foreign Broadcast Intelligence Service as an example. [14]

McCormack used his forum to push his plan for a "national intelligence authority" chaired by the secretary of state and including the secretaries of war and navy, as well as others serving on an ad hoc basis. This authority would plan intelligence programs, distribute responsibilities to appropriate agencies, and disseminate the final intelligence produced. In addition, there would be a number of interdepartmental working committees, chaired and staffed by the agency with primary interest, to oversee each principal field of intelligence. He stressed, however, that the proposed organization would "steer clear of domestic matters . . . because a foreign national intelligence organization has no business meddling in our domestic affairs." When asked about cost, he cited State Department budgeting in the field and asked rhetorically: "How much could we have afforded to pay for intelligence which would have averted war? . . . So I say that this country can afford to spend for good foreign intelligence a great deal more money than good intelligence will ever cost." [15]

It was hardly surprising that Donovan entered the intelligence debate with the zeal of a crusader and that, almost from the start, his views received wide notice. In September 1945 the New York Times reported his comment that the United States needed a permanent peacetime organization with approximately twenty-five hundred members to collect and analyze foreign intelligence. Later in the month, the newspaper's Washington bureau chief and premier political commentator, Arthur Krock, wrote an article favorable to Donovan's ideas.[16] At its National Encampment in October 1945, the Veterans of Foreign Wars passed a resolution calling upon the president and Congress to provide for "the early establishment of an independent agency for secret foreign intelligence and espionage in line with the recommendations of Major General William J. Donovan and the Joint Chiefs of Staff." The resolution further stated that such an organization was necessary "to perform adequately and fully our obligations as a leader of the United Nations" and to "protect the welfare of the American people." [17]

In a speech on September 16, 1946, to the Advertising Men's Post of the American Legion in New York City, Donovan denounced the NIA as "phony" and commented that it "contains the same log-rolling elements of the State Department, Army, and Navy that have made the intelligence service the 'Little Orphan Annie' of the Government since time began." He further declared that, since the Soviet Union had moved into "forward positions" in Europe, intelligence was the first line of American defense and again stressed the importance of an integrated service: "All we need is the American way of being on the level but not letting anyone push us around." [18]

Donovan's most detailed statement of views appeared in a long Life magazine article in September 1946. Most of the article dealt with what he considered the inadequacies of the prewar American intelligence system and a self-serving account of his own experiences in establishing the OSS. He was not sanguine about the postwar international scene, particularly relations with the Soviet Union, citing the recently exposed Soviet spy ring in Canada to illustrate his concern. The United States, he believed, required a strong foreign policy and adequate military strength for its own safety. Rather than maintain a huge military establishment, however, he urged a well-developed intelligence service to keep government leaders informed, forewarn of hostile actions by other nations, and strengthen foreign policy, since, to Donovan, the United States faced a dangerous future because of its deteriorated strategic position: "The rocket, the long-range bomber, the atomic bomb, bacteriological warfare and all the other paraphernalia of the 36-hour war have whittled down the wonderful defensive cushion of deep space which so far has always allowed us time to mobilize our productive resources for war while we had allies to fight delaying actions outside." But, in Donovan's opinion, the United States lacked the necessary intelligence organization for coping with this new threat. He condemned the system established by Truman in January as "makeshift" and unworkable because "it violates those precepts of intelligence which common sense and experience have handed down to us." His exposition of the necessary "precepts" summarized his proposal to Roosevelt in 1944.[19]

Doubtlessly inspired, and probably encouraged, by Donovan, other former OSS officials, although rarely identifying themselves as such, began to present their views on the postwar intelligence issue. Although their approach was often scholarly and, as a result, reached a much more limited audience than did the publicity-minded Donovan, it was an audience of considerable influence in making public policy. One such officer was David K. E. Bruce, former chief of the important OSS field office in London. In an article appearing in the summer 1946 edition of the *Virginia Quarterly Review*, he adopted much the same position as his former chief, although less stridently. He began by observing that, although the United States had committed itself to supporting the United Nations, it was essential "from the standpoint of our national security to keep informed regarding the strategic plans of other Governments." This could only be done "through a strong American foreign intelligence agency, relying upon its own citizens for the procurement and evaluation of information of major importance." He saw the prewar shortcomings of American intelligence culminating in the surprise at Pearl Harbor: "The attack on Pearl Harbor startled us like some dissonant firebell in the night of our false security. We felt betrayed and indeed we were. We were betrayed by the complete failure of our intelligence agencies. Any intelligence service worthy of name should have foretold this event." He then gave an account of the establishment of the COI and OSS, in the face of army and navy hostility, that was—unsurprisingly—warmly sympathetic to Donovan.

In measured language, Bruce examined the shortcomings of the system established by Truman's January directive. He felt that the lack of an independent budget prevented the CIG from recruiting and retaining competent individuals. He
believed that the three cabinet secretaries constituting the NIA, with administrative responsibilities for major agencies, could not devote the time needed for
positive direction of various operational intelligence agencies "which have, in
the past, displayed a disinclination to coordinate their activities, and no discern-
able ability to produce or to digest strategic information." He also believed that
the former OSS analysts were not being well utilized in the State Department
and worried over the proper direction of clandestine intelligence operations. He
concluded with a call for a strong intelligence agency as a first line of defense to
provide forewarning about hostile action against the United States: "The conduct
of espionage and counter-espionage organizations demands a degree of technical skill, of administrative ability, of knowledge of foreign languages, customs,
and history, such as is exacted by no other profession."[20]

Another former OSS officer to present his views was Sherman Kent. Because
he was still in government service, his article in the *Yale Review* was discreet about
policy but highly analytical about doctrine. He also took the view that the Pearl
Harbor attack had revealed "the inadequacy of our pre-war intelligence mechanism" and maintained that a repetition could only be prevented by "sharp,
timely, relevant knowledge of what is going on in the world." To Kent, this was
particularly true in the postwar world because the "existence of controllable
atomic energy and the dead certainty that others beside ourselves will soon pos-
sess the technical secrets, place a new and forceful emphasis upon intelligence
as one of the most vital elements in our survival."

Kent described the intelligence process as "close and systematic observation"
combined with a "continuous series of sorties" for data to test hypotheses. The
subject had two parts—"security intelligence" to identify "forces which are capable of jeopardizing national security" and "positive intelligence" to provide
government officials "with knowledge of those particular phases of life abroad
which will sooner or later affect our own national interest, and upon which we
should have a policy or be prepared to take action." Kent also defined three requirements for successful intelligence work: a "surveillance operation" to gather
information (by covert means, if necessary); a research and evaluation function;
and a coordination function. He emphasized the need for highly qualified and
well-trained personnel and went on to discuss the evolution of war and postwar
intelligence organization and the shortcomings of the system created by Truman
in January. He concluded by expressing the hope that the CIG would strengthen

itself to become "not merely the coordinator of departmental loose ends but also a positive complementary force in over-all intelligence."[21]

Other men of intelligence opted for book-length studies. One was George Pettee, a professor at Amherst College who, during the war, had done intelligence work for the Foreign Economic Administration and the Office of War Information. In October 1946 his work, *The Future of American Secret Intelligence*, was published by a small District of Columbia firm, the Infantry Journal Press. A short and rather pretentious book, it has since been hailed as a "pioneering classic" in the now-extensive field of intelligence writing.[22] Like other writers on the subject, Pettee emphasized prewar and wartime intelligence failures (specifically mentioning the surprise at Pearl Harbor and in the Ardennes in 1944) and pointed out the need for "an extraordinary competent strategic intelligence service" in the postwar period because "any square mile of the world can be attacked from any other square mile of the world," and because the United States "is already committed in many ways to accept active leadership of the world in seeking positive means to eliminate the causes of war." In addition, he urged the study of all aspects of foreign countries to secure the necessary information for national policy making. After a detailed discussion of doctrine, he considered organization. Although opposing complete consolidation, he called for substantial cooperation among all existing agencies and for a new, centralized organization to oversee the entire effort and to provide coordination and independent collection and analysis. Such an organization, wrote Pettee, should have highly trained personnel, freedom from public scrutiny, an independent budget, and the support of all executive agencies.[23]

A second major work to appear in 1946 was *Secret Missions*, the memoirs of veteran naval intelligence officer Ellis Zacharias. In his book, Zacharias described his long involvement in the field, the shortcomings he encountered, and the intelligence activities of the Germans and Japanese. He praised the British for their intelligence skills and emphasized the need that the United States would have in the future for high-quality foreign intelligence. He called upon Americans to put aside their bias against secret intelligence: "America, now rushing to its rendezvous with destiny, has much to learn in this field. Above all, it must learn to distinguish between the subversive espionage work which we may well leave to authoritarian regimes . . . and legitimate intelligence which every country vitally needs and is entitled to." (He did not define the difference.) Elsewhere, he wrote: "A highly effective intelligence organization is an inescapable necessity as a preventive of war. . . . Only intelligence makes possible a workable, fruitful diplomacy to prevent conflict—the vital function of diplomacy. We must now integrate and build and sharpen our intelligence organization as an implement of peace."[24]

As the veils of secrecy over the wartime activities of the American government began to lift, intelligence matters became a topic of journalistic attention, often in the form of articles describing the exploits of the OSS. Such accounts ranged from short features in *Time* to a lengthy series in *Collier's* in October 1945 and a detailed article in the March 10, 1946, edition of the *Washington Post* that was later reprinted in *Reader's Digest*. On some occasions these accounts concluded with appeals for some kind of postwar central intelligence organization. One of the best, written by John Chamberlain and probably inspired by Donovan himself, appeared in *Life* in November 1945. After presenting an informed and sympathetic account of the OSS in war, Chamberlain looked to the future, where he saw American intelligence planning as "somewhat nebulous." He did not like the division of the OSS between the War and State Departments because this was "going back to the same fragmentation and compartmentalization of intelligence that so bedeviled us in 1941." To Chamberlain, this was inefficient because the American army, "unlike an army in continental Europe, is not the nations's first line of defense," and the State Department, "which is enmeshed in protocol and officially devoted to the promulgation of justice and good works, lacks the operating coolness and objectivity needed in the gathering of strategic intelligence." He felt that a "good case" could be made for including a central intelligence organization within a future Department of Defense, but he preferred an OSS-type agency directly responsible to the president. He concluded on a suitably apocalyptic note:

> Certainly the republic needs its sentinels. Pearl Harbor resulted from bungled intelligence pooling. The blunder wasn't fatal, but if our next Pearl Harbor comes in the guise of atomic explosions set off by time fuses in the New York, Pittsburgh, Detroit and Chicago consulates of a conspiratorial foreign power, there will be no recovery from it. The *next* time our intelligence service must do its big job *before* the war. We need our new OSS, our new General Donovan, now.[25]

Perceived problems in the functioning of the CIG also generated journalistic commentary. Syndicated columnists Joseph and Stewart Alsop viewed this situation with the alarm that would become their trademark. In an April 1946 column they reported—erroneously—that Souers was considering the idea of turning over intelligence collection to the FBI. They observed grimly that only Spain, the Soviet Union, and prewar Germany and Japan had heretofore possessed "a secret service with the responsibility for both foreign espionage and internal security, and with the power of internal arrest." They concluded: "It would be folly to suggest that the FBI would in fact use its powers as they have been used in the totalitarian countries. Nevertheless, the pattern would be established and it would be a dangerous pattern."[26]

A considerably more measured account of the CIG's problems appeared the following month in the *New York Times*. Its author, Cabell Phillips, was a veteran, well-connected Washington correspondent who had been in contact with Donovan to prepare a history (never written) of the OSS. Noted Phillips: "That change comes slowly in a democracy is nowhere better illustrated than in our faltering efforts to create a peacetime foreign intelligence service." He commented that the CIG had benefited from cooperation among "the once highly competitive" military intelligence organizations, "virtually unlimited manpower resources," and funds from departmental budgets that were "not subject to Congressional scrutiny." Nevertheless, observed Phillips, the CIG's structure had been weakened by the ongoing threat of "interdepartmental jealousies" and "confused administration," while failing to meet the "need for centralized intelligence" because there was no provision for channeling raw intelligence "through a single agency where it can be combined, assessed, and analysed." In addition, the current arrangement not only did not guarantee professionalism but also did not "provide for an elite group of clandestine agents who can be called upon in emergencies." Finally, Phillips warned that lack of congressional oversight would be likely to be self-defeating, since, if Congress "gets wise" it could demand a public inquiry that "would prove embarrassing." Although Phillips was mildly critical of congressional failure to adequately fund intelligence efforts, he conceded that such reluctance reflected "the general air of suspicion and hostility with which a large segment of the American public continues to view anything connected with what it assumes to be the 'black arts' of espionage and secret intelligence."[27]

It is perhaps fitting that the most detailed—and possibly the most astute—journalistic presentation of the emerging postwar intelligence issue came from Hanson Baldwin. Late in 1945, the prestigious Council on Foreign Relations (of which Baldwin was a member) organized the Study Group on National Power and Foreign Policy, one of the first of the many "national security seminars" that would become commonplace in the postwar years. Baldwin was asked to chair the meetings that were held between October 1945 and April 1947 and were attended by some of the most prominent figures in government, business, science, the professions, and the military. As chairman, Baldwin also was charged with preparing a book embodying the results of the discussions. The outcome of his efforts was published in 1947 as *The Price of Power*, an impressive example of early thinking on cold war power politics, including an entire chapter on intelligence.[28]

In the book, Baldwin forcefully and articulately stated the "official" case for a strong postwar intelligence system:

> In the age of airpower, in the guided missile age where an atomic Pearl Harbor can mean complete destruction and absolute defeat, in the age of supersonic speeds, warning—that is, intelligence—is vital. . . . A sound intelligence service is, next to diplomacy and the foreign services, our true "first line of defense." Our military forces can act rationally only after our intelligence network has functioned and then only as a result of the facts collected by that network. . . . And war has proven the absolute indispensability of an organized system of fact-collection and fact-analysis. We have learned this lesson with difficulty; Pearl Harbor wrote in letters of blood the necessity of such a centralized system.[29]

With equal vigor, Baldwin described the principles around which the Central Intelligence Agency (his term) should be organized. It should collect as well as evaluate information, be the dominant agency in the intelligence community (but not engage in policy making), and be responsible for all foreign counterintelligence and countersubversive work while having no internal police functions. In addition, it should be independently funded by Congress, have a civilian director and a senior staff largely civilian in composition (since Baldwin argued military personnel "are rarely suited by training for the collection or evaluation of strategic or national intelligence"), and be able to hire and fire personnel "without publicity" and "without trial." In Baldwin's opinion, the CIA should be directly responsible to the National Security Council and be monitored by "a special congressional subcommittee, chosen for its wisdom and discretion." He also believed that the CIA should work in harmony with other intelligence organizations, particularly the FBI, which would be responsible for domestic counterintelligence and counterespionage work (with files open to the CIA).[30]

These discussions of the intelligence issue were not limited to the closed world of intellectuals or professional elites but had a certain resonance with the general public as well. In March 1946 a Gallup poll posited the question "Do you think Congress should provide money to maintain a large force of secret agents who would operate throughout the world to keep us informed of what other nations were doing?" The response was 77 percent to 17 percent in favor. The analysis noted that the veterans surveyed were "even more emphatic than the rest of the voting population in approving the idea." It also was observed that the issue had "taken on added importance . . . with the news stories of Russia's spying activities in Canada." According to the analysis, reasons for favoring such espionage activities included the following: "We have to keep abreast of world developments"; or "Present sources of information are not adequate"; or "There is only one way to keep prepared: keep informed"; or "All other countries are doing it, look at Russia"; or "It is a necessary safeguard against another Pearl Harbor"; or "We cannot trust other nations"; and "Since other nations don't allow access to the news, we have to go in and get it." Almost as an afterthought, the survey noted that those opposing the idea were "inclined to do so on moralistic or idealistic grounds of economy or ineffectuality" such as "We have no right to spy on other countries" or "We must build on the basis of trust, not intrigue." [31]

For its part, Congress also demonstrated an interest in intelligence matters as it increasingly focused on the issue of postwar national security organization. Such an interest derived from a general recognition that the Pearl Harbor attack had been such a devastating surprise because of intelligence failures. In September 1945 a joint resolution established a select joint committee to investigate the Pearl Harbor attack. Chaired by Democratic Senator Alben Barkley of Kentucky, it held extensive hearings from November 1945 to May 1946 and submitted a detailed final report the following July.

One of the report's conclusions called attention to the "imperfections and deficiencies of the *system* whereby Army and Navy intelligence was coordinated and evaluated." It also concluded that "the system of handling intelligence was seriously at fault and that the security of the Nation can be insured only through continuity of service and centralization of responsibility in those charged with handling intelligence." The War and Navy Departments were faulted for failing to appreciate the "professional character of intelligence work" and thus treating it as "just another tour of duty" that was "of secondary importance." The report therefore recommended that the War and Navy Departments select qualified men for intelligence work, keep them on duty for extended periods, and establish means "for intelligence to avoid all the pitfalls of divided responsibilities which experience has made so abundantly evident." [32]

Another major congressional statement on intelligence grew out of an investigation conducted by the House Military Affairs Committee. In October 1945 a special subcommittee, headed by committee chairman Andrew May, began an unpublicized investigation of postwar foreign intelligence activities. After extensive investigative work under committee General Counsel H. Ralph Burton, a confidential report was issued in December 1946. The flamboyantly written document made the usual statement that the American government required a strong intelligence system in the postwar years to avoid war and meet its enlarged global responsibilities. In discussing the centralization issue, Donovan was indirectly criticized, and the report concluded that a centralized agency for coordination and evaluation should not be involved in operational matters because it would be prejudiced in favor of its own information and would compromise and destroy other intelligence organizations. In the course of its work, the subcommittee considered a War Department proposal for establishing an Army Intelligence Corps, along the lines of the Corps of Engineers, with highly trained and experienced officers who would make foreign intelligence work their careers. The report, however, did not endorse this proposal.[33]

It did, however, recommend that the NIA be established by law, that the CIG have an independent budget and control of its own personnel, that the director of central intelligence be a civilian with a fixed term of ten years (although a military officer could also serve as DCI), and that he be confirmed by the Senate. The duties of the DCI would include the correlation, evaluation, and distribution of strategic intelligence within the government, and the performance of common intelligence services and other duties "related to intelligence affecting the national security" as directed by Congress or the NIA. The report was clear on one point: "It is specifically understood that the Director of Central Intelligence shall not undertake operations for the collection of intelligence. . . . One should not remove any intelligence operation from the agencies where day-to-day policies and decisions have to be made; the collection and basis [sic] analysis in each field of intelligence should be assigned to the agency having primary responsibility in that field."[34]

Although the report was a classified document intended for internal use and had not been officially accepted by the entire committee, it was leaked to the press by Burton on December 17 and received some journalistic attention. Two articles by William S. White in the New York Times on December 18 and 19 discussed the report, emphasizing the War Department proposal. On January 12, 1947, the Alsops referred to the report in a column advocating the creation of a centralized, professionally run, independently funded intelligence agency somewhat on the model of the British Secret Intelligence Service. The report also was used in a well-informed article by Fletcher Pratt in the September 1947 issue of Harper's Magazine that was critical of centralized collection (as opposed to analysis) and the service of a military officer as DCI.[35]

While this report was not used in the preparation of any specific legislation, it demonstrated that Congress was cognizant of the intelligence issue and would be receptive to executive branch proposals for considering it as part of any projected plan to overhaul the national security apparatus.[36] Such a proposal had in fact appeared in a special message to Congress from President Truman on December 15, 1945, which discussed the need for military "unification" and made several incidental references to the importance of intelligence. In response to Truman's message, the Senate Military Affairs Committee created a subcommittee comprising Vermont Republican Warren Austin and Democrats Elbert Thomas of Utah and Lister Hill of Alabama to prepare appropriate legislation. After long effort and eight rejected drafts, on April 9 a final bill was reported to the full committee, which approved it on April 23 and sent it to the full Senate. This measure, the Common Defense Act of 1946 (S. 2044), was sponsored by Senator Thomas and contained a section establishing a Central Intelligence Agency.[37]

In this legislation the CIA would be subordinate to the Council of Common Defense, and its director could be either a civilian or a military officer who would be appointed by the president and confirmed by the Senate. Incumbency by a military officer would not affect his service pay or other prerequisites of rank, and his salary as director was to be adjusted accordingly. Personnel were to be assigned to the CIA from other parts of the executive branch as recommended by the council and approved by the president. The CIA would be responsible for planning and developing a coordinated government-wide intelligence program, analysis of intelligence information, dissemination of finished "strategic and national policy" intelligence, coordination of various intelligence activities, making recommendations to the council for the establishment of overall "policies and objectives" concerning intelligence, and performance of "such other functions and duties relating to intelligence affecting the national security" as directed by the president and council. The director was specifically made responsible "for fully protecting intelligence sources and methods." Other government intelligence organizations would continue to operate, and the CIA was instructed to work with, and through, them. They, in turn, were instructed to make their facilities and services available to the CIA, whose director was authorized to inspect their operations and receive their intelligence output. The legislation also declared specifically that the CIA "shall have no police, subpoena, law enforcement, or internal security powers or functions; nor shall anything herein be construed as authorizing the making of investigations inside the continental United States or its possessions, except as provided by law."[38]

Although the provisions concerning the CIA were themselves unopposed in the Senate, the overall legislation fell victim to the disputes between the War and Navy Departments over the broader "unification" issue. S. 2044 contained many provisions opposed by the Navy Department, which persuaded the Senate Naval Affairs Committee to hold extensive hearings. In the course of these hearings, Navy Department spokesmen raised enough objections to block further consideration of the legislation.[39] Nevertheless, the presentation and consideration of the proposed law provided a dress rehearsal for later congressional action that would finally make central intelligence a reality.

7

Establishing a Structure

Following his appointment as DCI, Souers was asked by intelligence officer Thomas Braden: "What do you want to do now?" With a chuckle, Souers replied, "I want to go home."[1] Souers could hardly be faulted for such a view, since he had long neglected both his family and his business affairs in Missouri for government service in Washington. Nevertheless, Souers was determined not to return to private life until the matter of organizing a postwar intelligence system was in hand. Writing to an even more famous intelligence officer years later, he commented: "Because of my experience during the Second World War, my burning ambition was to see that we had a unified intelligence organization which would be able to supply the top policymakers in government and in the services the necessary intelligence."[2] It was to that end that he directed his efforts as DCI.[3]

Souers was, by nature, a low-key operator and consensus builder. Faced with a cautious mood in the White House, his own limited resources, and the determination of the State, War, and Navy Departments to maintain their own intelligence prerogatives, he readily recognized the need to proceed in a careful and deliberate fashion. On February 2, 1946, he addressed a memo to the NIA, requesting that "an initial personal authorization and an outline of organization should now be approved so that the Group may be activated and proceed with the pressing problems now confronting the National Intelligence Authority." In his view, the most immediate problems were producing "daily and weekly summaries of the most significant intelligence and operational information related to national security and foreign policy" for the president and NIA members, and carrying out "a survey of existing facilities for collecting foreign intelligence information, with a view to determining how these facilities may be better coordinated and improved." He included a draft enabling directive as an attachment.[4]

The NIA held its first meeting on February 5 to discuss Souers's proposed directive. Byrnes emphasized that it was his responsibility to furnish the president with foreign policy information for decision making. Admiral Leahy replied that the president wanted information from all departments in order to be kept fully informed.[5] Further discussion resulted in no action that day, but Souers's patience was rewarded on February 8, when the NIA, at its second formal session, approved Directive No. 1, entitled "Policies and Procedures Governing the Central Intelligence Group," based on his initial views of February 2. Under the directive, the CIG was to be "operated as a cooperative interdepartmental activity with adequate and equitable participation" by the State, War, and Navy Departments and, as requested by the DCI and approved by the NIA, "other Federal departments and agencies." The CIG would be responsible for furnishing "strategic and national policy intelligence" to the president, the JCS, the NIA members, and such "other governmental departments and agencies having strategic and policy functions related to the national security." The directive also set forth the membership and responsibilities of the Intelligence Advisory Board, which would serve to channel policy recommendations to the NIA through the DCI. Such recommendations, when approved by the NIA, would "govern the intelligence activities of the separate departments."

The directive also instructed the DCI to prepare a proposed organizational structure for the CIG and to estimate funds and personnel requirements from the departments for upcoming fiscal years. Following NIA approval, and "within the limits of available appropriations," the "necessary funds" would be made available "by arrangement between you and the appropriate department through its member on the Intelligence Advisory Board." The DCI also was authorized "to determine the qualifications of personnel and the adequacy of individual candidates. Personnel assigned to you will be under your operational and administrative control, subject only to the necessary personnel procedures of each department." Under the directive, the CIG would "utilize all available intelligence" in its work, and, in order to perform its mission, "all necessary facilities, intelligence and information in the possession of our respective departments" would be made available to the DCI through the Intelligence Advisory Board (IAB). Conversely, CIG facilities and the intelligence that it prepared would be available to the NIA and its members through the IAB. The DCI was further authorized to inspect the operations of departmental intelligence agencies for CIG planning purposes through the IAB and received the authority "to request of other Federal departments and agencies any information or assistance required" to meet its responsibilities.[6]

The NIA issued a second directive of February 8 concerning the initial organization and functions of the CIG, again based on Souers's earlier ideas. It set down its initial personnel authorization and confirmed Souers's plan to begin producing daily intelligence summaries and surveying existing intelligence facilities.

Administratively, the DCI was given responsibility for "all operations" of the CIG and could make personnel assignments. He also was instructed to name an assistant director "from each of the personnel contingents . . . , one of whom he may designate as his Deputy." According to the directive, the CIG would have an Administrative Section to perform its administrative and security responsibilities and serve as the secretariat for the NIA; a Central Reports Staff to carry out the correlation, evaluation, and dissemination of intelligence; a Central Planning Staff "for the coordination of intelligence activities related to the national security, and in preparing recommendations regarding the establishment of such over-all policies and objectives as will assure the most effective accomplishment of the national intelligence mission"; and Central Intelligence Services comprising "such operating agencies" as would be established in accordance with Truman's January 22 directive.[7]

These two directives inaugurated central intelligence, and Souers lost no time in tending to its nurture. Three days after Truman's directive, he had assembled a small cadre of planners from the State, War, and Navy Departments and, upon the official inauguration of the CIG on February 8, quickly began to develop its initial organizational structure. He instituted broad studies on the coordination of government intelligence activities, and on February 13 the first CIG daily intelligence summary appeared. The Central Reports Staff was formally established on April 19, and Souers expanded its work to include the preparation of a weekly summary to provide a broader interpretation of events; its first issue appeared on June 14. Souers proceeded to install basic administrative functions and endeavored to recruit outside expert consultants, including George Kennan, the recently returned Chargé from Moscow. Due to the work of his Planning Staff, he began urging the NIA to centralize under CIG oversight such "services of common concern" as the clandestine collection of foreign intelligence and the monitoring of foreign press and broadcasting. He also urged that the CIG's analytical responsibilities be extended to include basic research into such areas as economics, geography, sociology, and biographical studies. With some satisfaction, Souers could note in June that the "initial organizational and planning phase of CIG activities has been completed and the operation of centralized intelligence services should be undertaken by CIG at the earliest practicable date."[8]

Creating the new organization was slow work in other areas, however. In the face of postwar budget cuts, the three NIA departments were reluctant to surrender personnel; by June 1946, the CIG had only 84 of the 165 people that it had been authorized by the NIA. In a report to the NIA, Souers complained that the "reduction of Departmental funds and personnel for intelligence activities [has] made it difficult for Departments, despite their desire to cooperate, to furnish the necessary facilities to CIG. The inability of CIG to recruit personnel directly from civilian life, and the administrative complications of procuring personnel from the Departments, are likely to jeopardize effective conduct of CIG operations." He also struck a chord that would become increasingly familiar by noting that the "lack of enabling legislation making the CIG a legal entity has made it impossible to negotiate contracts which are required for many operations." He therefore urged that the NIA and CIG "should obtain enabling legislation and an independent budget as soon as possible" in order for the CIG to conduct "urgently needed central intelligence operations" effectively and efficiently and in order that the NIA and CIG "have the necessary authority and standing to develop, support, coordinate, and direct an adequate Federal intelligence program for national security."[9]

As DCI, Souers had laid the foundation for a postwar central intelligence structure. He had, however, agreed to serve as DCI only on an interim basis, and by mid-1946 his desire to return to private life could no longer be denied. Nevertheless, before departing, he demonstrated his good judgment in the selection of his successor: Army G-2 chief, Lieutenant General Hoyt Vandenberg. Only forty-seven, Vandenberg was a dashing, energetic officer who had already distinguished himself as a leader in the celebrated Ninth Tactical Air Command in northwest Europe during the war. Well respected both for his ability and for his capacity to work with others, he had been assigned to war planning when hostilities ended; in January 1946, Chief of Staff Eisenhower had appointed him chief of army intelligence as part of an Army General Staff reorganization. In that post, he had demonstrated his usual ability and drive, and Souers, who recognized that it was the army's "turn" for the DCI post (no thought was given to choosing a civilian in 1946), obviously realized that Vandenberg's talents would be essential for establishing the strong intelligence service that he desired. He was also quick to realize that Vandenberg's rank would help the CIG in bureaucratic wars and clearly recognized that being the nephew of the powerful Michigan Republican Senator Arthur Vandenberg would aid efforts to secure enabling legislation for the new organization. Overcoming the ambitious young general's initial reluctance to take the DCI post by pointing out that it was an excellent stepping-stone to his true career goal—command of the soon-to-be independent air force— Souers forwarded Vandenberg's name to Truman in April.[10]

Naturally enough, Chief of Staff Eisenhower was reluctant to lose one of his most promising officers; on April 27 he wrote the president to recommend Major General Charles H. Bonesteel, a competent but colorless officer, as Souers's replacement. In Eisenhower's view, Bonesteel had "a reputation for integrity, energy and administrative ability and, in addition, has a good personality." Despite his age (sixty-two), he was, said Eisenhower, "in splendid health and full of vigor and vitality" and was, moreover, "instantly available" for duty.[11] Souers would have none of it. Writing to Leahy on May 7, he noted that there was "nothing in the record of this officer to indicate that he has ever had any broad experience in intelligence matters. He has had no intelligence duties." Since, said Souers, the NIA was a "new concept in intelligence," it required "a breadth of view and a deep understanding of the entire field on the part of the Director of Central Intelligence. . . . To insure the most beneficial results in the Central Intelligence Group it is necessary that the Director be an officer whose specialists will look for leadership and guidance based on a thorough and comprehensive knowledge of this complex subject." Bonesteel, in Souers's view, "seems to have passed the peak of his career some years ago. His record, while honorable, is not too impressive." On the other hand, Souers felt that Vandenberg had "a fine war record, is regarded as an outstanding officer and is keenly interested in intelligence. His leadership in G-2 has been strong and determined. He has demonstrated his recognition of the necessity for the reorientation of the intelligence structure."[12]

Leahy agreed and wrote to Truman on May 9: "In my opinion, it is essential in the formative period of the National Intelligence Authority to have as Director of Central Intelligence an officer of proven ability in the collection and evaluation of intelligence who has also superior executive ability and an established prestige in the intelligence field as well as in the opinions of the Secretaries of State, War, and Navy." In Leahy's view, the only available officer meeting these requirements was Vandenberg, and he therefore recommended "that the Secretary of War be informed of the high importance that the President attaches to the successful completion of the development of the National Intelligence Authority and that he desires that General Vandenberg be made available for assignment as the Director of Central Intelligence . . . within the ensuing two months."[13] Truman, quick to concur, wrote Secretary of War Patterson on May 16 to order Vandenberg's release, commenting: "It seems to me that Lieutenant General Vandenberg is the proper person for this position—he knows it from 'A to Z,' he is a diplomat and will be able to get along with the State and Navy, as well as the War Department."[14] On June 7 Truman informed Vandenberg of his appointment, effective June 10, and officially notified Secretaries Byrnes, Patterson, and Forrestal of his action.[15]

Souers knew his man. Vandenberg, assuming his duties as DCI with his customary energy, soon acquired the nickname "Sparkplug." He had little sympathy for his predecessor's cautious, incremental approach to setting up an intelligence organization and boldly launched an empire-building campaign worthy of Donovan's grandest wartime efforts. Shrewdly exploiting the organizational retrenchments forced on government agencies by the end of the war, he actively sought new functions and responsibilities for the CIG wherever he could find them. Vandenberg's aim, like Donovan's, was to create an independent, self-sufficient intelligence service, and he went far toward actually setting up what Donovan had only conceptualized. Broadly interpreting his authority as DCI, Vandenberg moved the CIG from a coordinating role to a clandestine collector of intelligence and an organization responsible for conducting independent research and analysis. By the end of his short tenure, a central intelligence organization had come off the drawing board to become a functioning operation.[16]

Vandenberg wasted no time in initiating his quest for empire. On June 20, 1946, he submitted a lengthy position paper to the Intelligence Advisory Board that forcefully declared: "The former and present Directors of Central Intelligence are in agreement that the initial organizing and planning stages of the Central Intelligence Group have been completed and that the time has arrived to request that the National Intelligence Authority authorize the Director of Central Intelligence to undertake certain operations and functions of vital importance to the national intelligence mission." He therefore proposed that the responsibilities of the DCI, as set forth in Truman's January directive, be expanded to make him "executive agent" for the NIA "in coordinating and supervising all Federal foreign intelligence activities related to the national security," and that he be specifically authorized to conduct "all Federal espionage and counter-espionage operations for the collection of foreign intelligence information required for the national security" and "all Federal monitoring of press and propaganda broadcasts of foreign powers." In addition, the State, War, and Navy Departments were to "make available to the Director of Central Intelligence, upon his request, the necessary funds, personnel, facilities and other assistance required" for the performance of these responsibilities.

In justifying these proposals, Vandenberg noted that the DCI was responsible "for the accuracy, adequacy and timeliness of intelligence required for the national security" and therefore should have the authority "to undertake within the Central Intelligence Group basic research and analysis of original and unevaluated intelligence and counter-intelligence information from all available sources" in order "to ensure adequate coverage, from a national viewpoint of those fields which are of common interest to more than one agency, such as economics, science, biography, geography, sociology, etc." He also argued that his proposed "executive agent" role was necessary, since coordination and supervision of the system was important for "the effective execution of the national intelligence program." He then went on to justify exclusive control of foreign intelligence and counterintelligence operations by asserting that this approach would prevent embarrassment to other executive departments in conducting their regular "overt" activities, would serve "national" rather than individual departmental interests, would guarantee "maximum security" of such operations, would avoid the "danger of competition and confusion between agents of different agencies," and would make sure that the "interdependency and interrelationship between geographic areas and foreign countries" would be protected by "one agency with world coverage." Finally, he argued that the "difficult and specialized administrative problems involved in such operations make a single central agency more efficient and economical." Almost as an afterthought, he rationalized the DCI's control over foreign press and broadcast monitoring by noting the multiagency utility of this activity and the unwillingness and inability of the State, War, and Navy Departments to fund it.[17]

It was a compelling presentation, and no one put forward an alternative. As a result, it was basically enacted in NIA Directive No. 5 on July 8, which authorized the DCI to "undertake such research and analysis as may be necessary to determine what functions in the fields of national security intelligence are not being presently performed or are not being adequately performed" and, based on his findings, to "centralize such research and analysis activities as may, in his opinion and that of the appropriate member or members of the Intelligence Advisory Board be more efficiently or effectively accomplished centrally." In addition, the DCI was "authorized and directed" to act for the NIA "in coordinating all Federal foreign intelligence activities related to the national security to ensure that the over-all policies and objectives established by this Authority are properly implemented and executed." He was further directed to perform such "services of common concern" as the conduct "of all organized Federal espionage and counterespionage operations outside of the United States and its possessions for the collection of foreign intelligence information" and "all Federal monitoring of press and propaganda broadcasts of foreign powers" required for national security purposes. Funds, personnel, and facilities would be provided by the NIA departments "within the limits of their capabilities." Where the performance of his duties required "the liquidation, transfer, or integration of funds, personnel, or facilities," such actions would be carried out through "mutual arrangement between the DCI and the appropriate department or agency."[18]

Armed with this sweeping grant of authority, Vandenberg set out for new worlds to conquer. His most important objective was the clandestine foreign intelligence organization of the defunct OSS. Although assigned to the War Department by Truman's 1945 executive order as the SSU, the arrangement was recognized as a temporary measure. As a result, the army, undergoing a drastic peacetime reduction, was willing to abandon its espionage inheritance, and, at an early date, the CIG was recognized as a place to put it. On January 28, 1946, SSU officer Major General Stafford Irwin wrote Assistant Secretary John McCloy that transferring the SSU to the CIG "would furnish that agency with an organization in being for intelligence operations. . . . While transfer appears desirable, it must be done in such a manner as to retain assets without unduly compromising future operations of the intelligence section of the CIG." He concluded by urging that those parts of the SSU to be retained should be transferred to the DCI's control "under whatever designation he may prescribe." [19]

Action was also urged by SSU chief Magruder, who prepared a series of anguished memos to his superiors on the fate of the organization. Writing to War Department officials on February 14, he asserted:

> It will not be possible for the SSU much longer to continue effective operations in its present interim status. Lack of [a] specific directive permitting long-range plans and commitments [has] seriously affected its logical development. Personnel has [sic] already begun to melt away. . . . Furthermore, from the budget viewpoint, the War Department cannot continue to justify for any substantial period the maintenance of a provisional intelligence organization separate from its established Military Intelligence Division. Unless early disposition is made of the assets represented by SSU it will undoubtedly become necessary to effect curtailment if not liquidation of its remaining personnel and facilities.

Noting that the CIG "would, as one of its major functions, operate a clandestine service for the procurement of intelligence abroad," he recommended that the NIA transfer the SSU to the CIG, since the SSU "at present provides significant intelligence coverage in many parts of the world." Therefore, even though it was not "a complete or adequate worldwide clandestine intelligence agency," it remained "the sole operating agency not only in many geographical areas but in specialized functions it could profitably be employed by the CIG until replaced by, or incorporated into, a permanent organization." [20]

Souers, ever the cautious but calculating bureaucrat, responded on February 19 with a directive establishing a five-member committee to review the matter and recommend what SSU "resources, facilities, and operating functions" should be retained, what disposition should be made "of the preserved resources and facilities and what assignments should be made of responsibility for conducting the preserved operating functions" and what budgetary arrangements would be necessary.[21] The committee, headed by army Colonel Louis Fortier from CIG and including representatives from Army G-2, Army Air Forces A-2, ONI, and the State Department, submitted its report on March 14. After a detailed examination of the SSU's history, organization, and conduct, the committee unsurprisingly concluded:

> There is immediate need for the continued maintenance of foreign intelligence coverage throughout the world and for the implementation of clandestine and semi-clandestine operations in areas hitherto covered by the SSU. . . . No other intelligence authority has been established with appropriate directions to perform throughout the world the functions of the character performed by those of the SSU and there is no other operating unit presently directly available to the Director of Central Intelligence for the collection, evaluation and dissemination of clandestine intelligence, nor has any long term decision on policy and operations been made by the National Intelligence Authority.

Therefore, until such a long-term plan was developed, the committee felt that "the present SSU should be placed under the CIG and properly and closely supervised, pruned and rebuilt" and should "function under specific directives in selected and clearly defined fields of vital interest to the United States in which clandestine operations and planning for clandestine operations are deemed necessary."

In addition, the committee felt that "further consideration should be given to a plan which will permit the special development of purely clandestine intelligence operations under the CIG in close coordination with the total needs of CIG for foreign intelligence by whatever means obtained leaving more overt United States Government collection activities to other agencies prepared and authorized to act in the field with a minimum embarrassment to the United States." Concerning budget matters, the committee felt that the War Department should continue to fund the SSU for the immediate future, but that "at an early stage the CIG undertake the duty of preparing budgets, seeking funds and defending budgetary requests before the Bureau of the Budget and committees of Congress. The Committee does not believe that in the long run CIG can or should rely on other departments in such matters." It was adamant, however, that "so far as it is possible under the law the amount of governmental expenditures for secret intelligence and the nature of the items of expenditures should be concealed." It also emphasized "the necessity of removing all personnel of CIG from Civil Service control," recommended that the DCI assume control over SSU assets, and closed its report with the admonition that "all action taken hereunder be secret so far as permissible." [22]

Fortier's committee undoubtedly told Souers what he wanted to hear, and on March 26 he presented a draft proposal to the IAB for a phased liquidation of the SSU and the transfer of its functions, activities, and funds to the CIG. The IAB gave its concurrence without extended discussion,[23] and Souers forwarded his plan to Admiral Leahy on March 28. It became official policy on April 2, with the issuance of NIA Directive No. 4, "Policy on the Liquidation of the Strategic Services Unit," which formally transferred the SSU's responsibilities to the CIG.[24] On April 3 Acting Secretary of War Howard Peterson informed SSU chief General William Quinn (who had replaced Magruder on April 1) that he should proceed with the liquidation of the SSU under the direction of the DCI; the following day, Souers informed him that this phaseout should not be at the expense "of such operations, services and liaisons deemed essential" to support U.S. military and diplomatic activities and directed him to carry out "such collection missions, distribution and other intelligence services" as may be ordered by his representative, Colonel Fortier.[25]

Thanks to Souers's careful preparatory work, Vandenberg was left with only loose ends to wrap up. On July 11 he issued a directive officially establishing the Office of Special Operations (OSO) under Army Colonel Donald Galloway to carry out the secret intelligence activities mandated by NIA Directive No. 5 of July 8.[26] On September 12 Vandenberg informed Leahy that the SSU would be formally deactivated on October 19 and that the CIG's new OSO would "assume responsibility for the conduct of espionage and counter-espionage in the field for the collection of foreign intelligence information required for the national security. Every possible effort is being made to extend and develop foreign coverage. Only a limited number of carefully selected individuals formerly with the Strategic Services Unit will be employed to inaugurate the program under the new auspices." [27] Similar messages went to the other NIA principals, and, on the chosen date, Quinn issued SSU General Order No. 16 formally dissolving the organization.[28]

Vandenberg was quick to organize his legacy. In his enabling directive to Galloway on October 25, he declared that OSO's mission was to secretly conduct, "under the direct supervision of the Director, all organized Federal espionage and counterespionage operations outside the United States and its possessions for the collection of foreign intelligence information required for the national security." This intelligence information would be "put in usable form" and delivered to the CIG's analysts, or to other government agencies "when appropriate." OSO also was authorized to "maintain direct liaison with departments and agencies of the Federal Government on secret operational matters," and it would be responsible for "the collection, processing, and distribution of foreign counterespionage intelligence information and will be the repository for such information." [29] Vandenberg was clearly pleased with his handiwork. On February 25, 1947, in one of his periodic intelligence memorandums to President Truman, he boasted: "The clandestine intelligence operations of the Central Intelligence Group are being carefully established in the most critical areas outside the United States and are proceeding satisfactorily. These operations are already productive of results which are of considerable value to many government agencies." [30]

Perhaps Vandenberg's boldest initiative was one not even Donovan had dared to contemplate—the acquisition of the FBI's wartime intelligence network in Latin America. Although Director Hoover probably realized that the loss of his wartime foreign operations was inevitable with the return of peace, he was not a man who yielded power easily, and he feared CIG inroads on his domestic counterintelligence authority. Vandenberg would need to apply all his talent to overcome Hoover and his numerous bureaucratic allies. Vandenberg's ploy had been implicit in his June 20, 1946, memo to the IAB, and the FBI was quick to note it. Writing to Assistant Director Michael Ladd the next day, FBI officer C. H. Carson noted that the proposal, "of course, is the same super-colossus originally proposed by General Donovan"; he went on to note that, if it was approved and if the CIG was

> successful in setting up complete foreign coverage, the Bureau would undoubtedly be pushed into a "second-rate" position insofar as purely intelligence functions are concerned in the domestic field. Our law enforcement functions, of course, could not be touched by the Central Intelligence Group. It is inevitable that the Central Intelligence Group must enter into the domestic field picture insofar as intelligence is concerned because of the sources of *foreign* intelligence existing in that field. Also, it is impossible to separate entirely foreign intelligence and the domestic functions performed by the Bureau. . . . The sheer size of the foreign intelligence setup and its intimate relationship with powerful de-

partments in the United States Government would probably mean that the
Central Intelligence Group would be in a position to win out in any controversy as to action to be taken touching on the intelligence field.

Carson felt that, since Vandenberg's plan could not be directly opposed, the FBI's
primary domestic responsibilities be safeguarded by specifying that the DCI's
new coordinating and operational responsibilities be focused entirely "outside
the United States and its possessions."[31]

Not all FBI officers were so negative, however. In an addendum to Carson's
memo, Hoover's senior deputies, Edward Tamm and Clyde Tolson, disputed his
view, arguing that "a coordinated program for the exchange of information" between the CIG and the FBI "permitting a free and comprehensive exchange of
information in matters of mutual interest, will enable the Bureau to work in the
domestic field without interference from the Central Intelligence Authority [sic]
in the same manner that the Bureau works . . . with local police departments or
other government agencies within defined jurisdictional lines." Hoover himself
thought otherwise. In a handwritten comment he noted: "I am not as optimistic
as Tolson & Tamm. I think that it is inevitable that there will be a collision with
CIG over our domestic jurisdiction or rather their expansion into our intelligence
matters. It ought not occur but this new memo of CIG shows how greedy it is.
It is the Donovan plan almost in toto & is being slyly put over. It means we must
zealously guard our domestic jurisdiction & not yield an inch & be ever alert to
resist any encroachments."[32]

Vandenberg was quick to recognize his vulnerability. At an IAB meeting on
June 28, he expressed regret over any turmoil caused by his original proposal,
claiming that he was not trying to usurp departmental prerogatives but only
wanted to determine where deficiencies existed that he could correct.[33] On July 3
he wrote an ingratiating letter to Hoover, offering to cooperate closely in working out an "orderly transition" of intelligence assets in Latin America from the
FBI to the CIG.[34] Suitably mollified, Vandenberg's counterparts accepted his initiative as part of NIA Directive No. 5 of July 8. On July 19 Vandenberg wrote to
Hoover again to thank him for his cooperation and to suggest that the two "work
out immediately a program for the transfer of secret intelligence responsibilities
in Central and South America." He lavishly praised the FBI for its past intelligence
collection efforts in the region and then made his pitch: "Since our immediate
aim is to relieve FBI at the earliest possible date, I believe it essential that the accomplishments of FBI in gathering intelligence information and administrative
facilities be made available to CIG as far as is practicable. . . . It is my recommen-

dation that FBI personnel should remain at each field station for a time after the arrival of my representatives in order that the successors may enjoy the benefits of the Bureau's experience in each country." He also requested that FBI intelligence reports be made available to CIG officers and that the newly arriving CIG officers "be acquainted by your special agents with local contacts and sources of information which you have developed and arrangements worked out for the possible further utilization of these persons. Your advice on the handling of such informants and the safeguards against untrustworthy individuals will be greatly appreciated." [35]

Vandenberg's friendly words did not make Hoover a gracious loser. Although reconciled to the inevitable, he continued to resent turning over his intelligence assets and files in Latin America to what he considered a new and untried organization with possibly unreliable personnel. In August he began withdrawing his agents from Latin America faster than the CIG could replace them, alarming U.S. diplomats in the region. Reflecting their concerns, Acting Secretary of State Acheson wrote his NIA counterparts on August 5 to warn of the "grave danger" that "the excellent FBI organization in Latin America may disintegrate before it can be taken over by the new personnel from the CIG. This would be a major blow to the effectiveness of our security intelligence network in the Latin American field, from which it might take us many years to recover." Emphasizing the concerns of his ambassadors, he urged that the transfer of responsibility be done in an orderly fashion to prevent such disruption and that no FBI agents depart until a CIG replacement had arrived and become familiar with operational matters.[36] The issue was addressed by the NIA on August 7; it instructed the CIG representative, Colonel Galloway of OSO, to draft a letter to Attorney General Clark requesting that he direct the FBI to retain its personnel in Latin America until CIG officers could replace them and that a transition period be provided "so that the new organization could be properly oriented and be given contacts in each country." [37] A formal letter to this effect (signed by Leahy, Acheson, Patterson, and Acting Navy Secretary John Sullivan) was sent to Clark the following day.[38]

Several days of intense negotiations followed between Hoover, Clark, Leahy, the State Department, and the White House. Truman was insistent that the CIG assume the U.S. foreign intelligence role, and Clark instructed Hoover to meet with Vandenberg to work out an orderly schedule for replacing FBI agents with CIG officers.[39] On August 12 Leahy informed Vandenberg that both Truman and Clark wanted such replacement efforts to be expedited: "Granting that there will be a temporary reduction of efficiency by an early relief of FBI agents in Latin America, it is my opinion that the reliefs can be accomplished at a much earlier date than at present scheduled and it should be done."[40] Given their marching orders, Hoover and Vandenberg finally worked out transfer arrangements. On December 31 the CIG chief wrote the FBI director that his officers would start replacing FBI agents in the coming year, beginning with Rio de Janeiro on January 20, 1947, and concluding with Havana on April 14. Vandenberg concluded his message with "[I]t is anticipated that FBI representatives will remain at their posts for a sufficient period of time after the arrival of CIG personnel in order to insure orderly transfer of records, valuable assistance, and thorough guidance."[41] Such would not be the case, however. As CIA officer Richard Helms (then in OSO) later commented ruefully: "Hoover pursued a scorched earth policy. He cleaned out all the files, wouldn't allow his agents to talk to the new CIA [sic] people about sources. We got nothing worth having. He just cleaned the place out and went home in a sulk."[42]

Vandenberg, like other U.S. airmen, had a strong technological bent, which he demonstrated in pursuit of another target of opportunity—intelligence in the field of atomic energy. Although the newly established Atomic Energy Commission (AEC) was officially charged with overseeing U.S. nuclear policy, Vandenberg saw the CIG as being its intelligence staff.[43] Once again, Vandenberg proved that he was not a man to hesitate. On August 13, 1946, he wrote to the NIA, declaring that foreign atomic energy developments "constitute a paramount field of intelligence related to the national security" and a new area of responsibility for the NIA. He noted that the collection and evaluation of atomic energy intelligence was in the hands of the Foreign Intelligence Branch of the army's Manhattan Engineer District (MED), which was due to be taken over by the AEC. Therefore, asserted Vandenberg:

> It is considered appropriate at this time that the National Intelligence Authority should authorize and direct the Director of Central Intelligence to coordinate the collection by agencies subject to NIA coordination of all intelligence information related to foreign atomic energy developments and potentialities affecting the national security and to accomplish the correlation, evaluation and appropriate dissemination within the Government of the resulting intelligence. To accomplish this function, the personnel and working files of the Foreign Intelligence Branch . . . should be transferred to the Central Intelligence Group.

He attached a draft directive to serve this purpose.[44]

It was a sally worthy of Donovan's finest, and it was well timed. When the NIA took up the proposal on August 21, Patterson, faced with the prospect of drastic downsizing of the military establishment, strongly supported transferring the MED's intelligence function to the CIG. He was backed with some vigor by Forrestal and rather tepidly by Leahy. Acheson was skeptical, however, feeling that the plan undercut the AEC's responsibility. Vandenberg responded that it was not his intent to undercut the AEC and promised that he would furnish atomic energy intelligence information to it or any other agency as directed by the NIA. He also emphasized that the CIG could perform this mission most effectively, since it would utilize all sources. He added that other intelligence agencies were not cooperating with the MED and that its chief, General Leslie Groves, had admitted that his best source of information had been the SSU.[45] Despite Acheson's appeals for delay, the NIA prepared a directive giving Vandenberg the authority he requested, authorizing him to make arrangements with other intelligence agencies to utilize their collection facilities, and transferring the MED's Foreign Intelligence Branch to the CIG.[46] This draft directive was forwarded for approval in cable format to Truman, who was away from Washington. Truman, however, who did not wish to act until the new AEC was installed and its functions clearly defined, did not sign it.

As Vandenberg lobbied, support came from General Groves himself, who wrote the AEC on November 21, urging that Vandenberg's proposal be accepted. Recalling that he had established his own foreign intelligence unit because of the inadequacies of other intelligence agencies in the nuclear field, he declared that it was "vital to the security of the United States that foreign intelligence in the field of atomic energy be maintained and strengthened" and that the CIG "must be able to evaluate the capabilities of other nations to use atomic energy in the military field, and the best nucleus upon which to build this organization is the Foreign Intelligence Section [sic]." To continue its functions, he maintained, "in any other way except under the control of CIG would be very difficult," since it "has never had complete facilities or personnel to do its own collection" and had to rely on raw input from other agencies. In addition, said Groves, its dissemination capabilities were limited, and its liaison contacts had been restricted to military attachés, the U.S. Army command in Europe, and the British. He concluded: "I have long thought that the CIG has the best resources for this intelligence collection and dissemination and for procuring and retaining personnel capable of serving the Atomic Energy Program in the future. . . . This is especially true since CIG already controls the Strategic Services Unit and is assured of cooperation with British Intelligence." He ended by reaffirming that MED's intelligence unit "should be an integral part of the CIG."[47]

Vandenberg's persistence finally paid off in NIA Directive No. 9 of April 16,

1947, entitled "Coordination of Intelligence Activities Related to Foreign Atomic Energy Developments and Potentialities," which repeated the provisions of the draft directive of August 21, 1946, giving the DCI the authority that Vandenberg had sought.[48] To accommodate bureaucratic proprieties, on July 25 the NIA accepted a proposal from the chairman of the AEC to give that agency a permanent seat on the Intelligence Advisory Board.[49]

Other conquests by Vandenberg in his pursuit of empire proved less contentious. One was the acquisition of the Foreign Broadcast Intelligence Service (FBIS). Established in 1941 within the Federal Communications Commission, it was responsible for monitoring, translating, and analyzing foreign broadcasts and publications, especially newspapers. Legislation in May 1945, however, directed that the FCC discontinue its foreign monitoring activities within six months of the termination of hostilities, and, in December, the program was turned over to the War Department. FBIS was an unwanted foundling for the War Department, however. Faced with their own drastic budget reductions, its leaders argued that the information collected by FBIS was more political and economic than military and could not, therefore, be justified as a military expenditure. On March 5, 1946, the CIG initiated a study to determine what should be done with FBIS once the War Department gave up responsibility.[50]

The issue was discussed at an IAB meeting of May 9, where it was suggested the orphaned agency properly should be placed within the CIG. Cautious DCI Souers demurred, however, arguing that the CIG was not an independent agency and thus could not sign contracts, adding that it did not have the technical personnel available to run FBIS. Due to the nature of its work, he suggested that FBIS could be placed in the State Department. In response, the department's intelligence chief, William Langer, said that while the idea was logical, the State Department's administrative burdens were already so large that it could not assume new responsibilities.[51] When the IAB next met on June 10, Vandenberg was DCI, and he made clear his willingness to take over FBIS, subject to such administrative arrangements as were necessary with the War Department.[52] Meeting no opposition, he got his wish as part of NIA Directive No. 5 of July 8, 1946.[53] Later renamed the Foreign Broadcast Information Service, this organization became an unsurpassed collector of foreign intelligence.

Vandenberg was fully cognizant of the importance of "open" sources. He sought to develop cooperative relations with other government agencies for the collection of biographical intelligence in order to create centralized personality files at CIG. He also acquired responsibility for the Washington Document Center, a joint-service activity established during the war for translating captured documents, and made arrangements with the Librarian of Congress to procure foreign publications. In addition, he initiated plans to assume monitoring of the foreign-language press in the United States, which had been done by the OSS and taken over by the State Department.[54] His boldest stroke in the area of "open sources," however, was his "gentleman's agreement" with the *New York Times*. Recognizing that the newspaper was then unequaled in foreign news coverage, in December 1946 Vandenberg contacted publisher Arthur Sulzberger to seek access to the private reports and letters sent by overseas correspondents to their editors that contained information on events, trends, and personalities which had not made print. In February 1947 Sulzberger responded that "you and your representatives will always meet with the fullest cooperation" from the newspaper's staff. Vandenberg and Sulzberger both designated staff members to handle liaison arrangements; as a result, letters and documents (often sent by diplomatic pouch) ended up not only with *Times* editors but also with CIG officers, often without the knowledge of the writers themselves. Vandenberg also arranged to have CIG officers debrief *Times* correspondents returning from overseas assignments. In the words of the official history of the newspaper, this arrangement "became so conventional, so cut and dried, that after awhile it came to be regarded as completely normal and bureaucratic." [55]

Vandenberg also recognized the importance of collecting "foreign" intelligence in the United States from private citizens (particularly businessmen) returning from overseas, foreign travelers, and resident aliens. Organizing to do so, however, led to another sharp exchange with FBI director Hoover, a man ever alert against what he considered challenges to his domestic authority. On August 23, 1946, he pungently complained to Leahy that Vandenberg's proposal for domestic clandestine intelligence collection by the CIG caused him "considerable concern," since he regarded the idea as "an invasion of domestic intelligence coverage which, according to our laws, is the sole responsibility of this Bureau." He then noted grandiloquently: "We are sure you will agree that it is imperative that the present arrangements for domestic intelligence coverage should not be tampered with at this critical period" and concluded that initiating Vandenberg's plan "definitely would create considerable difficulty and would inevitably lead to confusion, duplication of effort and intolerable conditions to the detriment of the national well-being." He appended a copy of a letter that he sent to Vandenberg arguing that such a domestic mission for the CIG was in flat contradiction to Truman's January intelligence directive.[56]

At a meeting of the IAB three days later, the issue provoked sharp discussion between Vandenberg and Hoover's representative, C. H. Carson. Vandenberg argued that the CIG could best carry out this intelligence function, since it could focus more people on it and could avoid the problem of duplication. Carson responded that the proposal, as Vandenberg presented it, was too broad and could conflict with the FBI's domestic operations. He suggested that the groups or individuals to be contacted be defined or that the enabling directive be limited to U.S. business concerns. Vandenberg objected that it would be impossible to specifically define such groups or individuals. He went on to assert that, since the CIG would be collecting "foreign positive intelligence," it would not be interfering with the FBI's internal security, criminal, or counterintelligence responsibilities. Carson remained unconvinced, and, after more discussion, the IAB resolved to temporize, to allow the DCI and the FBI director to work out the matter themselves.[57]

Leahy sought to mediate the dispute. Writing to Hoover on September 4, he observed that a "careful reading" of the proposed directive "fails to find wherein it invades the domestic coverage that is the responsibility of your Bureau" and requested that he send a representative "who is qualified to explain your objections" so he could discuss the issue with the NIA.[58] Instead, Hoover replied sharply on September 6 that he was seeking to avoid "duplication or confusion in contacts with representatives of foreign language groups and non-governmental groups and individuals in whom the Federal Bureau of Investigation is primarily interested because of its responsibility in covering Communist activities within the United States." He had no objection to the CIG making contacts with representatives of U.S. business organizations operating overseas and urged that the proposed directive be so confined. In his view, under Vandenberg's plan, the CIG "would be authorized to contact and to 'exploit' foreign language groups and other individuals with similar connections or background, which 'exploitation' would be in addition to similar utilization of these channels by the Federal Bureau of Investigation and I fear that there would be inevitable duplication, confusion, misunderstanding and perhaps conflict which would operate to the disadvantage" of both the FBI and the CIG.[59]

Since Vandenberg's domestic collection plan enjoyed both the support of the military intelligence chiefs and the indifference of the State Department, he was able to accommodate the recalcitrant Hoover with promises to respect his domestic authority, and his initiative was approved by the IAB on October 1.[60] His final victory in the contentious battle was spelled out in CIG Directive No. 15 issued the same day, entitled "Exploitation of American Business Concerns and Scientific, Educational and Religious Organizations with Connections Abroad and American Residents Abroad as Sources of Foreign Intelligence Information."

The directive set forth policy for collecting raw intelligence from representatives of business and other nongovernmental organizations operating overseas, as well as from U.S. citizens traveling or residing abroad. The DCI was given responsibility for securing the cooperation of such individuals and protecting their confidentiality. Under the directive, he was also charged with coordinating the exploitation of such sources nationwide with other government agencies, particularly the armed services and the FBI.[61]

Dynamic operator that he was, Vandenberg quickly set about organizing his growing intelligence empire. Beginning in July 1946, a series of directives created four more major offices in addition to OSO, each under an assistant director: Office of Collection and Dissemination, to gather and distribute the foreign intelligence information required to produce "national" intelligence estimates and to oversee their proper dissemination; Office of Reports and Estimates, to establish requirements and prepare regular intelligence reports; Office of Security, to develop overall policies in that area for the CIG; and Office of Operations, to collect overt information. Applying his military approach, he also established an Executive Staff under an executive director who served as the DCI's "chief of staff" and oversaw such administrative functions as personnel, supplies, budget, legislation, legal matters, and security. In addition, Vandenberg set up an Interdepartmental Coordinating and Planning Staff with personnel drawn from various government agencies to supervise and coordinate the development and implementation of overall intelligence plans throughout the government, and to make sure that the CIG and other intelligence organizations received the raw intelligence information needed and that finished intelligence was promptly disseminated.[62]

Despite his success in empire building, Vandenberg had never made a secret of either his desire to return to military service or his overriding ambition to head the soon-to-be-independent air force. As early as February 1947 the NIA had been considering a successor, and the pending retirement in April of General Ira Eaker as chief of the Army Air Forces and Air Staff brought both to realization. On April 30, 1947, Truman wrote Vandenberg that he had agreed to a request from Chief of Staff Eisenhower to release him as DCI and thanked him for services "exceptionally well-performed." At Leahy's initiative, the NIA approved Admiral Roscoe Hillenkoetter, U.S. naval attaché in Paris, as his replacement. Truman concurred and, again on April 30, wrote the admiral, naming him DCI, effective May 1. Although primarily a line navy officer (having recently commanded the battleship USS *Missouri*), Hillenkoetter was not without some intelligence experience. In addition to Paris, he had also served as naval attaché in Madrid and

Lisbon; during the war, he had commanded the navy's Intelligence Center, Pacific Ocean Areas, in Hawaii, under Admiral Nimitz from September 1942 until March 1943.[63] The White House duly announced the change on May 1. In his farewell statement, Vandenberg asserted that the United States needed a vigorous intelligence organization "if we are to be forewarned against possible acts of aggression and if we are to be armed against disaster in an era of atomic warfare." He denounced the idea that there was something "un-American about espionage and even about intelligence generally," arguing that, as a world power, the United States had to have an intelligence system that was "self-sufficient."[64]

By the measure of his accomplishments, Vandenberg was fully entitled to blow his own horn. In his brief tour as DCI, he had gone far to create the postwar intelligence empire that Donovan had only contemplated; in the process, had even bested the formidable J. Edgar Hoover in bureaucratic combat. By the end of 1946, the CIG had grown from a small cadre under Souers to approximately eighteen hundred persons. About a third were overseas with the OSO; of those in Washington, half were involved in administrative support functions, a third were part of OSO, and the remainder were devoted to intelligence analysis.[65] Although still relatively modest in size, a central intelligence organization was now in place. All that remained was the legislation that would bring it into legal existence.

8

Legislating a New Order

Despite Vandenberg's highly successful empire building, the Central Intelligence Group remained essentially a transitional organization pending the creation of a permanent organization through legislation, as well as a compromise in the face of opposition within the government to any sort of centralized intelligence office.[1] Intelligence "professionals" were clearly dissatisfied. William Colby later noted that

> the general consensus of professional intelligence people was that the CIG was a disorganized assembly of parts, not a working machine, bigger but not much better than before. What was worse, it even failed to perform the specific function for which it was created. Separate intelligence reports from G-2, ONI, the State Department and a host of other agencies still flooded the President's desk. The CIG merely added one more, albeit an interesting one, to the unstanchable stream.[2]

Another "professional," Ray Cline, commented: "When attempts were made to prepare agreed national estimates on the basis of intelligence available to all, the coordination process was interminable, dissents were the rule rather than the exception, and every policymaking official took his own agency's intelligence appreciations along to the White House to argue his case. The prewar chaos was largely recreated with only a little more lip service to coordination."[3]

Upon becoming DCI, Vandenberg took up the cause. Irked by having to rely on the State, War, and Navy Departments for funds and personnel, he quickly became a strong advocate of legislation to provide an institutional mandate for his organization. To achieve his purpose, Vandenberg relied heavily on Lawrence Houston, a lawyer and OSS veteran who had continued in the SSU. Appointed CIG general counsel by Souers, he had been working on draft enabling legislation since February 1946.[4] It soon became clear that time also was of the essence. On June 13, 1946, Houston sent Vandenberg a memo pointing out that, whatever the thrust of Truman's January directive, legally the CIG had "purely a coordination function with no substance or authority to act on its own responsibility in other than an advisory and directing capacity." In Houston's view, therefore, the CIG lacked the power to take personnel actions, certify payrolls and vouchers, authorize travel, procure supplies, or enter into contracts. Therefore, said Houston, "the essential problem is that the CIG has no power to expend Government funds." Houston also pointed out that a recently enacted law (the Independent Offices Appropriation Act of 1945) declared that no funds could be made available to any agency that remained in existence for more than one year without a congressional appropriation during that year. Thus, concluded Houston woefully, "after 22 January 1947, Departments could not even furnish unvouchered funds to the Director, CIG, and it would be questionable whether the Departments could furnish personnel and supplies paid for out of vouchered funds."[5]

Thus motivated, the CIG got down to work. Vandenberg and the "intelligence professionals" were in full accord regarding what they wanted—a Donovanesque freestanding intelligence organization reporting directly to the president, with a seat on the projected national security policy-making "council," a separate budget, clearly defined responsibilities for the DCI, and authorization for the clandestine procurement, financial activities, and personnel actions deemed essential for the conduct of "secret operations." Primary drafting work on the proposed law fell to Houston and his deputy, John Warner, and responsibility for expediting its passage through Congress belonged to Walter Pforzheimer, the chief of legislative liaison. Although not a lawyer, he proved a crafty lobbyist.[6]

Vandenberg, meanwhile, took up the battle with the NIA. At its meeting on July 17, 1946, he complained that the CIG needed an "adequate and capable" staff to fully meet its responsibility to provide intelligence and that, under the present structure, it was proving "extremely difficult administratively" to hire the personnel needed to do so. He therefore felt that it was absolutely necessary for the CIG to be established as an agency by enabling legislation with its own funds. Byrnes and Patterson responded that the present structure had been intentionally established to avoid a separate CIG budget, since it was considered necessary, for security reasons, to conceal "the amount of money being spent on central intelligence." In response, Vandenberg commented that such considerations had to "be balanced against the administrative difficulties they caused." Admiral Leahy admitted that the CIG "eventually would broaden its scope" and thought that the NIA should get its own appropriation. Nevertheless, he also thought that primary funding should come through the three departments. After more wrangling over the CIG's budgetary and personnel problems, Leahy said that the matter had to "be approached very carefully" and deferred to Byrnes on it, due to his "Congressional background." He made clear, however, that the president considered the NIA to be the responsible agency for intelligence collection and coordination and that the DCI was "not responsible further" than to carry out its directives. He added that Truman was not in favor of presenting separate intelligence enabling legislation to Congress at that time. After more discussion about the CIG money issue, the NIA authorized Byrnes to approach the Budget Bureau about it.[7]

Subsequent discussions did not resolve the issue, and Vandenberg returned to it at the NIA meeting of February 12, 1947. Changing his tack, he complained that the uncertain status of the DCI was hindering the proper coordination of intelligence activities, since existing directives were unclear about his power to act on his own. This time his strategy worked, and his importunings received a more positive response. The NIA resolved that the DCI "shall operate within his jurisdiction as an agent of the Secretaries of State, War, and Navy and the necessary authority is hereby delegated by the Secretaries . . . so that his decisions, orders and directives shall be considered as emanating from them and shall have full force and effect as such, provided that any aggrieved agency may have access to that agency's Secretary and through him to the NIA."[8]

Vandenberg's toughest battle, however, proved to be with the White House. In overall discussions concerning national security reform legislation, Truman took little personal interest in the provisions concerning the proposed Central Intelligence Agency and left the matter to his staff, under the direction of Clark Clifford.[9] The politically astute Clifford knew even better than Vandenberg how to manipulate the levers of power. Unlike the general, who functioned within a rigid structure of command, Clifford operated in an environment of persuasion, manipulation, and compromise among people who could not be commanded. Since it was in this environment that legislation would be produced, Clifford was on his home ground. Replacing Vardaman as naval aide early in 1946, Clifford acquired increased power when, effective May 6, Truman closed down the White House Map Room, set up by Roosevelt in 1942 to serve as his wartime operations center. In announcing his action to the secretaries of state, war, and navy, and the DCI, Truman directed that material sent to the Map Room should be directed to the office of his naval aide for forwarding to him. Clifford's hold on power was civilianized and further consolidated the following month when he replaced Samuel Rosenman as counsel to the president. Because Rosenman's leave-taking had been an extended one, Clifford had been handling much of his business and had a firm grasp of Truman's programs and priorities.[10]

Thus, from the first, Vandenberg and his lieutenants had to deal with Clifford on the issue of intelligence legislation. It soon became apparent that Vanden-

berg and the "intelligence professionals" were out of step with the broad political consensus that had developed among policy makers in the executive branch
and legislators in Congress as a result of the extensive discussions on the issue
of national security reform that had occurred since 1944. Reputedly taken aback
when first presented with the CIG's sweeping initial proposals by Houston, according to one account Clifford exclaimed: "I thought you were to be a small
coordinating group!" To which Houston smugly responded: "No, we are to be
an operating agency." [11]

Clifford, however, held the high cards, since actual drafting of the enabling
legislation was done under his direction by a committee comprising presidential aide Charles Murphy, Deputy CNO Forrest Sherman, and Army Major General Lauris Norstad, director of Plans and Operations for the War Department.
In their work, the drafters followed the lines laid down in the past debates. Only
one section dealt with the CIA, and the drafters consciously intended it to be a
generalized statement showing how the CIA would be part of the overall administrative structure, pending a separate organic law for the CIA itself, which was
viewed as too extensive a piece of legislation to be included in the overall act and
therefore would be submitted at a later date. [12] Such an approach was hardly to
the liking of Vandenberg and the "intelligence professionals," however, who regarded it as something put together in a "scissors and paste" fashion from earlier
legislative proposals. [13]

Vandenberg, however, was not familiar with defeat, and he was quick to take
the offensive. Battle was joined on June 28, when he forwarded a copy of the
CIG's own draft proposals to Clifford for review. In true Donovanesque style, a
"declaration of policy" at the beginning stated grandly: "Experience in the two
world wars and the interim period between has shown that the acquisition of
foreign intelligence by separate departments and agencies is inadequate to inform properly the people of the United States and their elected representatives of
the events, trends and plans in foreign countries which, if known, might serve
to avert armed conflict. The lesson thus learned is that intelligence gathering and
analysis must be centralized so that all sources and facilities may be utilized to
their fullest potentialities. Accordingly, it is hereby declared to be the policy of
the people of the United States that in order to assure the common defense and
security, the processing, analysis, and dissemination of foreign intelligence shall
be centralized and its procurement coordinated so as to keep fully informed the
proper officers and departments of Government." The purpose of the legislation
was, therefore, to establish programs for coordinating the procurement of intelligence, its analysis and evaluation, and its dissemination, as well as "to take such

other measures in the field of foreign intelligence as will best serve to promote the national defense."

In accord with this glorious vision, the draft legislation would officially establish the NIA and create a Central Intelligence Agency under a director of central intelligence to be appointed by the president from either military or civilian life and confirmed by the Senate for a term of not more than seven years. Military officers so appointed would retain their service ranks and prerequisites. Military and civilian personnel from other government agencies could be assigned to the CIA, and it would be the duty of the CIA, under policies established by the NIA, "to plan, develop and coordinate the foreign intelligence activities of the United States in such a manner as to assure the most effective accomplishment of the intelligence mission relating to the national security." To carry out these objectives, the CIA would be authorized to correlate, evaluate, and disseminate intelligence information, make plans for the coordination of government intelligence activities, and perform "intelligence services of common concern," as well as "such other functions and duties relating to intelligence affecting the national security as the President or the National Intelligence Authority may from time to time direct." The draft denied the CIA domestic police powers and charged the DCI with the responsibility for protecting sources and methods. While other government agencies would retain their intelligence authority, the CIA would utilize their facilities and services, their intelligence production would be made available to the DCI, and their operations would be open to his inspection.

The proposal also gave the DCI sweeping powers. Without regard to other legislation, he was authorized to procure "necessary services, supplies, and equipment" upon "certification by the Director that such action is necessary in the interest of common defense and security or showing that advertising is not reasonably practicable" and to transfer "such sums as may be authorized by the Bureau of the Budget to other departments or agencies of the Government for the performance of any of the functions or activities authorized herein." All funds appropriated for the administration of the CIA and its personnel could be expended "without regard to the provisions of the law and regulations relating to the expenditure of Government funds or the employment of persons in the Government services"; "for objects of a confidential nature," such expenditures would be "accounted for solely on the certificate of the Director and every such certificate shall be deemed a sufficient voucher for the amount therein certified." [14]

At the White House, however, Clifford viewed the grand design of the "intelligence professionals" with considerable distaste. Clifford was a "power realist" and an increasingly hard-line cold warrior whose objections were based not on the sweeping grants of secret authority but on how far the proposal strayed from the parameters set by the White House and what, to his lawyerly mind, was sloppy drafting. In a trenchant response on July 12, he commented that in "several places the language seems difficult and unnecessarily repetitious," but "a more serious objection than that of the language . . . is the failure of the bill to define in clear terms the sense in which the word 'intelligence' is used." In Clifford's view, this failure of definition would "lead to the suspicion that the 'National Intelligence Authority' and the 'Central Intelligence Agency' will attempt to control, with the powers granted in this bill, the FBI and other intelligence activities." He then noted some "serious omissions" in the draft, such as the failure to define the functions and duties of the NIA and the failure to specifically establish the office of DCI. After enumerating a long list of specific errors, he concluded with a warning: "There are certain questions of policy about which I feel considerable concern, but I shall reserve comment on those unless you request it." [15]

Vandenberg had the sense to "request it," and on July 16 his assistant, James Lay, along with Houston, came to the White House to meet with Clifford and his deputy, George Elsey, on the legislation. Clifford opened the meeting by remarking that the draft he had received from Vandenberg went beyond the president's intentions by creating a separate and sizable new agency. When asked by Clifford why the original system established by Truman in January was unworkable, both Houston and Lay complained at some length about the personnel and fiscal problems that the CIG was having as the "step child [sic]" of three separate departments. They considered enabling legislation necessary to allow the CIG to function as an "integrated" operational organization with a large staff of intelligence experts. After considerable discussion, all agreed that the CIG needed to be reconstituted as a legally established and relatively large operating agency. Lay and Houston agreed to rewrite the legislation to accommodate Clifford's objections, and the meeting broke up with Clifford's admonition that careless drafting would arouse congressional objections. [16] Back at the CIG, Pforzheimer and his associates spent the following months redrafting and reorganizing their proposed bill; on December 2 they transmitted a revised draft back to the White House. More tightly written and better organized than its predecessor, it met the letter of Clifford's complaints but retained the broad authority given the DCI and ignored the White House's objection to creating a new, independent organization. [17]

The legislative process was not in the hands of Vandenberg and the "intelligence professionals" at CIG, however. Because the legislation establishing the centralized intelligence organization they desired was part of a broader enactment for national security reform, it was held hostage by the higher-profile wrangling between the War and Navy Departments over the future roles and structure of the armed forces in the new system. As a result, the intelligence issue went on the back burner as Secretaries Patterson and Forrestal sought to hammer out compromises on the "unification" question. Chafing at the delay, Vandenberg opted for direct pressure on Clifford to expedite matters. The December 2 draft had included a proposed statement on the importance of establishing a Central Intelligence Agency to be incorporated in Truman's 1947 State of the Union address.[18] On January 7, 1947, Vandenberg personally came to the White House to confront Clifford directly on the issue. Recalled Clifford: "Perhaps emboldened by the Republican victory in the Congressional elections [of November 1946], which had just made his uncle Chairman of the Senate Foreign Relations Committee [as well as president pro tem] Vandenberg expressed disappointment, verging on outrage, that the President was not going to recommend the creation of the CIA in his 1947 State of the Union message."[19] Clifford replied curtly that such a recommendation had been included in earlier drafts, but both Truman and Leahy had decided that it was "unnecessary and undesirable" to raise the matter with Congress as long as the interservice issues remained unresolved. Obviously miffed, Vandenberg said that he would raise the question of legislation with the NIA and report his actions back to Clifford.[20] Unintimidated, Clifford's deputy Elsey pigeonholed the CIG's draft bill with the laconic note: "To be filed, awaiting further advice from the National Intelligence Authority."[21]

Vandenberg was not the only aggrieved party in the development of intelligence legislation. The State Department, which had not been included in the drafting process, saw a threat to its own prerogatives in the creation of a Central Intelligence Agency responsible to a National Security Council on which the military services were heavily represented. Writing to Under Secretary Acheson on February 6, 1947, Office of Research and Intelligence chief William Eddy complained that the proposed legislation "would render more difficult the promotion of peaceful foreign relations by subordinating the political and economic intelligence activities of the Department of State to a Central Intelligence Agency completely dominated by the Armed Forces; and that it would further have the ultimate if not the immediate effect of placing the reporting activities of the Foreign Service under military control in time of peace as well as in time of war." Eddy noted that while the secretary of state chaired the NIA, he would be reduced to a level of equality with the members of the military establishment on the proposed NSC. Eddy also observed that the CIA "would be dominated by the military, with no indication that a representative of the Secretary of State would be accredited even as an adviser to the new Director of Central Intelligence, to whom it is proposed to give the salary and prerequisites of a 4-star general." Eddy further complained that these benefits would make the DCI favor military interests rather than "the civilian and peacetime interests of the Department of State."

Eddy continued by observing that, since nothing was said in the proposed legislation about unifying the various military intelligence units, its effect would be "the imposition of a new echelon above the Armed Forces and above the Department of State, with an intelligence agency whose powers are almost unlimited, an agency responsible to the National Security Council on which the Secretary of State occupies a position . . . exactly equal to that of one of the subsecretaries for Army, Navy, or Air." He predicted that, under such a system, "the facilities of the Department of State, both for collecting and evaluating foreign intelligence, will be subordinated to, if not actually controlled by, the Armed Forces establishment." He went on to point out that "at present our Government is served with foreign intelligence chiefly by the Foreign Service trained to preserve political and economic good relations with the rest of the world." Under the new act, however, said Eddy, "this worldwide coverage would be forced into the service of the military," which might be justified in wartime, but in time of peace, "the National Intelligence Service should be under genuinely civilian control and its estimates of political and economic situations abroad should be subject, as at present, to the preview [sic] by the Department of State which has the responsibility for our foreign policy." [22]

Through Acheson, Eddy's views reached Secretary of State Marshall, who apparently used them in a strong message to Truman on the following day in which he eloquently expressed his department's concern that an NSC dominated by the military would institute "a critical departure from the traditional method of conducting foreign policy." According to Marshall, under the proposed statute,

> [I]t would be the duty of the Council in carrying out the specific obligations imposed upon it and in exercising the authority granted to limit, in effect, this vital responsibility of the President in the first instance and at the same time markedly to diminish the responsibility of the Secretary of State. . . . The constitutional and traditional control of the President in the conduct of foreign affairs, principally throughout our history with the aid of the Secretary of State, is deeply rooted, I believe, in the sentiments of the people.

This view led Marshall to express concerns over the proposed establishment of a "central intelligence agency." Although not opposed in principle to some such organization, Marshall declared that the "Foreign Service of the Department of State is the only collection agency of the government which covers the whole world, and we should be very slow to subject the collection and evaluation of this foreign intelligence to other establishments, especially during times of peace. The powers of the proposed agency seem almost unlimited and need clarification." [23]

Marshall's views nonetheless went unheeded by Truman, who was committed to the broad executive-legislative consensus concerning national security reorganization of which he had been a part since his days in the Senate. Writing to the secretary on February 15, Eddy sought to put matters in their best light: "A central agency for national intelligence under civilian control is needed continuously in time of peace in addition to intelligence services in the several Departments." He observed that such an organization would be valuable for supplying intelligence "required by interdepartmental agencies . . . whose responsibilities extend beyond the province" of any single department; intelligence "on matters which may be of secondary interest to any one Department, and which would, therefore otherwise be neglected, but which may be of prime interest for national policy"; and "[u]nder-cover intelligence and espionage abroad which should not compromise the official representatives of the United States of America." He added: "Espionage, which is certainly needed, and which involves the employment of unofficial agents, both American and foreign, should be operated by an agency outside the Departments and with funds not subject to departmental accounting."

He continued by asserting that the CIG, under the proposed legislation, should be able to perform these "valuable services" and had "already made a good beginning." Nevertheless, it should avoid "entering the field of departmental intelligence where duplication would be wasteful. Only the Army and the Navy are technically equipped to direct their operational services; and only the Department of State, through its Foreign Service, attempts to cover the world with expert political and economic reports for its daily political and economic operations." In emphasizing the importance of operating a secret espionage service with its own "special agents and special funds," he concluded on a familiar note: "Of all the great nations of the world, the United States of America has lacked an efficient espionage service, which, in many critical parts of the world, is the only way to acquire indispensable information." [24] Marshall apparently agreed, for he took no further part in the legislative debate.

By February 1947 Patterson and Forrestal had resolved interservice disputes sufficiently to complete the drafting of the legislation. On February 26 Truman transmitted the proposed National Security Act of 1947 to Congress under a curt covering letter recommending enactment to Speaker of the House Joseph Martin and President Pro Tem of the Senate Vandenberg.[25] On February 28 it was introduced into the House as H.R. 2319 by Republican Clare Hoffman of Michigan and referred to his Committee on Expenditures in the Executive Departments. In the Senate it was introduced as S. 758 by Chan Gurney of South Dakota and assigned to his newly established Armed Services Committee.[26] The intelligence provisions were noncontroversial. The section dealing with the CIA was brief, merely establishing the new agency, subordinate to the NSC, under a presidentially appointed DCI. A second part permitted the service of a military officer as DCI without the loss of his prerequisites of rank. The last part provided that, upon the DCI's appointment, the NIA would cease to exist and that all funds, property, personnel, records, and duties of the CIG would be transferred to the CIA.[27] Nothing was said about the new agency's powers or restrictions upon it.[28]

These provisions, like the law itself, reflected the consensus that had developed since the war. Memories of Pearl Harbor and the unsettled international situation had strengthened the hand of the "reformers" who sought both a stronger system for national security management and a stronger intelligence capacity within it.[29] Their views were represented in a statement by Senator Thomas on March 14 that praised the measure and said of its central intelligence provisions:

> The significance of the collection, analysis, and evaluation of information concerning foreign countries is no less great now than it was during the war. The effective conduct of both foreign and military policy is dependent on the possession of full, accurate, and skillfully analyzed information concerning foreign countries. With our present world-wide sphere of international responsibility and our position among the world powers, we need the most efficient intelligence system that can be devised. . . . We have now a central intelligence agency established by executive action. Provision for such an agency should be made in permanent legislation. It seems entirely logical that such an agency should be placed in the framework of an agency that might be set up to coordinate military and foreign policies.[30]

Senate hearings began on March 18 and lasted for ten weeks. Although most of the committee's attention was focused on other issues and most of the discussions on intelligence were conducted in executive session, the proceedings produced a number of statements on the nature and conduct of foreign intelligence operations that clearly presented official thinking on a subject that was to become of critical importance in the postwar world. In virtually his last official act as DCI, Vandenberg vigorously promoted the legislation, visiting Senator Gurney and conferring with his powerful uncle, although what he said is unknown. He also took pains in drafting his prepared statement, relying on Pforzheimer, who reportedly told him that Congress "was loaded for bear" on the issue.[31]

On April 29 Vandenberg delivered his prepared statement to Gurney's committee on the importance of centralized intelligence. He endorsed the legislation, proclaiming that "a strong intelligence system is equally if not more essential in peace than in war" because: "Upon us has fallen leadership in world affairs. The oceans have shrunk until today both Europe and Asia border the United States almost as do Canada and Mexico. The interests, intentions, and capabilities of the various nations on these land masses must be fully known to our national policymakers. We must have this intelligence if we are to be forewarned against possible acts of aggression and if we are to be armed against disaster in an era of atomic warfare."

He went on to recall the disorganization of prewar intelligence work, which he felt had contributed to the surprise at Pearl Harbor; he believed that in the CIG and CIA "must be found the answer to the prevention of another Pearl Harbor." Referring to past dependence on the British, he observed: "Having attained its present international position of importance and power in an unstable world, the United States should not . . . find itself again confronted with the necessity of developing its plans and policies on the basis of intelligence collected, compiled, and interpreted by some foreign government." He concluded by emphasizing that the establishment of a permanent, centralized agency would promote "efficiency and economy" in all aspects of intelligence collection, evaluation, and dissemination; would retain many highly competent individuals in the intelligence field and secure the services of others; and would promote coordination and cooperation among the existing intelligence agencies.[32]

Expurgated from the official text placed in the record by Gurney on the following day was a section on the necessity for clandestine operations in which Vandenberg had asserted:

> I believe we should frankly acknowledge the need for and provide the means of collecting intelligence which can only be obtained by clandestine methods. In this we only follow, late by many years, the policy and example of every foreign nation. When properly provided for and established, these operations must be centralized in one organization. The ex-

perience of the British Secret Intelligence Service over hundreds of years proves this. The Germans violated this principle—as did the Italians and Japanese—with disastrous results for themselves.[33]

As the Senate deliberated, a ghost from the past reappeared. Because William J. Donovan had relied on presidential patronage to gain his ends as OSS chief, he had never bothered to develop a congressional constituency. As a result, he had been ignored on Capitol Hill as he had been in the Truman White House in the development of intelligence-related legislation. Nevertheless, due to his contacts with Wall Street colleagues working in Washington, he had kept generally abreast of legislative proposals for intelligence organization.[34] Not liking what he saw in the pending bill, he decided to undertake some direct lobbying.

Writing to Senator Gurney on May 7, he complained that the idea of putting the CIA under the NSC "not only perpetuates the existing evil of bad organization" but also "intensifies that evil" by making the CIA "not a central but a joint agency." In Donovan's view, for intelligence to be effective, "it must have parity of status," and the proposed legislation "would 'freeze' into law that which up to now has been a 'custom' devised out of service jurisdictional disputes and which can result only in fostering these disputes." His proposed solution was to have the new organization "report for administration and direction to the Secretary of National Defense [sic] but advise with the Security Council [sic] in the type and kind of information that is needed" and "to require that the Director of Central Intelligence be a civilian." Included with his letter was a long memorandum setting forth a version of his November 1944 proposal as detailed in his Life article of the preceding year.[35]

In a second letter to Gurney on May 19, Donovan changed his thrust:

> Strategic intelligence is not confined to the military but has a broader overall base. Therefore it would seem desirable in the public interest to take the central intelligence proposal out of the bill and deal with it on its merits, free from controversial service jurisdictional questions present in the unification bill. . . . Adequate information lies at the threshhold [sic] of our foreign policy. Why not start there and set up a proper intelligence machine on its own, the head of which would report directly to the President, until the Congress can decide whether there is some other way to give an intelligence organization the parity of position with other departments which it must have in order to be effective.[36]

Obviously taken aback by Donovan's gratuitous interposition, Gurney consulted with Pforzheimer on May 26. The cunning Pforzheimer, clearly recognizing that the pending legislation was the most he and his fellow "intelligence professionals" could expect, was not about to permit Donovan to derail the only opportunity available to create an independent central intelligence organization and gave his suggestions no support. He opined that placing the CIA under the military establishment would be unfair to the State Department and was not intended. He also saw no good reason for independent legislative action on the CIA provisions of the bill and complained that Donovan had not responded to Vandenberg's request to discuss the legislation. Thus reassured, Gurney continued on his present legislative course.[37]

Although Donovan was absent, his disciples were at hand to speak on his behalf. The most notable among them was Allen Dulles, Donovan's wartime spymaster in Switzerland. While at that time in private law practice, Dulles was nevertheless well on his way to becoming an intelligence legend in his own time, and the statement he submitted to Gurney on April 27 represented a major presentation by a leading "intelligence professional" of the nature of his craft. In Dulles's view, to create an effective CIA,

> we must have in our key positions men who are prepared to make this a life work, not a mere casual occupation. Service in the Agency should not be viewed merely as a stepping stone to promotion in one of the armed services or other branches of the Government. The Agency should be directed by a relatively small but elite corps of men with a passion for anonymity and a willingness to stick to that particular job. They must find their reward primarily in the work itself, and in the service they render their Government, rather than in public acclaim.

The CIA should be predominantly civilian, Dulles maintained, and its director should be a civilian with long tenure: "Appointment as Chief of Intelligence [sic] should be somewhat comparable to appointment to a high judicial office, and should be equally free from interferences due to political charges." The director, therefore, should be able to pick his own subordinates and have none imposed on him for "political" reasons, while his staff should be highly professional, long tenured, and devoted to intelligence work.

While not dismissing military participation entirely, Dulles believed that CIA leadership "should act in a civilian and not a military capacity" because peacetime intelligence work would differ greatly from wartime in techniques, personnel, and objectives. Problems would be not only military and strategic, thought Dulles, but also scientific, political, and social: "We must deal with the problem of conflicting ideologies as democracy faces communism, not only in the relations between Soviet Russia and the countries of the west, but in the internal political conflicts within the countries of Europe, Asia, and South America." As far as organization and functions were concerned, Dulles objected to the CIA being made subordinate to the NSC, which he regarded as being too large, ineffective, and dominated by the military. Instead, he preferred for the DCI to report to a smaller body, similar to the NIA, which would be composed of representatives of the secretaries of state and defense and the president.

While Dulles emphasized the importance of the State Department in collecting intelligence, he believed that the evaluation of intelligence should be the responsibility of the CIA. He maintained, however, that the CIA "should have nothing to do with policy" but should "try to get at hard facts on which others must determine policy." Dulles then noted six basic requirements for an effective intelligence agency: control of its own personnel and the right to co-opt personnel from other agencies for temporary duty; its own budget, with possible supplemental funds drawn from the budgets of the State Department and defense establishment to carry out unidentified "special operations" deemed necessary by the president and his national security advisers; "exclusive jurisdiction" for carrying out "secret intelligence" activities; access to intelligence information originated by any government agency, including that obtained by communications intelligence; recognition as the agency responsible for dealing with foreign intelligence organizations; and having "its operations and personnel protected by 'official secrets' legislation which would provide adequate penalties for breach of security." Calling intelligence the "first line of defense" in the future, he boldly concluded: "In this country we have the raw material for building the greatest intelligence service in the world. But to accomplish this we must make it a respectable, continuing, and adequately remunerated career. . . . With proper legislative backing, a correct technical set-up, and adequate leadership, all that is required for success is hard work, discriminating judgment and common sense. Americans can be found who are not lacking in these qualities."[38]

Less eminent than Dulles but no less articulate in his views was Charles S. Cheston, a former assistant director of OSS from 1943 to 1945 who had become an active lobbyist in his own right for a postwar central intelligence organization. In a memorandum placed in the record by Gurney on May 9, Cheston also emphasized the importance of a strong intelligence system in an age when atomic energy and long-range airpower had eliminated the defense of distance enjoyed by the United States. He therefore urged that the proposed agency be equal in status to the armed services and posited three basic tenets of its own for its proper functioning. The first was a civilian director to guarantee a broader range of subject-matter competence, continuity of leadership, and freedom for the agency from the "rigidities of the military system." The second was for a separate budget to guarantee the agency's independence, and the third (in sharp contrast to Dulles) was for the agency to be directly responsible to the secretary of defense. Like Dulles, however, he concluded by affirming that what was needed was "an effective, integrated single agency with clearly defined duties and authority to analyze and correlate information from all sources and, wherever necessary, to supplement existing methods of collection of information." [39]

The only discordant note was sounded in a statement by Frederick Libby, executive secretary of the National Council for the Prevention of War, submitted on May 7 and placed in the record two days later. According to Libby, the legislation, as a whole, would guarantee "brass hat control of our foreign policy" and "military 'Secret police unlimited' policing of the United States." He added that the bill set "no limits to the authority and functions" of the CIA either at home or abroad, and, under its provisions, the agency was "free to become a Gestapo at home and a universal spy system abroad." Libby's message called attention to the absence of a ban on internal police functions and expressed concern over the authorization for military officers to serve as director: "It would seem clear that no bill should ever be passed by Congress that would give the big brass unlimited police power." His statement concluded by suggesting that the CIA provisions of the defunct 1946 Senate legislation be used as a model on the subject. [40]

In the end, the senators stayed with the original version. On June 12 the committee approved the bill by a vote of 12 to 0 and sent it to the Senate floor. The report on the bill stated, concerning its intelligence provisions:

> In view of the fact that certain officers of the armed services have had wide experience in handling the type of intelligence with which this agency will be largely concerned, the provision of the bill to permit the Director of Central Intelligence to be appointed from the armed services as well as from civil life is most desirable. During the Agency's formative years, it is essential that its Director be technically the most experienced and capable obtainable, regardless of whether he is appointed from civilian or military life.

After floor debate concerning other provisions of the bill, it was passed by voice vote on July 12. [41]

In the House, hearings began on April 2 and continued until the end of June. It was ironic that so military-centered a piece of legislation could end up before a committee that usually focused on the administration of civilian agencies. Adding to the irony, Chairman Hoffman himself had no previous military service, no seat on any committee dealing with military matters, and no major military installations in his district. In addition, he had been a strong prewar isolationist, with little apparent interest in foreign or military affairs.[42] This irony would prove important, however. Although, as in the Senate, there was no dispute over the basic premise of establishing a central intelligence organization, the strong civilian orientation of the committee's responsibilities generated concerns ignored in the upper house and overlooked by proponents of the legislation: the question of civil liberties.

While a considerable amount of testimony was given in executive session, the open hearings proved surprisingly candid. Forrestal took the lead concerning the intelligence provisions and was closely questioned by several committee members during his appearance on April 25. J. Caleb Boggs, Republican of Delaware, felt that the intelligence provisions were among the most important in the bill, but he expressed "some fears" over their "generality" because he saw "no limitation" and no provision for Senate confirmation of the DCI. He believed that "there should be a provision with more care and more restriction" to "safeguard all of our rights here." Forrestal replied that "the President has in mind nothing contrary to that objective. The broad principle upon which this bill was written, for the framework in which it was conceived, was to avoid freezing it, limiting it too narrowly because . . . this is not a blueprint or a chart from which you can move to immediate results." He concurred with Boggs's view that the DCI should be confirmed by the Senate. In response to Boggs's suggestion that the DCI was important enough to be a member of the NSC, Forrestal replied: "I think that there is always some limit to the effectiveness of any organization in proportion to the number of people that are on it." He believed that intelligence information would be given to policy makers as a matter of course, adding that the normal functions of the NSC would require the frequent presence of the DCI. Boggs was not entirely convinced, so Forrestal was forced to conclude: "This thing will only work . . . if the components want it to work."[43]

The sharpest questioner proved to be Republican Clarence Brown of Ohio, who was particularly concerned over the fact that the proposed legislation merely enabled the new CIA to take over the CIG and nowhere defined the scope of the new agency's power. Brown professed himself to be "very much interested in seeing that the United States have as fine a foreign military and naval intelligence as they can possibly have, but I am not interested in setting up here in the United States any particular central policy agency under any President, and I do not care what his name may be, and just allow him to have a gestapo of his own if he wants to have it." He then added: "Every now and then you get a man that comes up in power that has an imperialistic idea." Forrestal replied that the new organization would be "limited definitely to purposes outside this country, except for the collation of information gathered by other Government agencies" and added that Vandenberg had relied on collaboration with the FBI for "domestic operations." When asked if this was stated in the law, Forrestal admitted that it was not, and Brown responded: "That could be changed in 2 minutes and have the action within the United States instead of without." Forrestal answered that such action could be taken only with "direct and specific" presidential approval, causing Brown to rejoin that "even then it could be done without violation of the law by the President or somebody who might write the order for him and get his approval, and without the knowledge and consent or direction of the Congress." He then asked Forrestal rhetorically: "Do you think it would be wise . . . to at least fix some limitations on what the power of this individual might be, or what could be done, or what should be done, and all these safeguards and rights of the citizen may be protected?" Forrestal dodged a direct answer and was rescued from the Ohioan by the chairman's call for adjournment.[44]

Brown persisted in his concerns. In further hearings on June 12, he commented that he wanted "to write a lot of safeguards into this section that deals with the Central Intelligence Agency. I want to make certain that the activities and functions of the Central Intelligence Agency are carefully confined to international matters and to military matters and national security. We have enough people now running around the country looking into other people's business without establishing another agency to do so." He added: "What we ought to do is eliminate 90 percent of the present snoopers instead of adding to them. I do not think it would be the Central Intelligence Agency's right, authority, or responsibility to check on the ordinary domestic activities of the average American citizen, and yet they could have the power and authority to do it under this bill as written."[45]

By now it became clear to the "intelligence professionals" that Brown's strongly held views posed a challenge to their legislative goal, and Pforzheimer once again moved to reclaim control of the situation. After the June 12 hearing, he talked privately to Brown, who vowed that further safeguards would be written into the bill.[46] To avoid unwanted amendments, Pforzheimer launched an end run around the Ohioan's objections. On June 19 he met with Representative James Wadsworth of New York, a member of the committee long identified with the internationalist wing of the Republican Party and in general sympathy with the administration's legislative approach. Alluding to Brown, Pforzheimer expressed concern "regarding the feelings of certain members of the Committee and some witnesses appearing before it that we were, or might become an incipient Gestapo, or interested in domestic intelligence of any sort." He then told Wadsworth that the CIG leadership was considering addressing a letter to chairman Hoffman suggesting that a provision be included in the bill to prohibit any police, internal security, or law enforcement powers. Wadsworth strongly endorsed the idea, although he thought the sentiments of concern to the CIG were "not very general." Pforzheimer later met with Hoffman, who said that he would gladly receive such an amendment, introduce it, and "give it every consideration."[47]

Other testimony concerning the legislation by administration spokesmen was relatively routine. Secretary of War Patterson testified on April 2, 24, and 29 but added little of substance. In the course of his appearances, he explained to Representative William J. B. Dorn, Democrat of South Carolina, that the CIA would not be on the military establishment's policy council in order to protect its independence; he assured Pennsylvania Republican Mitchell Jenkins that the CIA would have only the responsibilities of the CIG and would not replace the military and naval intelligence services. Testifying on May 8, Chief of Staff Eisenhower spoke of the proposed CIA with approval and, in response to a question from Democrat John McCormack of Massachusetts, emphasized the importance of permanence and a strong intelligence background as requirements for any future DCI. On June 24 the committee heard from Dr. Vannevar Bush, the engineer and eminent technocrat who had headed the wartime Office of Scientific Research and Development and was, in 1947, the chairman of the War and Navy Department's Joint Research and Development Board. He, too, spoke of the postwar need for high-quality intelligence but, in response to questions from Republican Walter Judd of Minnesota and Henry Latham of New York, said that a civilian would be more appropriate to head the CIA, since a military officer would have a career outside intelligence work to pursue. He also thought there would be "no danger" of the CIA becoming a "Gestapo," since it would be dealing with foreign matters.[48]

As in the Senate, there were some discordant voices. Retired Admiral Zacharias, in a prepared statement of June 19, commented that the CIA proposal was "inadequate in every respect in that it fails to provide specifically for a well integrated and efficient organization," but he declined to discuss specific alternatives in open hearings.[49] The most pungent criticism came from Merritt Edson, a marine brigadier general who had chosen early retirement in order to freely criticize the entire unification bill. In a statement of June 17, he declared that the legislation "opens the door toward a potential gestapo or NKVD in the Central Intelligence Agency, and then invites its domination by the military." In a discourse with Representative Jenkins and Democrat Chet Holifield of California, Edson emphasized that the CIA should have no domestic police power, that it should have a civilian director, and that Congress should "definitely set forth" the scope of its powers and functions.[50]

House hearings ended on July 1. The concerns voiced in those hearings had influenced the committee, and the CIA section of the bill was drastically amended by the time it reached the House floor on July 16. The chamber resolved itself into a Committee of the Whole on July 19 to consider all amendments and approved the measure by voice vote that same day. The Senate, however, was initially unwilling to accept the amendments and, on July 21, called for a conference. In conference, the Senate concurred in the House amendments on July 24 and so voted that day, while the House accepted the conference decision on July 25.[51]

The section of the National Security Act of 1947 that created the CIA drew heavily on the Thomas-Austin-Hill draft legislation of the preceding year. The act abolished the NIA and CIG and created, as the official successor to the latter, a Central Intelligence Agency. The new agency was responsible to the NSC and was to be headed by a director appointed by the president and confirmed by the Senate. The DCI could be either a civilian or a military officer, but in the latter case he was removed from all military chains of command, although retaining all prerequisites of rank. The DCI was specifically charged with protecting intelligence "sources and methods" from "unauthorized disclosure" and was empowered, at his discretion, to remove any agency employee "whenever he shall deem such termination necessary or advisable in the interests of the United States."

The responsibilities of the agency were generally described as follows: coordinating government intelligence activities, advising the NSC on intelligence matters, evaluating and distributing intelligence information, performing services of "common concern" in the intelligence field as determined by the NSC, and "such other functions and duties related to intelligence affecting the national security" as directed by the NSC. The law was clear that "the Agency shall have no police, subpoena, law enforcement powers, or internal security functions," but it omitted the ban on domestic investigations included in the 1946 bill. Other government agencies were permitted to continue their intelligence role, but, at NSC direction, the DCI was authorized to inspect such intelligence and have it made available to the CIA for its work. In apparent deference to FBI director Hoover, requests for FBI intelligence information from the DCI had to be made in writing.[52]

The legislative process was colorfully completed on July 26. Following formal finalization by Speaker Martin and President Pro Tem Vandenberg, the National

Security Act was rushed under police escort from the Capitol to Washington National Airport, where Truman waited in his presidential aircraft, delaying for seventeen minutes his departure to Missouri to attend his dying mother. Upon signing the bill, Truman issued Executive Order 9877, setting forth the missions of the armed services and nominating Forrestal to be secretary of defense. Within two hours of its arrival in Congress, the Senate Armed Services Committee approved the nomination, and, in executive session, the chamber confirmed the appointment by voice vote before adjourning.[53]

The CIA's inaugural was considerably less dramatic. On August 29 the White House announced that Hillenkoetter would continue as DCI and that Souers would become executive secretary of the NSC. On September 26 they were sworn in at a ceremony in the White House attended by Truman and Forrestal.[54] Thus did postwar central intelligence begin its legal existence. When Donovan read of the enactment in the New York Times, he reputedly noted the brief reference to the CIA and remarked: "I see they finally made intelligence respectable."[55] Nevertheless, again it was a Times journalist who caught the significance of the event. Writing in early August, reporter Samuel Tower commented: "One of the final steps before adjournment, largely overlooked in the avalanche of last-minute legislation, was the stamp of approval Congress placed on the creation, for the first time in American history, of an effective world-wide American intelligence service of its own. . . . Now, with America playing a major independent role in world affairs, this country has also embarked on the hidden game of international and national security."[56]

9

The Emergence of Central Intelligence

In accordance with the provisions of the National Security Act, the Central Intelligence Agency officially opened for business on September 18, 1947.[1] Writing a number of years later, Truman professed satisfaction with the improved methods that had been developed to furnish him with foreign intelligence information. The DCI was his first caller every day to present a digested intelligence report of the global scene. Also present would be Admiral Leahy and, upon his retirement, Souers, in his capacity as national security adviser.[2] The CIA's first "intelligence estimate," entitled "Review of the World Situation as It Relates to the Security of the United States," was published by the Office of Reports and Estimates on September 26.[3]

Hillenkoetter moved to build the appropriate bureaucratic bridges between his organization and the new national security apparatus. On September 11, 1947, he sent a memo to the secretaries of state, war, and navy, noting that when the National Security Act came into effect, the NIA would disappear and the CIA would pass under the authority of the NSC. He therefore suggested that, when the NSC met, all NIA and CIG directives continue in force until the NSC reviewed them and that the DCI be instructed to prepare draft directives to bring them up to date, according to the National Security Act. He further suggested that, because of the NSC's size, a subcommittee be established "to furnish the active direction" of the CIA. Concluding, he wrote:

> The Director of the Central Intelligence Group sat as a non-voting member of the National Intelligence Authority, and, while I believe it is presumptuous and awkward on my part to suggest that he so sit with the National Security Council, still it would be of the utmost assistance if he could attend all meetings of the National Security Council in some capacity, either as an observer, counsel or advisor in order to keep informed of what the thoughts of the National Security Council may be. In addition, by being present, the Director of Central Intelligence would also be available for such direct questions as may be propounded.[4]

On September 19, the day after the NSC's official inauguration, Hillenkoetter submitted a second memo, requesting that the NSC approve the continuance "in full force and effect" of all NIA and CIG directives until repealed or amended. He also requested that he, as DCI, be authorized to submit to the NSC, within sixty days, new authorizations supplanting NIA directives and specifying his functions and those of the CIA in accordance with the National Security Act.[5] The NSC held its first meeting on September 26, with Truman himself presiding. Also in attendance were Forrestal, Acting Secretary of State Robert Lovett, Secretary of the Army Kenneth Royall, Secretary of the Navy Sullivan, new Secretary of the Air Force Stuart Symington, National Security Resources Board chairman Arthur Hill, Souers, and Hillenkoetter. The council quickly approved Hillenkoetter's suggestions regarding the former directives and authorized the DCI to sit in its meetings as an "observer and advisor."[6]

On December 12 the NSC issued its first intelligence directive to implement the provisions of the National Security Act. It established a new Intelligence Advisory Committee (consisting of representatives from the State Department, the armed services, the JCS, and the AEC)[7] and authorized the DCI "to make such surveys and inspections of departmental intelligence material . . . as he may deem necessary" to meet his responsibilities for advising the NSC and coordinating intelligence activities. The directive declared explicitly that such coordination "should be designed primarily to strengthen the overall governmental intelligence structure. Primary departmental requirements shall be recognized and shall receive the cooperation and support of the Central Intelligence Agency." Recommendations to the NSC by the DCI would, when approved, be issued as directives to be implemented, as appropriate, by the intelligence components of the government. For his part, the DCI was directed to ensure the implementation of NSC directives by issuing supplementary directives that would be subject to review by the IAC and the NSC in areas of dispute among agencies. The DCI was also directed to "produce intelligence relating to the national security [but] not duplicate the intelligence activities and research" of other government agencies, "make use of existing intelligence facilities," and "utilize departmental intelligence for such purposes." The directive further authorized the dissemination of finished intelligence and other information between the CIA and other government agencies and added the elastic responsibility "to perform . . . such services of common concern . . . as the National Security Council determines can be more efficiently accomplished centrally." The directive concluded by setting down provisions for liaison and intelligence exchange between the CIA and other agencies.[8]

American central intelligence was now operating. In the course of the following year, the NSC issued other directives reaffirming and developing the DCI's authority to conduct all foreign espionage and counterespionage operations, monitor foreign press and broadcasting, exploit nongovernmental organizations and individuals within the United States as sources of foreign intelligence, and prepare and disseminate intelligence analysis on a wide variety of political, economic, scientific, and biographical topics.[9] It is not the purpose of this chapter to present a comprehensive account of the early years of the CIA.[10] Instead, it will focus on certain key developments that transformed the nature and purpose of the CIA. These developments (the agency's growing pains and the investigations they prompted, the invention of covert operations, the enactment of long-sought enabling legislation in 1949, and the change of leadership in 1950) resulted in the CIA's metamorphosis from what it was intended to be by Truman's policy makers into the freestanding intelligence empire—a postwar OSS—that William J. Donovan had championed.

It would be stressing the obvious to observe that this transformation was catalyzed by the world situation. The collapse of the grand alliance, the brutal Sovietization of Eastern Europe, the increasingly minatory nature of the Soviet policy toward Western Europe, and escalating instability in the Far East ended optimistic visions of postwar international comity and fully alarmed U.S. policy makers. While, with the benefit of hindsight, it is clear that their sense of threat far exceeded the actual degree of menace—in the late 1940s or ever—posed by the war-ravaged and perpetually backward Soviet Union, the danger seemed real enough at the time. Since the closed, xenophobic nature of the Soviet system isolated the American embassy in Moscow and eliminated normal sources of information, the need for new and unconventional ways of acquiring knowledge on which to base policy decisions gave new significance to the concept of "secret intelligence" collected by a centralized organization.[11]

These international events provided the background for the natal years of the CIA. Like any other new organization, it suffered growing pains that were perhaps intensified by the rapid growth of the CIG due to Vandenberg's empire building. As one astute intelligence writer put it:

Expansion and obfuscation characterized the infant CIA's history between 1947 and 1950. . . . Few people knew the precise extent and nature of the expansion. . . . Only among the cognoscenti did an increasingly sophisticated if deliberatively secretive discussion occur. Officials and experts concluded that the avoidance of Pearl Harbor–type surprise attacks was not enough; they developed a theoretical framework for intelligence; they introduced the notion of "national intelligence estimates"; and they debated the place of intelligence in overall U.S. strategy.[12]

This debate was a protracted one, but very early Washington's national security managers realized something was amiss. On October 24, 1947, Secretary of Defense Forrestal met with FBI director Hoover, the armed services' intelligence chiefs, Hillenkoetter, and Souers to discuss the "present and widespread belief that our Intelligence Group [sic] is entirely inept."[13]

Criticism of the new order of things had, in fact, begun even before the enabling legislation was on the books. In February 1947, upon hearing that Vandenberg was to be replaced by Hillenkoetter, State Department intelligence chief William Eddy wrote to Under Secretary Acheson: "In the thirteen months of its existence, the Central Intelligence Group already has had two directors, each a Service representative. Should there be a continuation of the policy of selecting directors from one of the Services, there is always the danger that the demands of the appointee's department may result in similar early shifts in the directorship." After emphasizing the need for leadership continuity in such a "new and growing organization" like the CIG, he added that the nature of such an organization "requires that its director be . . . untouched by any departmental bias or influence. Under such circumstances a Service director will always and inevitably be torn between absolute objectivity and natural allegiance to his own Service." This led him to conclude that "continuity and objectivity of leadership can best be assured by a director drawn from civilian ranks and not subject to demands from or allegiance to a single department." He was particularly concerned over this point, since, under the proposed legislation, the NIA would be replaced by the NSC: "Since the composition of the Council is weighed heavily on the side of the Armed Forces, it is important that the national, as opposed to the military, character of its central intelligence agency be emphasized in the form of a civilian director."[14]

Eddy's concerns also were felt in the new "national military establishment" itself. On October 30, 1947, Robert Blum, deputy to Forrestal's special assistant John Ohly, wrote his boss to outline several serious problems that he saw concerning the CIA's relations with the rest of the defense establishment. These included the relationship between the JCS intelligence organization (the Joint Intelligence Committee) and the CIA, the lack of "systematic arrangements" needed in order that the DCI "may be appraised of strategic planning so he may adjust his intelligence objectives accordingly," the status of communications intelligence, the proper method of producing intelligence estimates, and the "predominance of military personnel" in the top CIA leadership. He also suggested that the armed services should be canvassed to determine "their relations with CIA and of the service which CIA is giving them." He added that he was told by an unidentified State Department intelligence official "that from their point of view the position is very unsatisfactory as CIA is trying to do much more than it is qualified to do; in his opinion its chief usefulness comes out of secret operations for which it has exclusive responsibility." Nevertheless, he concluded, the conduct of such operations, and their relationship to future military activities, also needed to be addressed.[15]

As Forrestal's adviser on intelligence matters, Ohly shared his deputy's concern. In December he observed to Blum that there was a lack of "an intelligence concept which has been carefully thought out and which serves as a clear guide to the various collection agencies and sources, and which permits and requires the establishment of priorities as to areas and subjects." He felt that collection efforts were disorganized and scattered, and "some collection agencies are going pretty much their own way collecting what they want to collect without reference to what is most needed." He, too, was concerned about the heavy military presence in the CIA, noting: "I have strong reason to suspect that, on the average, military intelligence agencies have drawn the least qualified rather than the most qualified" personnel for assignment to the CIA, and such individuals, often close to retirement, who "have no incentive to do a good job even if they could, and who lack imagination, energy and broad perspective." In addition to violating what Ohly felt was the legislative concept of "a largely civilian intelligence agency," he commented that the effects of their presence "on the many able civilians underneath are also most unfortunate." He concluded by complaining about the "conflict between CIA and the other intelligence agencies which is the product of organizational and personal jealousies, lack of mutual confidence, and, I suppose, a variety of other factors."[16]

Because Vandenberg had been so active in his efforts to acquire the responsibility for collecting scientific intelligence, particularly in the field of atomic energy, the CIA's activities and reputed shortcomings in that area came in for particular attention, especially from the Research and Development Board (RDB), the scientific arm of the national military establishment. On December 2, 1947, David Beckler, chief of the RDB's Intelligence Section, noted in a memo to Ralph Clark, director of the Programs Division, that his counterparts in the AEC considered themselves in an "awkward position," since atomic energy intelligence "at present is handled almost exclusively by CIA." Because the NSC was still in the process of developing the CIA's relationship with other intelligence agencies, reported Beckler,

> the present confusion is causing considerable embarrassment to the newly created Intelligence Division of the AEC, and greatly impedes its operations. Since the directives as finally decided upon may affect the nature and scope of intelligence operations, the Army, Navy, and Air Force Departments as well as the CIA—while agreeing in principle to cooperation with the AEC—are deferring actual exchange of information until the AEC-CIA relationship is crystallized. Considering the conflicting directives which have been proposed—this may take considerable time.

Beckler concluded that there was "considerable difference of opinion as to the type of CIA organization that would be best suited to implement the provisions and spirit of the National Security Act. Until CIA specifically delineates its objectives and responsibilities and defines its terms and mission, it is doubtful that the best organizational pattern can be decided upon." This situation posed a serious problem for the RDB, Beckler thought, since it was "completely dependent upon CIA for strategic as well as scientific intelligence which are the sine qua non for carrying out Board responsibilities under the Act. The extent of the CIA's ability to produce such intelligence will largely be determined by the outcome of the present negotiations." [17]

Clark thought enough of Beckler's views to forward his memo to RDB chief Vannevar Bush on the following day, noting in his own covering message that the "difficulty seems to be fundamental differences in philosophy between the two groups in that the heads of the operating agencies feel that CIA should be a small, high-level strategic intelligence integrating organization, evolving what they call 'national intelligence' from information supplied by the operating agencies, while the CIA proposes to be a conglomerate of operating and evaluating functions with considerable authority over the other operating intelligence agencies." This impasse, thought Clark, was hindering RDB's efforts to recruit and organize its scientific staff and to obtain "any useful intelligence" from the CIA. Therefore, he suggested to Bush: "Someone at the highest level should define the objective of CIA in relation to the production of strategic intelligence in support of the activities of the Security Council and delineate the relationships between CIA and the operating agencies in such manner that the work of producing information, detailed intelligence, and integrated strategic intelligence can proceed." [18]

The nuclear intelligence issue was, indeed, reaching the "highest level." On

March 28, 1948, Ohly noted to Blum that he was becoming "increasingly concerned about our intelligence set up for the handling of nuclear energy matters." He saw a double problem of both making sure that collection capacity was "the best possible obtainable" and that the consumers of the collected intelligence became convinced "that the intelligence furnished them is, in fact, worth considering." He added, however: "At the present time, I am told the consumers have absolutely no confidence and have every reason for lacking confidence." Because of the critical nature of the subject, he proposed that the issue be brought to Forrestal's attention for consideration by the NSC.[19]

An especially sharp criticism of the CIA's management came as a parting shot from Stephen Penrose, a retiring CIA officer and former OSS man, included as part of a report prepared for the secretary of defense early in 1948. Penrose strongly faulted Galloway's direction of clandestine intelligence collection activities, lamenting the loss of experienced personnel, due to "inept and unimaginative policies." He also criticized ORE for the poor quality of its intelligence reports and its cumbersome publishing process. The Office of Collection and Dissemination and the Office of Operations were similarly reproached for their "ineptitude" and their "mechanical and inflexible" procedures in developing and utilizing other agencies as well as private organizations and organizations for intelligence collection. Similarly, Penrose scored internal arrangements for analyzing scientific intelligence and maintained that the lines of communication between the analysts and clandestine intelligence collectors were inadequate. Throughout the report, he complained about too much power being in the hands of military officers inexperienced in intelligence matters.

Penrose then concluded forcefully:

> The disturbing situation which has been described is the more alarming because it occurs at a time when . . . the government needs an effective, expanding, professional intelligence service. On the contrary, the CIA is losing its professionals, and is not acquiring competent new personnel who might gain experience in the only rapid way possible, namely by close association with those professionals. It is dependent in most working branches for imaginative and energetic direction upon career military men of a type which is not apt to be either imaginative or energetic as regards non-military intelligence or procedures. . . . Other departments feel no assurance that they can rely upon CIA to perform intelligence functions which they will privately admit could and probably should be performed centrally. Without that assurance they will continue . . . to operate their intelligence services in a manner which cannot but nullify the prin-

ciples of coordination and centralization which were implicit in establishing the CIA.[20]

Early in 1949, in a message to Louis Johnson, Forrestal's successor as secretary of defense, Ohly also addressed a problem that never seemed to go away. Noting that "the greatest weakness of CIA stems from the type and quality of its personnel and the methods through which it is recruited," he deplored the tendency "to staff virtually all the key jobs in CIA with military personnel, mostly discarded personnel." Not facing this problem, he felt, would mean "accepting a poor to mediocre intelligence operation virtually in perpetuity." Ohly noted that the situation had, in his view,

> resulted in a complete deterioration of morale among some of the better qualified civilians who would like to make CIA a career and has meant the loss of many extremely able individuals who simply could not stand the situation, and who unfortunately cannot be replaced with persons of comparable talent. . . . Most of the able people left in the Agency have decided that unless changes occur within the next several months, they will definitely leave. With this cadre of quality lost, the Agency will sink into a mire from which it will be difficult, if not impossible, to extract it.[21]

Since it is virtually impossible to keep secrets for long in Washington, the travails of the CIA became public knowledge fairly soon. Unsurprisingly, the well-informed Hanson Baldwin described them in a lucid and comprehensive series in the New York Times in July 1948[22] and boldly summed up his conclusions in The Price of Power. He asserted that the CIA "has been beset from its beginnings with frictions . . . and particularly by the natural resentment of the older agencies, a resentment always pronounced in Washington, a city obsessed with the struggle for power. A bitter behind-the-scenes fight . . . has been waged, with the nation's security the ostensible issue, but personal power and service prestige are the real ones."[23] Such strictures were not limited to elite opinion but were present in the popular media as well. An example was an article by Frank Gervasi appearing in Collier's magazine late in 1948 pointedly entitled "What's Wrong with Our Spy System?" After excoriating the CIA and its OSS parent in lurid detail, the article concluded: "If the recent war and troubled peace that followed taught us anything, it taught us the value of foreknowledge. . . . It is not enough to uncover enemy spy rings in our own country. We must also set up our own systems in other nations."[24] Such views did resonate with the public. A steady stream of letters came to the White House and the NSC calling for an "independent" intelligence service. Some even suggested placing Donovan at its head. All received a courteous, pro forma response that included a reference to the role of the CIA.[25]

The CIA's internal problems and its difficult relations with other intelligence agencies became enmeshed in the larger issue of the perceived weaknesses of the national military establishment and the overall matter of administrative reform in the federal bureaucracy as a whole. In 1947 Congress created the Commission on Organization of the Executive Branch of the Government, chaired by former president Herbert Hoover. It included a task force on intelligence, headed by Ferdinand Eberstadt (and including Hanson Baldwin as one of its members). The task force focused considerable attention on intelligence issues. Eberstadt contacted Souers on May 31, 1948, to initiate consultations. Souers, in turn, designated his deputy, James Lay Jr., as his liasion to the Hoover Commission (as the new group quickly came to be called). Always the wily political operator, he readily agreed to discuss the CIA from his own perspective, but suggested that Eberstadt contact DCI Hillenkoetter directly as well. For his part, Hillenkoetter also designated a liasion officer, navy Captain W. C. Ford.[26]

In the following weeks, the Eberstadt panel conducted wide-ranging but entirely nonpublic hearings, consulting members of Congress, Souers, Leahy, Vandenberg, Forrestal, and Hillenkoetter, who made an eloquent presentation on the importance of "our foreign information collection activities conducted by clandestine or semi-clandestine means."[27] In keeping with the "national security" mind-set of the times, the comments in the task force's published report, which appeared in 1949, were relatively general. It ritualistically declared that intelligence was "the first line of defense in the atomic age" but found many "disturbing inadequacies" in the American intelligence system. Internally, the report noted, the CIA still had "too many disparate intelligence estimates," which often had been "subjective and biased," and therefore more comprehensive collection, better coordination, and "more mature and experienced evaluation" were "imperative." The report also called for greater attention to medical and scientific intelligence collection and recommended that a board solely devoted to intelligence evaluation be created within the CIA. The report was emphatic on CIA relations with other intelligence organizations: "The relationships of this agency to some of the other intelligence agencies of Government . . . have been and still are unsatisfactory. . . . The Central Intelligence Agency deserves and must have a greater degree of acceptance and support from old-line intelligence services than it has had in the past."[28]

The Eberstadt task force also produced a lengthy classified report on U.S. national security organization that included a chapter on the CIA. This section was a seminal statement on government intelligence policy that should be examined at length. In the area of intelligence analysis, the report noted that the CIA "has yet fallen short" of becoming a "major source of coordinated and evaluated intelligence," since its product "does not presently enjoy the full confidence of the National Security Organization [sic] or of the other agencies it serves and has not yet . . . played an important role in the determinations of the National Security Council." Like its published counterpart, the report faulted "inadequacies" in the collection of scientific intelligence and acknowledged that the CIA's evaluative abilities were undermined by the disorganized and subjective collection activities of other (particularly military) intelligence agencies: "Out of this mass of jumbled material, and harassed often by the open and covert opposition of the older agencies, CIA has tried to make sense. That it has not always succeeded has not been entirely the fault of CIA."

The report was more opaque in discussing the CIA's clandestine operational activities, but it commented that the officials who testified on the topic were "fairly well satisfied with the necessarily slow progress in this field, although there was a distinct feeling that progress could be more rapid." Nevertheless, the report noted, "this limited satisfaction is not echoed in lower ranks." Because these activities were a service of common concern, "there is little doubt that they should all be treated together as a single unit." The report then commented: "Too great a dependence upon the Foreign Service for 'cover,' communications, and facilities is fatal to any intelligence service and dangerous to the Foreign Service, which would be compromised and embarrassed in case of discovery. . . . Other 'cover' devices must be found if a clandestine service is to be efficient."

Concerning organization, the report concluded that the CIA, as a "coordinator and evaluator," was "properly placed" under the NSC and deprecated the idea of placing it under the State Department or defense establishment (since its "functions and interests transcend both") or putting it directly under the president (because it was "doubtful whether . . . he has time to pay much attention to it"). On the issue of CIA personnel, the report observed: "During the course of a much too rapid expansion of the organization which took place under a previous Director, mistakes in personnel procurement were made." Despite improvements, however, "Time, experience, and training are necessary, probably requiring years, to build up a fully competent staff for all offices and echelons of the CIA." As far as the CIA's future organizational needs were concerned, the report again emphasized the "imperative" to "improve all facilities for evaluating and stimulating the collection of scientific intelligence" and suggested that its operating offices be grouped under a deputy director "who should have considerable, though not unlimited, independence." In the report's view, however, the "greatest need" was for "the establishment at a high level of a small group of highly capable people, freed from administrative detail, to concentrate upon intelligence evaluation. . . . A small group of mature men of the highest talents, having full access to all information, might well be released completely from routine and set thinking about intelligence only."[29]

The work of the Hoover Commission served as a benchmark for policy makers and encouraged initiatives among Truman's national security managers for a sweeping internal review of the government's foreign intelligence apparatus.[30] Souers and Ohly discussed the idea of examining the CIA's organization and functions at a meeting on December 31, 1947. Souers suggested that such an investigation should be conducted by Allen Dulles, since, Souers believed, he was well qualified and his selection would remove the issue from politics. In reporting the discussions to Forrestal, Ohly noted: "I believe such an investigation is desperately needed unless the [National] Security Council is prepared to initiate reforms on its own. Many of the best civilians are now leaving CIA and the military domination of the agency is becoming very serious."[31]

Forrestal readily fell in with the idea, hoping that such a survey would lead to changes that would end the bickering and rivalries within the intelligence establishment and bring about higher professional standards. He discussed the idea at length with Souers, suggesting that the former DCI direct such a study. Souers declined, however, recalling later: "I called his attention to the fact that if I had wanted to continue to run Central Intelligence I would have remained at that job and I did not wish to supervise it as Executive Secretary of the NSC."[32] Forrestal also raised the issue with Truman, writing him on February 28, 1948, that "the emergence of this new boss has not been entirely accepted by the traditionally secretive and autonomy-minded military intelligence groups. I have consistently taken the position that CIA should be strengthened, and its coordinating authority recognized by the service groups, but in a field like intelligence, such objectives cannot be accomplished by fiat."[33]

In accordance with such thinking, on January 13, 1948, the NSC resolved "that a group of two or three specially qualified individuals not in the Government service should make a comprehensive, impartial, and objective survey of the organization, activities, and personnel of the Central Intelligence Agency." This committee was instructed to report back to the NSC and make recommendations on the "adequacy and effectiveness" of its organization structure, the "value and efficiency" of its existing activities, their relationship to those of other agencies, and the "utilization and qualifications" of CIA personnel. It also "authorized and directed" the DCI and other intelligence chiefs to provide the group "access to all information and facilities required for their survey, except details concerning intelligence sources and methods." [34] The NSC also readily accepted Souers's idea of having Dulles head the study, and he himself was quite ready to take the lead. At that time the veteran spymaster was serving as an adviser to presidential aspirant Governor Thomas Dewey of New York, whose nomination was certain in 1948 and whose election seemed assured against the supposedly unpopular Truman. According to Dulles's biographer, Peter Grose, Dewey had confided to Forrestal that, when elected, he would put national intelligence work into "professional" hands. Thus, according to Grose, Dulles, always ambitious to head the new CIA, agreed to present this study in early 1949 in order to be "convenient to the timetables of the election and the installation of a new administration," since, having "accepted a role in defining the intelligence capabilities of the United States," he "was assured that he would be the one calling the plays." [35]

Forrestal drew upon his network of connections to complete the panel. Joining Dulles was New York lawyer William H. Jackson, who had worked with Dulles in the OSS in France during the last months of the war, and his former Navy Department aide, Mathias Correa, a nominal Democrat. [36] On February 13 Souers formally empowered the three to proceed with their survey, and to expect full cooperation from the government's intelligence organizations. [37] Souers was well pleased with these developments, and his own role in initiating them, writing later: "Allen Dulles was selected largely because we had a Republican Congress and he was a Republican and we wished to keep Central Intelligence entirely out of party politics. Bill Jackson was selected because Forrestal had a very high regard for him because of his experiences with the British intelligence organization and the Imperial Defense Council [sic]. Correa was selected because of his close tie to Mr. Forrestal and also the fact that he was fairly familiar with the FBI Operation and the work of ONI." [38]

Souers presented the three with a formal NSC enabling memo on February 13, based on the council resolution of the preceding month. [39] As their work got under way, Souers followed up with a second memo on March 17, further clarifying their mission. Their survey, said Souers, "will comprise primarily a thorough and comprehensive examination of the structure, administration, activities, and inter-agency relationships of the CIA." It would "also include an examination of such intelligence activities of other Government Departments and Agencies as relate to the national security in order to make recommendations for their effective operations and overall coordination, subject to the understanding that the group will not engage in actual physical examination of departmental intelligence operations (a) outside of Washington or (b) in the collection of communications intelligence." Souers, as NSC representative, would seek the cooperation of those agencies not on the council that had an intelligence role. Staff assistance would be supplied by Forrestal's office, and cleared staff members would "be given access to information and facilities required for the survey in the same manner as provided for your group in the Council's resolution." Funding would come from NSC and CIA resources, and it was "contemplated that the survey will be completed and the final report submitted on or before January 1, 1949."[40]

The committee labored for the remainder of 1948, and Dulles presented its report—entitled "The Central Intelligence Organization and the National Organization for Intelligence"—to Forrestal at a luncheon meeting on New Year's Day, 1949. The defense secretary praised the report, comprising 193 pages and presenting fifty-seven specific conclusions and recommendations, as a "guidebook" for a "long time to come"; he wrote Dulles on February 24 that it was a model for how a report should be prepared.[41] Although the entire document remains classified and has not yet been released to the public,[42] its thrust was apparent in the vigorous executive summary, which began by reviewing the CIA's responsibilities under the National Security Act of 1947 and asserted that while no amendments relating to its provisions were "required at this time," action "to give effect to its true intent" was needed.

The report then reviewed problem areas, beginning with the CIA's responsibilities to "coordinate intelligence activities," and concluded that "this coordination function . . . is not being adequately exercised," since NSC directives "defining the scope and limits of departmental activities" had "not gone far enough." As a result, "the absence of coordinated intelligence planning . . . remains serious," especially in the areas of scientific and technological collection (including atomic energy), as well as "domestic intelligence and counter-intelligence." It declared that such coordination "can most effectively be achieved by mutual agreement among the various agencies," and, with "the right measure of leadership" from the CIA, "a major degree" of coordination could be accomplished. Continuing on this issue, the report then addressed the "long-felt need for the coordination, on the highest level, of intelligence opinion relating to broad aspects of national policy and national security," which was "probably the principal moving factor" in bringing about the creation of the CIA and the lack of which "was one of the most significant causes of the Pearl Harbor intelligence failure." Nevertheless, in the report's judgment, the CIA "has not yet carried out this most important function."

The fault, concluded the report, rested with ORE, which was given responsibility for "national intelligence" production but had "been concerned with a wide variety of activities and with the production of miscellaneous reports and summaries which by no stretch of the imagination could be considered national estimates." Since ORE's reports were regarded as its own product and not fully coordinated works representing the views of all agencies, the report recommended that the CIA establish a "small group of specialists" that would be tasked "to review the intelligence products of other intelligence agencies," as well as the CIA, and "draft estimates for interagency consideration." Once approved, such estimates "should be clearly established as the product of all the contributing agencies in which all share and for which all take responsibility. It should be recognized as the most authoritative estimate available to the policy-makers."

The report then looked at "services of common concern," which it divided into "static services, consisting of intelligence research and production on certain assigned subjects which do not fall exclusively within the function of any one existing agency," and "operating services, consisting of certain types of intelligence collection and related secret operations." These "static" services could be dealt with by establishing an office for conducting intelligence research and analysis separate from that doing "national estimates." Within such an office should be a unit undertaking scientific and technological analysis that could draw upon the expertise of all government agencies. As far as "operating" services (espionage and secret operations) were concerned, the report was quite specific. Since these functions were "unique because of their secrecy and consequent security requirements," they "should have common administrative services separate from those of the balance of the Central Intelligence Agency" and "should be responsible to one official charged with their direction." This proposed Operations Division would be "self-sufficient as to administration and semi-autonomous. This would, to a large extent, meet the criticism frequently voiced, and with a good deal of merit, that it is essentially unsound to combine in a single intelligence agency both secret operations and over-all cooordinating and estimating functions."

The report was particularly harsh concerning the issues of aims and leadership. It considered the CIA's "principal defect" as being "its direction, administrative organization and performance" not showing "sufficient appreciation" of its assigned functions, and, as a result, it "has tended to become just one more intelligence agency producing intelligence in competition with older established agencies of the Government departments." Here, too, it quickly placed blame: "Since it is the task of the Director to see that the Agency carries out its assigned functions, the failure to do so is necessarily a reflection of inadequacies of direction." It therefore concluded that the CIA was "over-administered in the sense that administrative considerations have been allowed to guide and, on occasion, even control intelligence policy to the detriment of the latter." To rectify the matter, the report recommended that the heads of the proposed new divisions be included on the DCI's staff, so that "the Director, who at present relies chiefly on his administrative staff, would be brought into intimate contact with the day to day operations of his agency and be able to give policy guidance to them." The authors then strongly concluded: "While organization charts can never replace individual initiative and ability, the Central Intelligence Agency, reorganized along the functional lines indicated in this report, should be able more effectively to carry out the duties assigned it by law and thus bring our over-all intelligence system closer to that point of efficiency that our national security demands."[43]

Although the report generated some defensive rumblings within the CIA itself,[44] its initial impact on policy makers was anticlimactic. As Dulles's biographer observed: "Instead of a blueprint for reform that Allen could implement under President Dewey, the study landed almost irrelevantly on the crowded desks of the reelected Truman administration."[45] Forrestal, who might have vigorously acted on it, had stepped down, following discord with Truman and a mental breakdown that led to his suicide in May 1949. His successor, Louis Johnson, referred the report to his management adviser, General Joseph McNarney, who, with State Department officer Carlisle Hummelsine, prepared joint implementing recommendations for the NSC. On July 1, 1949, the NSC approved most of the proposals piecemeal but did not completely accept the assertions of the CIA's leadership and policy shortcomings, but rather attributed most of its problems to its newness and the lack of mutual understanding between the CIA and departmental intelligence agencies over their respective missions.[46]

Nor was Hillenkoetter the man to launch major initiatives. On July 12 he informed his senior staff that the NSC had accepted much of the original report but did not lay out a plan of action for the CIA to follow.[47] On December 27 he submitted a report to Souers on its implementation. He noted that, effective January 1, an Office of Scientific Intelligence had been established "as one of the major offices" in the CIA and was "being well staffed and is now devoting its time to matters of scientific intelligence in cooperation with other government agencies." On matters of domestic intelligence, he noted that OSO was "working closely" with the FBI "where their respective interests are related." He also emphasized that, in regard to counterespionage activities overseas, the degree of cooperation between the CIA and FBI "at the present time is close, effective, and mutually advantageous." He also described a series of measures designed to exploit the intelligence potential of aliens, defectors, and foreign nationality groups and organizations within the United States. He added that actions had been taken in cooperation with the Army "which has resulted in appreciable improvement" in covert intelligence operations in occupied areas. Not ignoring analysis, he also described a series of reforms made in ORE to strengthen its ability to prepare national estimates.[48] There matters rested for the remainder of Hillenkoetter's tenure.

Although the proposals of the Dulles-Jackson-Correa report were not immediately acted upon, the quest for administrative reform that had inspired it, combined with the troubled international scene, helped bring about one of the most long-sought goals of the "intelligence professionals": separate enabling legislation that explicitly spelled out the CIA's authority. Not even the introduction of the National Security Act had deterred this effort. On March 17, 1947, George Elsey wrote acidly to Clark Clifford: "CIG is up to its old tricks again. It has submitted 'informally' the draft of a proposed bill to be submitted to Congress very similar to the two previous drafts which Vandenberg sent to you in recent months and which you filed without further action." He noted that he, himself, had been contacted by a Budget Bureau representative for advice on how to deal with CIG's importunings: "I suggested that CIG be informed that there was no necessity for such legislation in view of the sections concerning Intelligence which are included in the Unification Bill."[49] Efforts nonetheless persisted. On May 14 the NIA formally directed DCI Hillenkoetter to prepare drafts of enabling legislation for future use,[50] and, in a June 26 report to the NIA on CIG activities, Hillenkoetter stated: "The continued absence of legislation continues to hamper the soundest development of CIG in several directions, both within and without the Government."[51]

Policy makers' attitudes changed relatively quickly, however, as the cold war confrontation between Washington and Moscow intensified. The desired legislation was introduced in mid-1948 and approved in executive session by the Armed Services Committees of both houses. It passed the Senate on June 19, but no action was taken on a companion bill in the House before adjournment. On November 6, 1948, Truman circularized all agencies about their legislative programs for the upcoming congressional session. In response, Hillenkoetter submitted a revised draft of his proposed legislation to Budget Bureau director James Webb on December 15. Following Budget Bureau review, Hillenkoetter formally presented his draft legislation to the House and Senate on February 11, 1949.[52]

The House Armed Services Committee again considered the bill in executive session and reported it favorably on February 24, with minor stylistic changes. The legislative report that accompanied the bill noted blandly: "The purpose of the proposed legislation, in general, is to grant to the Central Intelligence Agency necessary authority for its proper and efficient administration. . . . A few provisions are unusual in nature, but nevertheless are essential to the successful operation of an efficient intelligence service." The report then concluded that it "does not contain a full and detailed explanation of all the provisions of the proposed legislation in view of the fact that much of such information is of a highly confidential nature. However, the Committee on Armed Services received a complete explanation of all features of the proposed measure. The committee is satisfied that all sections of the proposed legislation are fully justified." [53] The entire House took up action on the bill, along with other defense measures, at the beginning of March, under rules barring amendments not offered by the Armed Services Committee and limiting debate to one hour. The *New York Times*, in covering the legislative action, observed that committee members said the "spy bill" was "so vital and so confidential that almost nothing can be told of its aims." [54]

Some congressmen found such secrecy excessive. One was House minority leader Joseph Martin, a conservative Republican from Massachusetts, who complained that it was "difficult to see why it is so secret if the members of the committee and 100 others know about it. In Washington, if three people know anything, everybody does." Nonetheless, he was chided by fellow Republican Clarence Brown of Ohio, who said that it would be "damn foolishness" to discuss the bill publicly "so a lot of people from all over the world would get information on our intelligence service." Martin was also rebuked by Armed Services Committee chairman Carl Vinson, Democrat of Georgia, who added: "When you are in the spy business you can't go shouting about it from the house tops." [55] House rules were suspended to take up the bill under conditions permitting no amendments and requiring a two-thirds vote for passage. Representative Dewey Short of Missouri, ranking Republican on the Armed Services Committee, declared that it would be "supreme folly" to debate the legislation, and the House, at committee insistence, went along. The act was approved on March 7 by a vote of 348 to 4, without discussion. Among the dissenters was radical Vito Marcantonio, of New York's American Labor Party, who forced a roll call and complained that the secrecy was unprecedented. Rejoined Short: "We spent $2,000,000,000 on the atomic bomb before anyone around here knew anything about it." [56]

Senate action was even more cursory. The Armed Services Committee reported the bill on March 10, also stating that the purpose of the legislation was "to grant the Central Intelligence Agency the authorities necessary for its proper administration. . . . Further, it protects the confidential nature of the Agency's functions and makes provisions for the overseas administration of the Agency."[57] On May 27 the full Senate passed the bill unanimously and without debate. Its sponsor, Senator Millard Tydings, a Democrat from Maryland, admitted that it granted the CIA a degree of secrecy unparalleled in peacetime, but he said such measures were indispensable for protecting the "most dangerous" espionage work. He praised the Truman administration's "candor" in seeking formal legislative authorization for a system usually "disguised" by other governments. He also asserted that had such an organization as the CIA existed in 1941, the Pearl Harbor disaster might not have occurred.[58] Because the two houses had approved slightly different bills, a conference committee met, and the House agreed to accept the Senate version on June 6. The final legislation was sent to Truman for signature.[59]

The executive branch likewise expedited enactment. On June 9 Hillenkoetter requested Truman's signature, and the State Department gave its concurrence on June 10. After a review, the Budget Bureau recommended approval on June 16. Truman signed it on June 20 with no ceremony.[60] The CIA Act of 1949 was everything that the "intelligence professionals" wished it to be. Virtually unaltered from its original draft, the law provided for various mundane but necessary administrative functions (such as establishing procurement authority and providing for the training and travel of employees), but it also gave the CIA and its director sweeping independent authority. The CIA was authorized to transfer and receive funds with other government agencies "without regard to any provisions of law limiting or prohibiting transfers between appropriations." Such funds could also be expended by the CIA "without regard to limitations" previously placed upon them. The DCI was made "responsible for protecting intelligence sources and methods from unauthorized disclosure" without defining either, thus giving him broad powers to control the flow of information. The CIA also was exempted from all laws requiring "the publication or disclosure of the organization, functions, names, official titles, salaries, or numbers of personnel employed by the Agency," and the Budget Bureau was prohibited from reporting to Congress on these subjects. The DCI was also authorized to admit up to one hundred aliens per year "for permanent residence without regard to their admissibility under immigration or any other laws or regulations, or failure to comply with such laws or regulations." In establishing the authority of the CIA to expend appropriated funds, the law was emphatic: "The sums made available to the Agency may be expended without regard to the provisions of law and regulations relating to the expenditures of Government funds; for objects of a confidential, extraordinary, or emergency nature, such expenditure to be accounted for solely on the certificate of the Director and every such certificate shall be deemed a sufficient voucher for the amount therein certified." [61] The CIA now had the legislative mandate that gave it the power to wage secret war.

No activity has done more to transform the CIA than the practice of covert action. Covert action—Donovan's "subversive operations abroad"—is officially defined as "[a]n operation designed to influence governments, events, organizations, or persons in support of foreign policy in a manner that is not necessarily attributable to the sponsoring power; it may include political, economic, propaganda, or paramilitary activities." [62] Although only a part (albeit sometimes the predominant part) of the CIA's overall responsibilities, the "acquisition of this mission had a profound impact on the direction of the Agency and on its relative stature within the government." [63] While the practice was not directly addressed in the National Security Act of 1947, Clark Clifford maintains that it was authorized by the "catchall" provision concerning "such other functions and duties" to be carried out at NSC direction:

> The "other" functions the CIA was to perform were purposely not specified but we understood that they would include covert activities. We did not mention them by name because we felt it would be injurious to our national interest to advertise the fact that we might engage in such activities. . . . In light of the continuing controversy over the role and activities of the CIA, it bears emphasizing that it was by act of Congress that the CIA was established and exists today, and it was by act of Congress that covert operations were authorized.[64]

Despite attempts to give covert action a venerable lineage,[65] it derives from OSS precedents and is primarily a product of the unique circumstances arising during the early years of the cold war. Donovan was an activist by nature and, in the words of one scholar of intelligence, had been "captivated by the power and potential of subversive warfare. . . . His mistaken belief that the Nazis were particularly adept at intelligence and subversive operations led him to overestimate the importance of shadow warfare and underestimate the significance of conventional weapons and economic factors in the Second World War." [66] Mistaken or not, however, he made sure that his creation—the OSS—possessed the capacity for covert political, psychological, economic, and paramilitary activities. Donovan's disciples, who had engaged in these activities, were a group of able and articulate men, near or within the corridors of power, claiming for the OSS "great expertise in shadow warfare" and pointing to what they asserted "was a glorious record of operational triumph in World War II." [67]

Such a cadre would be of potent influence as American policy makers addressed the increasingly unstable situation in Europe. By late 1946 the impact of the communizing and Sovietizing of Eastern Europe, the civil war in Greece, Soviet pressure on Turkey and Iran, and the activism of Sovietized Communist parties in economically prostrate Western Europe ended hopes for a cooperative relationship with the Soviet Union and raised the specter of the USSR as a threat to U.S. security—a new "evil empire." The Communist coup in Czechoslovakia in February 1948 was a shock to senior policy makers like Marshall and Forrestal, who were already obsessed with the Soviet Union's reputed skill at subversive activities. Their immediate attention focused on Italy, a country struggling to overcome the effects of war, military defeat, and foreign occupation, and where a large, well-organized Communist Party was making a bid for political dominance. The CIA contributed to the growing official concern with a grim assessment of the Italian situation issued on February 16, 1948.[68] Truman and his foreign policy advisers, "feeling that since the Soviets did not play fair, provision had to be made for carrying out dirty tricks,"[69] sought a similar capacity for the United States. Because they wished to avoid the implications of exposure and accountability, however, they turned their attention to the secret resources of the CIA.[70]

Policy-maker interest first focused on "psychological operations," a covert activity defined as "[p]lanned psychological activities in peace and war directed towards enemy, friendly, and neutral audiences in order to create attitudes and behavior favorable to the achievement of political and military objectives. These operations encompass those political, military, economic, ideological, and information activities designed for achieving a desired psychological effect."[71] On December 12, 1946, the NIA received a report on "psychological warfare" from the State-War-Navy Coordinating Committee (a consulting body left over from the war that would eventually be replaced by the NSC), which emphasized its importance as "an essential factor in the achievement of national aims and military objectives in time of war, or threat of war as determined by the President." The report nevertheless noted the improvised and disorganized way such activities were carried on during the war and therefore advocated "the immediate establishment of a committee with full-time representation from appropriate governmental agencies to serve as an agency charged with preparation of psychological warfare policies, plans, and studies for employment in time of war, or the threat of war."[72] Souers himself addressed the issue in a memorandum to Forrestal on October 24, 1947, in which he recognized "the need for psychological warfare operations to counter Soviet-inspired Communist propaganda, particularly in

France and Italy." In his view, the problem could be dealt with by strengthening the overt public information activities of the State Department, assigning "the conduct of covert activities to the Central Intelligence Agency, since it already has contacts and communications with appropriate organizations and agents in foreign countries," and establishing an interdepartmental board to develop policies and coordinate operations "under the chairmanship and supervision" of the State Department, with military and CIA cooperation.[73]

On December 9 Souers submitted a report entitled "Coordination of Foreign Information Measures" to the NSC. In it, he noted that the Soviet Union was "conducting an intensive propaganda campaign" aimed at undermining U.S. prestige and policy and weakening non-Communist elements in foreign countries "to a point where effective opposition to Soviet designs is no longer attainable by political, economic or military means." The United States, however, was "not now employing *coordinated* information measures to counter this propaganda campaign or to further attainment of its national objectives. . . . None of the existing departments or agencies of the U.S. Government is now charged with responsibility for coordinating foreign information measures in furtherance of the attainment of U.S. national objectives." The report concluded with recommendations for the "immediate strengthening and coordination of all foreign information measures of the U.S. Government" and for charging the secretary of state "with formulating policies for and coordinating the implementation" of all such measures in close cooperation with other appropriate government agencies.[74]

Souers was clearly preaching to the choir. His concerns resulted in an NSC directive to the DCI on December 17, 1947. After noting that "the vicious psychological efforts of the USSR, its satellite countries and Communist groups to discredit and defeat the aims and activities of the United States and other Western powers" required that the U.S. government's foreign information activities "must be supplemented by covert psychological operations," and observing that the "similarity of operational methods involved in covert psychological and intelligence activities and the need to ensure their secrecy and obviate costly duplication renders the Central Intelligence Agency the logical agency to conduct such operations," the NSC directed the DCI "to initiate and conduct, within the limits of available funds, covert psychological operations designed to counteract Soviet and Soviet-inspired activities which constitute a threat to world peace and security or are designed to discredit and defeat the United States in its endeavors to promote world peace and security."[75]

Hillenkoetter then acted to bring the NSC's decision to life. On December 22 he informed OSO chief Galloway of the NSC's action and assigned OSO the responsibility for carrying it out: "It is desired that you take immediate steps to prepare a plan for the conduct of covert psychological operations utilizing wherever practicable existing facilities of your office and other offices of this Agency."[76] An interim Special Procedures Branch was organized within OSO on February 24, 1948,[77] and Hillenkoetter followed up with more detailed instructions to Galloway on March 22 to establish within OSO a unit for the "performance of covert psychological operations outside the United States and its possessions." Such operations would include "all measures of information and persuasion short of physical," and the "originating role of the United States Government will always be kept concealed." These measures would be "kept entirely distinct" from overt foreign information activities of other U.S. government agencies, and their objectives would be "to undermine the strength of foreign instrumentalities, whether governments, organizations or individuals which are engaged in activities inimical to the United States" and "to support U.S. foreign policy by influencing foreign public opinion in a direction favorable to the attainment of US objectives."[78] On March 29 Galloway promulgated a directive establishing a Special Procedures Group organized to accomplish these ends.[79]

A Rubicon had been crossed. Once the concept of covert psychological operations had been accepted, it was only a short step to full-scale covert political activity. This step was promptly taken by George Kennan, who, in 1948, headed the State Department's newly established Policy Planning Staff.[80] On May 4, demonstrating the intellectual fecundity he had shown earlier in his famous "long telegram" of 1946 on the nature of Soviet international conduct, he prepared a lucid memo for presentation to the NSC concerning the "inauguration of organized political warfare," which he defined as "all the means at a nation's command, short of war, to achieve its national objectives." He then observed that the U.S. government "has, of course . . . , been conducting political warfare. . . . Having assumed greater international responsibilities than ever before in our history and having been engaged by the full might of the Kremlin's political warfare, we cannot afford to leave unmobilized our resources for covert political warfare. We cannot afford in the future, in perhaps more serious political crises, to scramble into impromtu covert operations." He then described various types of useful actions, such as organizing committees to promote the "liberation" of Soviet-dominated Europe, support for "indigenous forces combatting communism" in non-Communist states, and preventive "direct action." Kennan then recommended the prompt establishment of a "directorate of political warfare operations" under the NSC, with a director picked by, and responsible to, the secretary of state, with "complete authority over covert political warfare operations conducted by this Government" and "the authority to initiate new operations and bring under its control or abolish existing covert political warfare activities."[81]

Like those in his "long telegram," Kennan's ideas quickly reached a receptive audience, particularly Marshall and Forrestal, his two main patrons in the national security establishment. Although there was no disagreement over the perceived need for an instrumentality to conduct the kind of covert political operations envisioned by Kennan, its placement in the bureaucracy was an open question. Since Marshall did not want responsibility for such activities to be lodged in the State Department, lest their exposure cause diplomatic embarrassment and possibly compromise the conduct of U.S. foreign policy, attention once again turned to the CIA. Because OSO was primarily an intelligence collection unit (despite its new "psychological operations" responsibilities), creating an entirely new organization quickly gained favor. Further issues to be resolved were whether the head of such an organization should come from the CIA and the extent to which the secretaries of state and defense, as well as the JCS, would be involved in its conduct. Resolution of these issues gave birth to NSC 10/2 on June 18, 1948.

Drafted primarily by Kennan, NSC 10/2 was one of the seminal documents in the history of the CIA and the larger history of U.S. foreign policy conduct during the cold war. After ritually deploring the "vicious covert activities" of the Soviet Union, its satellites, and political action groups against the United States and other countries, the document declared that "the overt foreign activities of the U.S. Government must be supplemented by covert operations." Because of its existing overseas intelligence mission, the NSC felt that it was "desirable, for operational reasons, not to create a new agency for covert operations, but in time of peace to place the responsibility for them within the structure of the Central Intelligence Agency and correlate them with espionage and counter-espionage operations under the over-all control" of the DCI. The NSC therefore directed that a new Office of Special Projects be created within the CIA "to plan and conduct covert operations; and in coordination with the Joint Chiefs of Staff to plan and prepare for such operations in wartime." The secretary of state was to nominate a "highly qualified person," acceptable to the DCI and approved by the NSC, to head the new organization. Although this individual would "report directly" to the DCI, for "purposes of security and flexibility of operations, and to the maximum degree consistent with efficiency," the new office "shall operate independently of the other components" of the CIA.

The DCI was directed to ensure "through designated representatives of the Secretary of State and of the Secretary of Defense, that covert operations are planned and conducted in a manner consistent with U.S. foreign and military policies and with overt activities." Disagreements were to be resolved by the NSC. Plans for "wartime covert operations" were to be drawn up in cooperation with the JCS and closely supervised and coordinated by the military in "active theaters of war where American forces are engaged." The DCI also was directed to inform "agencies of the U.S. Government, both at home and abroad (including diplomatic and military representatives in each area) of such operations as will affect them" and to conduct covert operations "pertaining to economic warfare" under "the guidance of the departments and agencies responsible for the planning of economic warfare." The document authorized the DCI to seek supplemental funds to conduct covert operations in fiscal 1949, but, thereafter, "funds for these purposes shall be included in normal Central Intelligence Agency Budget requests."[82]

Despite this sweeping grant of power, the CIA was initially cautious in approaching its new mandate. Nearly a year earlier, on September 25, 1947, General Counsel Houston had written Hillenkoetter on the CIA's legal authority "to engage in black propaganda or the type of activity known during the war as SO [secret operations], which included ranger and commando raids, behind-the-lines sabotage, and support of guerrilla warfare." In his view, those provisions of the National Security Act authorizing "services of common concern" and such "other functions" as directed by the NSC could be construed as providing such authority. Nevertheless, he provided a caveat: "Taken out of context and without knowledge of history, these Sections could bear almost unlimited interpretation, provided the service performed could be shown to be of benefit to an intelligence agency or related to national intelligence." He then added that a

> review of the debates indicates that Congress was primarily interested in an agency for coordinating intelligence and originally did not propose any overseas collection activities for the CIA. . . . We do not believe that there was any thought in the minds of Congress that the Central Intelligence Agency under this authority would take positive action for subversion and sabotage. . . . It is our conclusion, therefore that neither MO ["morale operations," i.e., covert propaganda] or SO should be undertaken by the CIA without previously informing Congress and obtaining its approval of the functions and the expenditure of funds for these purposes.[83]

Kennan, however, was not a man to worry over such legalisms. With NSC 10/2 formally promulgated, he presented a list of proposed nominees to head the new organization to Under Secretary of State Robert Lovett on June 30. Heading that list was Frank Wisner, a former OSS officer serving in the State Department's Office of Occupied Territories, of whom Kennan rather offhandedly wrote: "I have placed Wisner at the head of the list on recommendation of people who know him. I personally have no knowledge of his ability, but his qualifications seem reasonably good, and I think that it would be relatively easy to spare him for this purpose." On August 6 Kennan met with Wisner, Souers, Hillenkoetter, and Defense Department representatives Robert Blum and Colonel Ivan Yeaton to discuss implementation. All agreed on the importance of political warfare as a foreign policy instrument and accepted the view that the hybrid organizational arrangement was necessary to assure maximum oversight of operations while also assuring their maximum flexibility and freedom from regular administrative standards. Wisner's appointment was approved by the NSC on August 19, and, on August 27, the CIA issued an administrative directive establishing the new organization, renamed the Office of Policy Coordination (OPC). On October 1 Lovett wrote to Forrestal, requesting that the military establishment give OPC full cooperation in carrying out its activities. In his response of October 13, Forrestal promised that it would do so.[84]

Faced with reality, Houston did his lawerly duty and drafted the appropriate legal justification for a policy already decided upon. In a long memo to Hillenkoetter on October 19, exploring the DCI's responsibilities under NSC 10/2, he observed that

> the intent of the Council is to look to the Director for the proper functioning of covert operations. He is specifically held responsible for their control, which presupposes the right to initiate and to veto projects, subject only to NSC rulings in the event of dispute. As the funds involved are to be CIA funds, unvouchered expenditures will, by law, be the Director's personal responsibility. To carry this out, he must have power to set controls for all such expenditures and provide means . . . to insure that the funds are properly expended and regulations laid down by him.

Houston therefore maintained that NSC "intended no limitation" on the DCI's operational control and that he would be "guided" but "not controlled" by the JCS and the State Department in matters of foreign and military policy. He stated categorically "that responsibility for 'conduct' of OPC activities was specifically placed in the Director of Central Intelligence." Thus, he recommended that, if NSC 10/2 "was intended to carry the meaning its present wording appears to bear, there should be specific and detailed acknowledgement that the Director, in carrying out his mandate to conduct and be responsible for covert operations, has full administrative control of personnel and supplies, final authority over the expenditure of funds, and the right to initiate and veto projects." If such was not the intent of NSC 10/2, reasoned Houston, it "should be carefully amended" to make "quite clear" what the respective roles of the State Department, JCS, and DCI were to be.[85]

The victory of the Christian Democrats and their allies in the April 1948 Italian elections—following a major covert propaganda and political action campaign in which the CIA, according to various accounts, played a major role—seemed to confirm the value of covert activities,[86] and, in Frank Wisner, the times and the man had met. By all accounts an extremely able, imaginative, hard-driving, and driven man, Wisner, who, as an OSS officer, had witnessed the brutality of Soviet conduct in Romania, approached his new task with the zeal of a crusader. In the words of William Colby, who knew him well: "Wisner landed like a dynamo, read all the intelligence and set out to form a clandestine force worldwide. By hard work and brilliance, and by reaching widely for similarly activist OSS alumni, he started operating in the atmosphere of an order of Knights Templars, to save Western freedom from Communist darkness—and from war."[87] He drew in men such as himself: "determined interventionists," well educated, internationalist, comfortable with the concept of an activist government, possessed of a liberal sense of mission, often (but not inevitably) veterans of the OSS, and as committed as he to fighting a new "evil empire."[88] As one intelligence writer has observed: "The OPC was America's first peacetime covert organization. But no one in Washington, including the president, thought 1948 was peacetime."[89] Thus did Wisner and his associates come to preside over what became a growth industry for the CIA.[90]

The final key factor in determining the CIA's evolution was leadership. Although he had successfully presided over the transition of the CIG into the CIA, Hillenkoetter remained a seaman at heart. He was out of his element either as a player in the Washington bureaucracy's power game or as a spymaster. He lacked the status, professional prestige, and political influence to deal effectively with the service intelligence chiefs and had the misfortune to be caught in the rancorous feud over foreign and national security policy between Secretary of Defense Johnson and Secretary of State Acheson. Opined Walter Pforzheimer in later years: "They ate him alive."[91] In addition, Hillenkoetter had little empathy with the insular and arrogant world of the "intelligence professionals," many of whom shared Wisner's opinion that he was "an amiable lightweight."[92] Most seriously, he bore the stigma of reputed "intelligence failures" by the CIA: the failure to "predict" the Communist coup in Czechoslovakia and the riots in Bogotá during the inter-American conference attended by Secretary Marshall in 1948; the detonation of the Soviet atomic bomb and the fall of China to the Communists in 1949; and the outbreak of the Korean War in 1950. It was therefore hardly surprising that Hillenkoetter increasingly expressed the wish to return to sea duty.[93]

Souers insisted that Hillenkoetter could not step down, however, until a successor had been designated. A number of names were broached, without success, until Souers suggested General Walter Bedell Smith to Truman in May 1950. Smith, highly regarded as Eisenhower's chief of staff in Europe during the war, had recently completed a tour as ambassador to the Soviet Union. Respecting Souers's judgment, Truman concurred with the idea, although he was probably aware of Smith's formidable reputation as an organizer and manager, and likely recognized that Smith's rank (lieutenant general) and his prestige would guarantee his predominance over the intelligence establishments of the armed forces.[94] Whatever the basis for his choice, however, it was one with momentous consequences for the CIA.

Smith was an American original. Born in Indianapolis in 1895 and self-educated, he had enlisted in the Indiana national guard in 1911, did frontline service in World War I, and secured a commission in the Regular Army in the immediate postwar period. His natural ability was recognized by Chief of Staff Marshall, who, when the United States went to war again and began to plan for overseas deployments, recommended him as chief of staff to European commander Eisenhower. In this capacity, Smith soon demonstrated an enormous level of energy and ability, as well as a degree of drive that earned him the cognomen of "the American bulldog" from Winston Churchill. Although a gracious and engaging man personally, Smith cultivated a fearsomely intimidating public persona to get the most effort from his subordinates. He drove himself every bit as hard and suffered from massive ulcers as a result. Smith, however, did not wish the position. Having declined it on several occasions for health reasons, he was interested in retiring from the army to seek a career in business or a university presidency. The outbreak of the Korean War in June 1950 catalyzed the situation. After determining that Smith's health was satisfactory (he had been undergoing treatment for his ulcers), Truman ordered him to take the position. Smith, always the good soldier, obeyed.[95] Once again, the times and the man had met. Noted one admiring old agency hand in later years:

> The Korean War was the final blow needed to force the United States to revitalize its defense establishment and to build a modern intelligence system. If the CIA was to survive the bureaucratic battles and emerge as the strong keystone of the federal intelligence structure, it was at this time

that it needed a powerful hand at the helm. Smith had what was needed. He was tough, forceful, dynamic. . . . But, most important of all, Bedell Smith knew that his country had to have the best intelligence service in the world to survive and he gave everything he had to build that system.[96]

Smith's appointment was announced on August 18 and submitted to the Senate on August 21. After he made a brief appearance before the Armed Services Committee on August 24, his appointment was unanimously confirmed by the full chamber on August 28.[97] Noting the event, Time magazine observed that Smith "had no illusions about the difficulties of operating an all-seeing intelligence eye," quoting him on his new assignment that the "American people expect you to be on a communing level with God and Joe Stalin and I'm not sure that they are so much interested in God. They expect you to be able to say that a war will start next Tuesday at 5:32 P.M."[98] Completing his recuperation and winding up his affairs, Smith arrived in Washington on October 1 and called at the White House the next day to announce, "I came down per orders yesterday and reported for work and am feeling fine. Just wanted to tell the President to know I'm on the job."[99]

Hillenkoetter then took his leave, to assume command of a cruiser squadron in the Far East. On October 6 he wrote Truman: "I wish to thank you for acceding to my request to return to active sea duty with the Navy and to inform you that on tomorrow, 7 October 1950, I shall turn over the duties of Director of Central Intelligence to General W. B. Smith, whom you have designated as my successor." Truman responded graciously: "I cannot allow you to return to sea duty . . . without assuring you of my heartfelt appreciation of the splendid service you have rendered as Director of Central Intelligence. . . . With foresight, tenacity, and discretion you performed manifold duties in a manner designed to serve the national interest rather than that of any particular group. So I say to you as you return to active service with the Navy: Well done."[100] On schedule, Smith assumed his post as DCI the following day.

Smith assumed his new office with both a mandate and a personal inclination to bring about major changes in the CIA. Having read both the Hoover Commission report and the findings of the Dulles-Jackson-Correa study, he had clear ideas about what needed to be done and the personal force to gain his ends. Enthused one CIA insider in retrospect: "He was a shrewd, dynamic man with broad experience and absolutely no tolerance for fools. It was often said he was the most even-tempered man in the world—he was always angry. . . . For the first time since Donovan, central intelligence was in the hands of a man with vision and drive, a man with the prestige persuasive to military commanders, ambassadors, and Congressmen, and, finally, a man who had the full support of a President who wanted action." [101]

The CIA's difficulties were fully clarified for Smith in a lengthy report from the ever-officious Houston on August 29, 1950, that described "basic current problems facing CIA." Houston's report noted that the CIA was having difficulties in producing "adequate" intelligence estimates due to the failure of other agencies "to honor CIA requests for necessary intelligence information, departmental intelligence, or collection action," and that it was experiencing similar difficulties in distributing these estimates due to delays and dissents by other agencies. In addition, complained Houston, other intelligence agencies "resist the grant of authority to CIA to issue directives affecting the intelligence field in general and their activities or priorities in particular on the ground that it would violate the concept of command channels"; that the "status of CIA in relation to the President and NSC must be redefined and clarified"; and that the "relationships between CIA . . . and the Department of Justice—particularly the FBI . . . , must be improved and clarified." Houston was particularly exercised that difficulties "imposed by NSC directives in the field of unconventional warfare must be eliminated, particularly the policy control over CIA granted to the Departments of State and Defense." To Houston, the division "of clandestine operations into two offices within CIA creates serious problems of efficiency, efficacy and, above all, security," and "the failure of coordination of overt intelligence in the field" made it "necessary for CIA to take a strong position in the field of overt collection abroad." Houston concluded by asserting that the solution to these problems "lies in a grant of [adequate] authority to the DCI and CIA, and use of that authority to achieve the necessary coordination by direction rather than placing reliance in a spirit of cooperation and goodwill." [102]

Smith's initial step was to regularize the position of deputy director of central intelligence (DDCI), a post that had technically existed since 1946 but had been filled only intermittently. Remarking to Souers, "I know nothing about this business. I shall need a Deputy who does," [103] he persuaded William Jackson to serve in that capacity. Jackson, however, lasted only ten months, resigning in August 1951 to return to private business. Smith replaced him with Allen Dulles. It was a fateful appointment. Dulles, of course, was well qualified, but the relationship was not a happy one. There were sharp personality differences between the rigid self-made general and the urbane, cosmopolitan lawyer. Deeper differences, however, would shape the course of American foreign intelligence activities. Smith felt that Dulles's paramount focus on covert action undermined his capacity to manage other aspects of intelligence.[104] As Dulles's biographer has astutely noted: "Though respectful of Allen's experience and expertise in a field that he himself did not always understand, Smith nevertheless saw through the veneer of integrity; he simply did not trust Allen's capacity for judgment or self-restraint in the exercise of powers that, by their secret nature, had to operate beyond the normal discipline of accountability."[105]

To tighten up management practices, in December 1950 Smith established a deputy director for administration to oversee such support services as logistics, finance, and personnel; after a year of spotty cooperation (particularly from the clandestine operations units), he made it clear to his senior deputies that the new official would be responsible for all of the CIA's administrative support functions. Having developed an interest in intelligence analysis from his contacts with OSS analytical personnel in London during the war, he likewise moved to organize the CIA's analytical efforts by naming Loftus Becker deputy director for intelligence, effective January 1, 1952. Under Becker's authority were the existing Office of Collection and Dissemination, Office of Research and Reports, and Office of Scientific Intelligence, as well as a newly created Office of Current Intelligence and, later, the Office of Operations, responsible for collecting "open source" information.[106]

Smith, who believed strongly in the importance of preparing long-range, in-depth analyses of specific issues based on information from all sources, further acted to realize a long-sought goal of reformers by establishing an Office of National Estimates as the capstone of the new analytical structure, under the supervision of a Board of National Estimates that drew its membership from civilian and military specialists throughout the government. To head the new organization, Smith persuaded William Langer to leave Harvard University. Langer organized a staff of about sixty and developed the organization Smith envisioned. By the time he stepped down to return to Harvard in January 1952, he felt that the Office of National Estimates had become "a going concern of real stature in the government." He was replaced by his deputy, Sherman Kent, who had left Yale (again at Smith's behest in 1950) and, unlike Langer, remained at the CIA.[107]

The most vexing problem for Smith was the chaotic state of the clandestine services. Although both the Dulles-Jackson-Correa report and NSC-50 had called for the integration of OSO and OPC, and although Smith had named Dulles deputy director for plans in January 1951 (prior to his appointment as DDCI in August) to oversee them, relations between the two groups were marked by friction, rivalry, and lack of cooperation. On a functional level, OSO's conventional spies regarded OPC's risky operations as a threat to its sources, security, and cover. These "tradecraft" problems were exacerbated by tensions arising over competition for funds, personnel, and other resources and the ill feelings generated when OPC officers advanced more rapidly than their OSO counterparts. Nor was the freewheeling independence of OPC from the DCI's management authority something that Smith would long tolerate. Smith was not a man to temporize in the face of such problems, and, soon after becoming DCI, he solved them with a bureaucratic coup d'état.[108] Acting boldly, he directed Wisner to inform the representatives of the State and Defense Departments and the JCS that, in the future, all policy guidance and direction for OPC would be through his office, rather than directly to Wisner. Wisner did so at a meeting on October 11, 1950. Neither Forrestal nor Kennan was around to challenge the flinty general, and their successors had no stomach for doing so, giving Smith an easy victory.[109]

Smith then acted to consummate an OPC-OSO "merger" advocated by Houston and others. In a memorandum to his senior staff on July 15, 1952, he announced a new organizational structure for the CIA's clandestine service, to become effective on August 1. Under this plan, there would be a "single overseas clandestine service" with "a single chain of command and a single set of administrative procedures," as well as a "single chain of command from Washington Headquarters to the chiefs of the merged field organization." The deputy director for plans would be the DCI's "deputy for all CIA clandestine activities." The DDP would have a chief of operations "with responsibility for the direction of operations, for coordinating the efforts of and eliminating duplication among all staff elements under DD/P, and for insuring prompt and effective compliance with operational directives, including those which establish priorities for clandestine operations." The memo also mandated the establishment of "staff elements specializing in secret intelligence and counter-espionage, political and psychological warfare, paramilitary operations, technical support and administration," and it laid out procedures for implementation.[110]

Smith's new order came fully into effect with the creation of the Directorate of Plans later in 1952. With Dulles now elevated to DDCI, Wisner became its deputy director, with Richard Helms from OSO as his deputy, to promote an "integrated" structure. Smith was also quick to make clear to the "intelligence professionals" that he would not countenance the insolence from them suffered by his predecessor, telling the new spy chief, "Wisner, you work for me."[111] Wisner was intimidated by Smith and readily got the message. Nevertheless, he and his colleagues were fortunate in their master. Whatever doubts Smith may have had about covert operations, both he and the president he served saw a utility for Wisner's black arts in those bleak early days of the cold war and allowed them virtually free rein.[112]

A final reform by Smith had the ultimate effect of eliminating the long-criticized problem of excessive military influence in the CIA's professional staff. As a self-made man, Smith strongly believed in professional training and immediately took steps to make CIA service a professional career. Overcoming bureaucratic resistance with his usual vigor, he appointed a director of training and instituted a rigorous, centralized yearlong training program for newly recruited personnel to ground them in intelligence methodology and procedures. Although primarily focused on training clandestine operations officers, Smith conceptualized this program broadly enough to include those doing intelligence analysis as well, feeling that a real professional could be effective in both areas.[113] In a report to the NSC on April 23, 1952, he boasted: "Continuity of high caliber personnel, possessing specialized training and experience, is essential for the conduct of the Agency's activities. Accordingly, plans for a career service within the Central Intelligence Agency are being worked out and the first groups of prospective junior career officers are in training." He added that "it will be possible eventually to select senior officials of the Central Intelligence Agency from among their number."[114] And eventually it was. With the passage of time, this career training program, with many revisions, did succeed in providing the CIA with its professional cadre.

Smith had been the drillmaster of the CIA. When the Eisenhower administration came into office in 1953, he was named under secretary of state. In his tenure as DCI, he had changed history and finally brought about the intelligence empire that Donovan had envisioned. As a result of his initiatives, the CIA had been finally transformed into a vigorous, independent organization. Under his successor, Allen Dulles, it played an active and often autonomous role in the conduct of American foreign affairs and became a key power center in Washington. Thanks to the work of Smith, the CIA was fully positioned to enter its halcyon days as a player in the new "great game," never realizing that all good things must come to an end.

10

Ends and Beginnings

With Smith's reorganization in place, the CIA assumed its present structure.[1] For the remainder of the cold war, it provided the United States with an instrument for maintaining its posture as a world leader and superpower. In assuming this role as a clandestine combatant in the struggle against a new "evil empire," the CIA metamorphosed into the shape of its OSS parent. As James Reston, the keenest political observer and analyst of his day, observed, during the Eisenhower administration the CIA changed "from an intelligence-gathering and analyzing instrument to an operating arm of the military services."[2] Making this change gave Donovan the ultimate victory in the battle over the nature of the postwar American intelligence system. Although the OSS chief never achieved the position of postwar intelligence overlord that he so coveted, he lived long enough to see the empire that he envisioned in 1944 come into being. His OSS disciples from Allen Dulles to William Casey—by professing to know how to deal with "evil empires"—also dominated the CIA for the entire cold war and had a major impact on the conduct of American foreign policy.[3]

Nevertheless, Donovan's victory was only a partial one. The CIA never came to dominate the U.S. government's intelligence apparatus, as Donovan had sought, but remained only one member (albeit an influential one) of a congeries of organizations devoted to foreign intelligence activities. Believers in unique departmental expertise and missions, and in competitive overlapping analysis, effectively held their own against actual "centralism," and from its first days the CIA has had to contend with the interests and ambitions of powerful bureaucratic baronies beyond the control of the DCI. The Defense Department went far beyond its individual service intelligence components to create a huge internal intelligence establishment, particularly in the field of technical intelligence collection, that dwarfs the CIA. New emphasis on "low-intensity conflict" has also allowed it to expand its paramilitary special operations capacity. Similarly, the perception of terrorism and international crime as "national security" threats has enabled the FBI to expand its operational presence overseas. Nor has the State

Department ever abandoned its view that it is the proper instrument of government for analyzing and interpreting global issues—whether country-specific, regional, or functional. The complex political, strategic, and economic issues now confronting American policy makers in the aftermath of the cold war have become so enmeshed that the degree of interagency cooperation required to deal with them is slowly reviving the "collegial" system conceptualized in 1946 by Alfred McCormack.

During the course of the cold war, the CIA had its "contributions" to make in the struggle against the "evil empire" and those perceived by American policy makers to be its allies: clandestine intelligence collection operations, the development of overhead reconnaissance technology, the production of independent analysis for use by American leaders, and covert actions (often of a military nature) designed to promote American foreign policy objectives.[4] Nevertheless, it is only conjecture to speculate that the wartime and early postwar bureaucratic struggles over intelligence organization produced the most effective system, since no other system was ever tried. Donovan's disciples were fortunate to be in the right place at the right time. Had a second "evil empire" not appeared so soon after the demise of the first, it is likely that the evolution of the CIA would have been quite different, and might have more resembled the general coordinating body favored by Donovan's opponents.

Although the CIA came into being during the early years of the cold war, the basic premises underlying the organization preceded its onset. Although the need for an instrumentality to collect and analyze foreign intelligence was recognized by all, it was a concatenation of events that gave the CIA missions, such as "subversive operations abroad," that it otherwise might not have acquired. Of the four men most responsible for creating the CIA—Souers, Forrestal, Clifford, and Vandenberg—only the latter seemed to share Donovan's grandiose vision of a freestanding intelligence empire thanks to ambition and energy equal to Donovan's. Yet all (as well as the president they served) were willing to borrow Donovan's ideas when they perceived the necessity of engaging world politics in a clandestine fashion.

Over time, however, those responsible for bringing the CIA to life came to question what it had become. Reflecting in his memoirs, Clark Clifford felt that "over the years, covert activities became so numerous and widespread that, in effect, they became a self-sustaining part of American foreign operations. The CIA became a government within a government, which could evade oversight of its activities by drawing the cloak of secrecy around itself."[5] Similarly, George Kennan complained to a congressional committee in 1975 that "clearly, in recommending the development of a covert action capability in 1948, policymakers intended to make available a small contingency force that could mount operations on a limited basis. Senior officials did not plan to develop large scale continuing covert operations. Instead, they hoped to establish a small capability that could be activated at their discretion."[6] Sidney Souers had similar feelings. Writing to former president Truman in 1963, he observed: "Allen Dulles caused the CIA to wander far from the original goal established by you, and it is certainly a different animal than I tried to set up for you. . . . It would seem that its principal effort was to cause revolutions in smaller countries around the globe. . . . With so much emphasis on operations, it would not surprise me to find that the matter of collecting and processing intelligence has suffered some."[7] Truman himself, after years of private grumbling about CIA conduct, let fly a blast of his own in an article for the North American Newspaper Alliance in 1963: "For some time I have been disturbed by the way CIA has been diverted from its original assignment. It has become an operational arm and at times a policy-making arm of Government. . . . I never had any thought when I set up the CIA that it would be injected into peacetime cloak-and-dagger operations."[8]

The utility and effectiveness of the CIA's "contributions" have been, and will remain, matters of strenuous public debate and controversy that go well beyond the scope of this study. One thing is nevertheless certain. The CIA's secret life, fueled by unaccountable funds and unobserved by either institutionalized legislative oversight or public scrutiny, stigmatized it as alien to American political institutions and culture and subversive to the integrity of the American government itself. Again, it is the perspicacious Reston who best noted this impact: "From the Bay of Pigs fiasco under President Kennedy all the way through the Vietnam War under Johnson and Nixon and the Iran-Contra scandals under Reagan the CIA did more to break down confidence in the government's statements than anything else. And the problem was made worse by the fact that during the Reagan administration the head of the CIA authorized secret activities that even the president said he knew nothing about."[9]

That such a turn of events could transpire represents a serious failure of the American political process, since official warning had been given early and publicly of such risks. In 1955 the second Hoover Commission established a special task force on intelligence headed by retired General Mark Clark. In its final report, it emphasized its concern "over the absence of satisfactory machinery for surveillance of the stewardship of the Central Intelligence Agency. . . . Because of its position, the CIA has been freed by Congress from outside surveillance of its operations and fiscal accounts. There is always a danger that such freedom from restraints could inspire laxity and abuses which might prove costly to the American people." [10] Due to the exigencies of waging the cold war, however, such warnings were ignored, and Congress contented itself with leaving any oversight to the personal relationships of individual congressional oligarchs with CIA directors until the Vietnam conflict brought about the collapse of the cold war consensus. [11]

Just as the onset of the cold war served to realize Donovan's imperial vision for the CIA, its end—along with the demise of the Soviet Union itself in 1991—served to terminate it. These events altered both the way the American government addresses the world and the way in which the American people view their government's international conduct. For the CIA, they have turned the wheel of history full circle. In 1945, with the defeat of the Axis "evil empire," Donovan's OSS ceased to have a purpose and went out of existence. Only the prompt emergence of a new "evil empire" permitted its unintended resurrection as the CIA. Because the ramshackle Soviet commonwealth imploded of its own accord in 1991, without foreign assistance, America's unexpected "victory" was one of default, and one that permanently altered not only the global landscape but also the role of intelligence in the conduct of American foreign policy. [12]

The end of the cold war took with it the grand strategy of "containment" that drove American international action for nearly fifty years. Also rendered obsolete were a half century of bureaucratic policies and missions, as well as an entire intellectual mind-set, that the containment strategy underpinned. Nowhere has this sea change been more apparent than in the domain of foreign intelligence. As one intelligence writer aptly put it: "Intelligence, as it has been understood since the end of World War II, is a dying business. The end of the Cold War brought with it the destruction of a world where each intelligence agency had clear targets, broadly understood the nature of the threat, and had a clear role and technical means to combat it. Today there is no such security." [13] Emerging issues of post–cold war global concern—terrorism, international crime, weapons proliferation, regional instability and conflict, economic and societal upheaval—have made the international threat environment more diffuse and complicated. Not only have efforts to understand, and cope with, the increasingly disordered world scene caused intelligence priorities and the interests of policy makers to shift rapidly and dramatically, but the nature of the new threats and the revolution in information acquisition and dissemination have thrown traditional ways of intelligence organization, collection, evaluation, and distribution into question. [14]

Because the end of the cold war was accompanied by massive scandals within the CIA, it left behind not a sense of triumph but a sense of foreboding and of being confronted with unprecedented challenges to the agency's utility and even its very existence.[15] While the need for institutional change has been officially recognized, there has been little agreement over the nature, structure, and scope of such changes.[16] With no prospects for the emergence of a third "evil empire" in sight, the CIA has entered its second half century of existence striving to avoid the fate of its OSS parent. In the process, it is groping for new missions and purposes while blighted by the legacy of its past derelictions, and while operating amid a rapidly changing global environment and technological revolution that are rendering its sources, methods, organization, and mystique obsolete. As the once-threatening issues of the cold war recede into the historic distance and fade in memory, Donovan's ultimate victory in the battle to shape the structure of postwar central intelligence looms ironic. Because the CIA eventually became what Donovan wished it to be, it remains encumbered with the massive burden of its own past as it searches for new relevance now that the world that gave it its former relevance has vanished.

Notes

Introduction

1. Clark Clifford, *Counsel to the President: A Memoir* (New York: Random House, 1991), p. 146.

2. The most complete study of the national security reform movement is Demetrios Caraley, *The Politics of Military Unification* (New York: Columbia University Press, 1966).

3. U.S. Senate, Select Committee to Study Government Operations with Respect to Intelligence Activities, *Final Report: Supplementary Detailed Staff Reports on Foreign and Military Intelligence*, book IV, 94th Cong., 2d sess. (Washington, D.C.: USGPO, 1976), p. 1. Hereafter cited as Senate History.

4. Department of Defense, *Dictionary of Military and Associated Terms* (Washington, D.C.: Joint Chiefs of Staff, 1974), p. 75.

5. Central Intelligence Agency, *A Consumer's Guide to Intelligence* (Washington, D.C.: CIA Office of Public and Agency Information, 1995), p. 42.

6. The literature on intelligence policy and methodology is enormous and growing. The following books constitute only a representative sampling. The published views of the doyen of American spies on his chosen profession is Allen Dulles, *The Craft of Intelligence* (New York: Harper and Row, 1963). One of the earliest—and surprisingly thorough —journalistic examinations of the CIA and intelligence community is David Wise and Thomas Ross, *The Invisible Government* (New York: Random House, 1964). The publication of this book so agitated the CIA that it mounted a rather ludicrous, albeit illegal, domestic covert operation to suppress or discredit the work. The classic, but now outdated, academic study is Harry Howe Ransom, *The Intelligence Establishment* (Cambridge, Mass.: Harvard University Press, 1970). More recent studies include Walter Laquer, *A World of Secrets: The Uses and Limits of Intelligence* (New York: Basic Books, 1985); Phillip Knightly, *The Second Oldest Profession: Spies and Spying in the Twentieth Century* (New York: W. W. Norton, 1986); Scott Breckinridge, *The CIA and the U.S. Intelligence Community* (Boulder, Colo.: Westview Press, 1986); Angelo Codevilla, *Informing Statecraft: Intelligence for a New Century* (New York: Free Press, 1992); Jeffrey T. Richelson, *A Century of Spies: Intelligence in the Twentieth Century* (New York: Oxford University Press, 1995); and Loch Johnson, *Secret Agencies: U.S. Intelligence in a Hostile World* (New Haven, Conn.: Yale University Press, 1996).

7. Bradley F. Smith, *The Shadow Warriors: OSS and the Origins of the CIA* (New York: Basic Books, 1983), p. 391. As Smith correctly observes, the primary exponent of the "founding myth" is intelligence writer and former intelligence officer Thomas Troy in his *Donovan and the CIA: A History of the Establishment of the Central Intelligence Agency* (n.p.: CIA Center for the Study of Intelligence, 1981). This book is a pioneering study in the field of intelligence history, and the author, a highly competent scholar and diligent researcher, has unearthed an enormous amount of information of great value for those who come after him (including this writer). Nevertheless, his book does not deliver what the title advertises. Working as a CIA contractor, he wrote for the purpose of indoctrination. As a result, his book is an account of Donovan's adventures in the wartime Washington bureaucracy that ignores the larger policy context. Several relatively superficial chapters on the postwar, post-Donovan period are essentially an afterthought. Equally unfortunate is Troy's infatuation with his subject, which causes him to pass from scholarship to hagiography with too much ease.

Although Troy's work was originally prepared for internal CIA use, a commercial edition was published in 1981 by the University Press of America in Frederick, Maryland.

1. The Dual Road to Central Intelligence

1. Recent readable and comprehensive histories of the role of intelligence in American history are Christopher Andrew, *For the President's Eyes Only: Secret Intelligence and the American Presidency from Washington to Bush* (New York: HarperCollins, 1995); and George J. A. O'Toole, *Honorable Treachery: A History of U.S. Espionage and Covert Action from the American Revolution to the CIA* (New York: Atlantic Monthly Press, 1991). The "intelligence community" in its contemporary context is described as the "aggregate of the executive branch organizations and agencies involved in intelligence activities" (Central Intelligence Agency, *A Consumer's Guide to Intelligence*, p. 54). Today, this "community" comprises the CIA as well as the State Department, the numerous intelligence components of the Defense Department, the FBI and other offices in the Justice Department, and the Treasury and Energy Departments. A large and elaborate staff oversees "community relations."

2. The history of ONI is recounted in Jeffery M. Dorwart, *The Office of Naval Intelligence: The Birth of America's First Intelligence Agency, 1865–1918* (Annapolis, Md.: U.S. Naval Institute Press, 1979); and Dorwart, *Conflict of Duty: The U.S. Navy's Intelligence Dilemma, 1919–1945* (Annapolis, Md.: U.S. Naval Institute Press, 1983). For the history of army intelligence, see Bruce Bidwell, *History of the Military Intelligence Department of the Army General Staff: 1775–1941* (Westport, Conn.: Greenwood Press, 1986); and Marc Powe, *The Emergence of the War Department Intelligence Agency: 1885–1918*, published for *Military Affairs*, the journal of the American Military Institute, by Kansas State University, Manhattan, Kansas, 1975. These military intelligence organizations are not to be confused with those service components responsible for the interception and breaking of codes in the prewar years, the War Department's Signals Intelligence Service and the navy's Office of Naval Communications. The best overall history of cryptology is David Kahn, *The Codebreakers* (New York: Macmillan, 1996).

3. Useful accounts of the "old" (i.e., prewar) State Department are Henry Maddox, *Twilight of Amateur Diplomacy: The American Foreign Service and Its Senior Officers in the 1890s* (Kent, Ohio: Kent State University Press, 1989); and Robert D. Schulzinger, *The Making of the Diplomatic Mind: The Training, Outlook, and Style of United States Foreign Service Officers, 1908–1931* (Middletown, Conn.: Wesleyan University Press, 1975). The State Department also had its code-breaking unit, Herbert Yardley's "black chamber." In 1930 Secretary of State Henry Stimson, supposedly remarking that "gentlemen do not read each other's mail," ordered it closed. Stimson, a great public servant, has been unfairly maligned for this view, which represented a high-minded concept of international conduct that has been eroded by ideological conflict and total war.

4. The best study of the FBI as an institution remains Sanford Ungar, *FBI* (Boston: Little, Brown, 1975). For an overview of the FBI's prewar "intelligence" role (mostly one of counterespionage and countersubversion), see Frank Rafalko, ed., *A Counterintelligence Reader: American Revolution to World War II* (n.p.: National Counterintelligence Center, n.d.), pp. 111–127, 157–163, 169–181, passim.

5. Ray S. Cline, *Secrets, Spies, and Scholars: Blueprint of the Essential CIA* (Washington, D.C.: Acropolis Books, 1976), pp. 9, 13–16.

6. Troy, *Donovan and the CIA*, p. 6.

7. Despite the passage of time and the onward march of scholarship, the best histories of American foreign policy during this critical period remain two books by William Langer and S. Everett Gleason, *The Challenge to Isolation: 1937–1940* (New York: Harper and Brothers, 1952), and *The Undeclared War: 1940–1941* (New York: Harper and Brothers, 1953). Some years after the publication of these books, there was a stir in academe over the fact that both authors were senior CIA officers.

8. Troy, *Donovan and the CIA*, pp. 11–13; Cline, *Secrets, Spies, and Scholars*, pp. 18–19.

9. A copy of this document is to be found in Folder 1, Non-COI: 1940, Background Papers for *Donovan and the CIA*, Record Group 263, Records of the Central Intelligence Agency, National Archives. Hereafter cited as Troy Papers.

10. Ungar, *FBI*, p. 225.

11. A copy of this agreement is in Folder 31Q11, 3-1-41 thru 5-31-41 (4-2-35), Army Intelligence Decimal File, 1941–1948, Record Group 319, Records of the Army Staff, National Archives. Hereafter cited as NA.

12. A copy of this agreement is in Folder 1, Non-COI: 1940–1941, Troy Papers, RG 263, NA.

13. Ungar, *FBI*, p. 225.

14. A copy of this agreement is in Folder 31Q11, 3-1-41 thru 5-31-41 (4-2-35), Army Intelligence Decimal File, 1941–1948, RG 319, NA.

15. There is a shrine to Donovan, complete with a life-size statue, in the entrance lobby of the original CIA Headquarters building at Langley, Virginia. It is the product of DCI William Casey, who served in the OSS in Europe, knew Donovan, and saw himself as the OSS chief's direct descendant in battling the Soviet "evil empire" as Donovan battled its Axis counterpart. Thomas Troy gives literary apotheosis to Donovan by declaring him "a

giant whose personality, prestige, power, and push shook every rafter in the house of intelligence, to the delight of his followers and the anger of his foes" (Troy, *Donovan and the CIA*, p. 214).

While Donovan's biographers do not deify the man as Troy does, they tend to share his veneration. The best biography is Richard Dunlop, *Donovan: America's Master Spy* (Chicago: Rand McNally, 1982). Too important to be ignored is the biography by the controversial British intelligence writer Anthony Cave Brown, *The Last Hero: Wild Bill Donovan* (New York: Times Books, 1982).

16. This profile of Donovan is based on Dunlop, *Donovan: America's Master Spy*, pp. 9–273, passim.

17. Ibid.

18. Donovan to Knox, 26 May 1941, "Central Intelligence, 1941–1950," Vol. 1, Papers of William J. Donovan, U.S. Army Military History Institute, Carlisle Barracks, Pennsylvania.

19. Dunlop, *Donovan: America's Master Spy*, pp. 274–354 passim; and Troy, *Donovan and the CIA*, pp. 40–208 passim. The various documents involved in the creation of the COI and OSS are reprinted as Appendixes A through J in Troy, *Donovan and the CIA*, pp. 417–438.

20. In addition to the Dunlop and Troy works, see R. Harris Smith, *OSS: The Secret History of America's First Central Intelligence Agency* (Berkeley: University of California Press, 1972); and Bradley Smith, *The Shadow Warriors*. Declassified "official" histories include Kermit Roosevelt and associates, *War Report of the OSS* (New York: Walker and Company, 1975); and Anthony Cave Brown, ed., *The Secret War Report of the OSS* (New York: Berkley Medallion Books, 1976).

21. Calvin Hoover, *Memoirs of Capitalism, Communism, and Nazism* (Durham, N.C.: Duke University Press, 1965), p. 196.

22. No adequate study exists concerning the relations of the OSS and other components of the wartime "intelligence community." The freewheeling style of both Donovan and his organization, as well as the OSS chief's unsubtle ambitions for the future, aggravated many of his counterparts. Army and navy officers frequently viewed OSS personnel as civilian amateurs in uniform. For its part, the State Department was quick to resent another agency collecting, processing, and evaluating information related to foreign affairs. Noted William Langer: "Few officials in the State Department welcomed the incursion of intelligence specialists, since they were firmly convinced that, reading the diplomatic traffic, they knew all they needed to know about foreign affairs" (William Langer, *In and Out of the Ivory Tower* (New York: Neale Watson Academic Publications, 1977), pp. 199–200).

The attitude of FBI director Hoover (whose grim eminence hovered over the foreign intelligence field until the day he died) is complicated. All biographies of Hoover emphasize his animosity toward both Donovan and the OSS. His hostility toward Donovan was likely based on his distrust of Donovan's ambitions, his discomfort with Donovan's operating style, his suspicions about some of the people recruited into the OSS, and memories of personal discord going back to his service with Donovan in the Coolidge administration. Hoover was not a man who let go of grudges easily, and he rarely relished giving up any power once it was granted to him. In my judgment, the most useful study of Hoover is Athan G. Theoharis and John Stuart Cox, *The Boss: J. Edgar Hoover and the Great American Inquisition* (London: Harrap, 1988), passim. See also Curt Gentry, *J. Edgar Hoover: The Man and His Secrets* (New York: W. W. Norton, 1991), pp. 267–268; and Ungar, *FBI*, pp. 107–108, 225.

Good accounts of OSS operations overseas include Kermit Roosevelt, *War Report of the OSS: The Overseas Targets* (New York: Walker and Company, 1976); Joseph Persico, *Piercing the Reich: The Penetration of Nazi Germany by American Secret Agents During World War II* (New York: Viking, 1972); Max Corvo, *The OSS in Italy, 1942–1945* (New York: Praeger, 1990); and Maochun Yu, *OSS in China: Prelude to Cold War* (New Haven, Conn.: Yale University Press, 1996).

23. These figures are found in JCS 965/5, 15 September 1945, File 334.3 (5-1-42), Section 3, ABC Decimal File: 1942–1948, Plans and Operations Division, RG 319, NA.

24. Langer, *In and Out of the Ivory Tower*, p. 181.

25. Hoover, *Memoirs of Capitalism, Communism, and Nazism*, pp. 196–197; emphasis in the original.

26. Smith, *The Shadow Warriors*, pp. 390–391; Troy, *Donovan and the CIA*, pp. 218, 227.

27. A copy of this paper is in Folder 40, Post-War Plans: Antecedents, Troy Papers, RG 263, NA.

28. Copy in ibid.

29. General John Magruder, "Organization for Intelligence," 11 September 1943, ibid.

30. William Langer, "Post-Hostilities Intelligence in Occupied and Liberated Countries in Europe," 13 July 1944, ibid.

31. A copy of this publication is located in File ABC 334.3, OSS Sec 4 (5-1-42), ABC Decimal File: 1942–1948, Plans and Operations Division, RG 319, NA.

32. Dean Acheson, *Present at the Creation: My Years in the State Department* (New York: W. W. Norton, 1969), p. 158.

33. Cline, *Secrets, Spies, and Scholars*, pp. 18–19; and Acheson, *Present at the Creation*, p. 745.

34. Caraley, *The Politics of Military Unification*, pp. 3–122.

35. Admiral Ellis M. Zacharias, *Secret Missions: The Story of an Intelligence Officer* (New York: G. P. Putnam's Sons, 1946), p. 292.

36. Troy, *Donovan and the CIA*, p. 211.

37. Miles to Marshall, 22 May 1941, Folder 310.11, 3-1-41 thru 5-31-41 (4-2-35), Army Intelligence Decimal File, 1941–1948, RG 319, NA.

38. Walter Millis, ed., *The Forrestal Diaries* (New York: Viking Press, 1951). Troy's comment about King's viewpoint is interesting: "If Forrestal and King were referring to Donovan's [November 1944] plan, as they probably were, then they misconceived it. Donovan wanted in one agency centralization of clandestine activities and coordination of otherwise independent agencies or autonomous departments. To him this meant not a single *service* but a single *system*" (Troy, *Donovan and the CIA*, p. 276; emphasis in the original). The plan to which Troy himself refers will be discussed in detail in the following chapter.

39. JIS 89, 23 October 1944, CCS 334 (12-6-42), Section 1, Records of the Combined Chiefs of Staff, Record Group 218, Records of the U.S. Joint Chiefs of Staff, NA.

2. *General Donovan Proposes* . . .

1. Miles to Marshall, 8 April 1941, Folder 31Q11, 3-1-41 thru 5-31-41 (4-2-35), Army Intelligence Decimal File, 1941–1948, RG 319, NA.

2. "Discussion by Brigadier General Donovan . . . ," OPD 210.31 SOP (Section I) (Cases 1–73), Operations Division (OPD) Decimal File, 1942–1945, Record Group 165, Records of the War Department General and Special Staffs, NA.

3. Smith, *Shadow Warriors*, p. 394.

4. Donovan to Smith, 17 September 1943, File "Central Intelligence, 1941–1950," Vol. 1, Papers of William J. Donovan, U.S. Army Military History Institute, Carlisle Barracks, Pennsylvania.

5. Donovan to Marshall, 4 August 1944; BB to Marshall, undated; Marshall to Donovan, 10 August 1944; all in ABC 334.3, OSS Sec 4 (5-1-42), Plans and Operations Division, ABC Decimal File: 1942–1948, RG 319, NA.

6. Donovan to Roosevelt, 7 November 1944; Folder "Office of Strategic Services," President's Secretary's File; Papers of Franklin D. Roosevelt, Franklin D. Roosevelt Library, Hyde Park, New York. Hereafter cited as PSF:OSS, Roosevelt Papers, FDRL.

7. Troy, *Donovan and the CIA*, pp. 220–221; Cline, *Secrets, Spies, and Scholars*, p. 82.

8. Donovan to Roosevelt, with attachment, 18 November 1944, PSF:OSS, Roosevelt Papers, FDRL.

9. Roosevelt to Leahy, 22 November 1944, ibid. Leahy to General A. J. McFarland, 25 November 1944, CCS 334 CIA (12-6-42) Section 1, Records of the Combined Chiefs of Staff; RG 218, NA. JCS 1181, 25 November 1944, ibid. Memorandum from Col C. R. Peck to Joint Intelligence Committee, 27 November 1944, ibid.

10. JIS 96, 9 December 1944, ibid.

11. JIS 96/1, 9 December 1944, ibid.

12. JIS 96/4, 9 December 1944, ibid.

13. JIC 239/3, 28 December 1944, Minutes of JIC Meeting Number 121, 22 December 1944, ibid.

14. Donovan to Roosevelt, 26 December 1944, PSF:OSS, Roosevelt Papers, FDRL.

15. JIC 230/5, 1 January 1945, CCS 334 CIA (12-6-42), Section 2, Records of the Combined Chiefs of Staff, RG 218, NA.

16. JCS 1181/1, 20 February 1945, ibid., Section 2.

17. *Washington Times-Herald*, 9 February 1945. Trohan's memoirs, *Political Animals* (Garden City, N.Y.: Doubleday, 1975), pp. 157–185, give a caustic account of his wartime relations with the Roosevelt administration.

18. *Washington Times-Herald*, 9 February 1945.

19. Ibid., 10 February 1945.

20. Ibid., 11 February 1945.

21. *New York Herald Tribune*, 10 February 1945.

22. *New York Times*, 10 and 13 February 1945. Hereafter cited as NYT.

23. *Washington Star,* 16 February 1945.

24. *Washington Post,* 16 February 1945. Hereafter cited as WP.

25. Donovan to the JCS, 15 February 1945, PSF:OSS, Roosevelt Papers, FDRL.

26. For documentation on the investigation, see CCS 334 CIA (12-6-42), Section 3, Records of the Combined Chiefs of Staff, RG 218, NA.

27. The political officers at the British embassy in Washington who had observed the wartime political scene with keenness and detachment had kept abreast of this issue as well. On February 17, 1945, they reported to London that the leak had "caused a good deal of heartburnings in the Administration which fears that Congress might take fright." The embassy saw the plan as a sensible one, "designed to provide primarily for carrying on OSS's work after the war and for co-ordinating the sundry political intelligence carried on more or less independently" by other government agencies. In the British view, Donovan's proposal would "give the United States a more extensive political intelligence service than it has had hitherto." The report concluded that "the principal reason for drafting the proposals now seems to have been that Donovan, who has no intention of seeing his creation die with the war, is keen to hold on to his best recruits who are threatening to drift away to more permanent jobs. It may indeed be that the *Times-Herald* leakage will queer the pitch but schemes for more adequate protection of American interests against the wily British and unscrupulous Russians would normally find a not unfriendly reception in Congress these days" (H. G. Nicholas, ed., *Washington Despatches, 1941–1945: Weekly Political Reports from the British Embassy* [London: Weidenfeld and Nicholson, 1981], pp. 518–519).

28. Quoted in Dunlop, *Donovan: America's Master Spy,* pp. 464–465.

29. Marshall to the JCS, 22 February 1945, CCS 314 CIA (12-6-42), Section 2, Records of the Combined Chiefs of Staff, RG 218, NA.

30. General A. J. McFarland to Donovan, 28 February 1945, ibid.

31. JCS 1181/2, 2 March 1945, ibid.

32. Donovan to Roosevelt, 23 February 1945, PSF:OSS, Roosevelt Papers, FDRL.

33. Donovan to Roosevelt, 9 March 1945, ibid.

34. *Complete Press Conferences of Franklin D. Roosevelt* (New York: Da Capo Press, 1972), vol. 25, 1944–1945, pts. 82, 104.

35. See, for example, William Colby, with Peter Forbath, *Honorable Men: My Life in the CIA* (New York: Simon and Schuster, 1978), p. 59; and Cline, *Secrets, Spies, and Scholars,* p. 85.

36. Clifford, *Counsel to the President,* p. 165.

37. Dunlop, *Donovan: America's Master Spy,* p. 464.

38. Theoharis and Cox, *The Boss,* p. 189.

39. See the relevant item in "Personality Parade" in the syndicated Sunday magazine *Parade,* 30 April 1978.

40. Dunlop, *Donovan: America's Master Spy,* p. 464.

41. Troy, *Donovan and the CIA,* p. vi.

42. Phillip Meilinger, *Hoyt S. Vandenberg: The Life of a General* (Bloomington: Indiana University Press, 1989), p. 226 n. 26.

43. Roosevelt to Donovan, 5 April 1945, Foreign Intelligence File, Papers of Edward R. Stettinius, Jr., Alderman Library, University of Virginia, Charlottesville, Virginia. CCS 334 CIA (12-6-42), Section 2, Records of the Combined Chiefs of Staff, RG 218, NA; Donovan to the JCS, 6 April 1945, ibid.; Donovan to Roosevelt, 6 April 1945, PSF:OSS, Roosevelt Papers, FDRL; Donovan to Henry Stimson, 6 April 1945, OPD 350.05, Section XI, Cases 314–333, Operations Division Decimal File, 1942–1945, RG 165, NA.

44. This account of the meeting is based on Francis Biddle, In Brief Authority (Garden City, N.Y.: Doubleday, 1962), pp. 359–360; and General Clayton Bissell to General John Hull, 13 April 1945, OPD 350.05, Section XI, Cases 314–333, Operations Division Decimal File, 1942–1945, RG 165, NA.

45. Folder "1945 Apr 8–14 Record Vol. VI, Section 9," State Department Personal File, Papers of Edward R. Stettinius, Jr., Alderman Library, University of Virginia; Dunlop, Donovan: America's Master Spy, p. 465.

With Roosevelt dead, rejection of Donovan's plan by the State, War, Navy, and Justice Departments became largely a formality. In a crisp memo informing him of the April 12 decision, Secretary of War Stimson commented that, although there was a need for a "vigorous and coordinated system of intelligence" after the war, he did not consider Donovan's proposal "sound," but rather as running counter to the "strong system of intelligence for national security" envisioned by the War Department. He believed that the secretaries of state, war, and navy had primary foreign intelligence responsibility and therefore "should either themselves constitute the coordinating authority, or acting jointly they should directly create and supervise the coordinating authority." In his view, Donovan's proposed agency "would subject departmental intelligence operations to the control of officers outside the departments and not responsible to the heads of those departments." This, Stimson thought, was "dangerous and impractical." In addition, Stimson maintained, "the coordinating authority should not itself engage in intelligence operations, since it would then naturally tend toward enlarging its own operating functions at the expense of the operating agencies subject to its coordination." He also found the idea of an independent budget "objectionable," since the coordinating agency should concern itself only with interdepartmental operating relations, and therefore "any budgetary support should be a function of the departments" (Stimson to Donovan, undated, OPD 350.05, Section XI, Cases 314–333, Operations Division Decimal File, 1942–1945, RG 165, NA). By the time Donovan returned to Washington at the end of April, responses from the other executive branch agencies had trickled in as well. Except for the FEA, all were either negative or noncommittal (Troy, Donovan and the CIA, pp. 268–269).

3. . . . And Harry Truman Disposes

1. This assessment of Truman in 1945 is based on Richard F. Haynes, The Awesome Power: Harry S. Truman as Commander-in-Chief (Baton Rouge: Louisiana State University Press, 1973),

pp. 14–27 passim; John Ranelagh, *The Agency: The Rise and Decline of the CIA* (New York: Simon and Schuster, 1986), p. 97; Senate History, pp. 6–7; Smith, *The Shadow Warriors*, p. 392; and Rhodri Jeffreys-Jones, *The CIA and American Democracy* (New Haven, Conn.: Yale University Press, 1989), p. 29. An account of the tumultuous international scene at the time Truman assumed office is provided by J. Robert Moskin, *Mr. Truman's War* (New York: Random House, 1996).

2. WP, 27 April 1945.

3. Nicholas, *Washington Despatches*, p. 566.

4. Harry S. Truman, *Memoirs: Years of Trial and Hope* (Garden City, N.Y.: Doubleday, 1956), pp. 56–57; Sidney Souers to L. L. Montague, 13 August 1970, Papers of Sidney W. Souers: General Correspondence, 1953–1972, Harry S. Truman Library, Independence, Missouri. Hereafter cited as HSTL. According to Souers, because he had presented the JCS plan to Truman, the president mistook it for a navy plan, and so described it in his memoirs.

5. Donovan to Truman, 30 April and 25 August 1945, Rose Conway File: Office of Strategic Services (Donovan-Intelligence Services), Papers of Harry S. Truman, HSTL.

6. President's Secretary's File: Daily Sheets—May 1945, Papers of Harry S. Truman, HSTL.

Despite the fact that no one was present except the two principals, Donovan's primary biographer, Richard Dunlop, has written a colorful account of this meeting. According to Dunlop, Truman began by praising the wartime work of the OSS but then went on to say that "such an organization can have no place in an America at peace." When Donovan interrupted to say that the OSS could play an important postwar role, Dunlop relates that Truman exploded: "I am completely opposed to international spying on the part of the United States. It is un-American. I cannot be certain in my mind that a formidable and clandestine organization such as the OSS designed to spy abroad will not in time spy on the American people themselves. The OSS represents a threat to the liberties of the American people. An all-powerful intelligence apparatus in the hands of an undisciplined president can be a dangerous instrument. I would never use such a tool against my own people, but there is always a risk, and I cannot entertain such a risk." According to Dunlop, an angry Donovan argued the merits of a peacetime OSS, but to no avail, and later commented: "Mr. Truman was very quiet, and when I left, there was no question in my mind that the OSS would be dissolved at the end of the war" (Dunlop, *Donovan: America's Master Spy*, p. 468). Unfortunately, Dunlop provides no citation for this account, and no record of it could be located in the working papers for his book that are held by the Army History Institute.

7. On January 13, 1946, Donovan, now a private citizen, wrote presidential counselor Samuel Rosenman: "The President told me that he was working on a central intelligence agency and that he would like to have my views before any decision is made. . . . During the last five years it has been my duty to give considerable attention to this and, more than most men, perhaps I know the dangers and pitfalls that must be avoided. . . . I am glad to hear that you are setting up your own organization. This is the decision I had to make for myself fifteen years ago. It is the way you will be happiest." Rosenman responded with a

polite brush-off on January 16, saying only that Truman had "been working on a central intelligence agency" but adding disingenuously that "I do not know that he has come to any conclusion about it." This exchange of correspondence is found in Alphabetical File (C–T), Donovan, William J., Papers of Samuel I. Rosenman, HSTL.

8. Clifford, *Counsel to the President*, p. 165.

9. Clifford interview with Thomas Troy, 6 November 1975, Notes in Folder 56, Interviews and Letters . . . , Troy Papers, RG 263, NA.

10. Braden's and Murphy's comments are quoted in Ranelagh, *The Agency*, p. 100; Colby's comment is quoted in Mark Riebling, *Wedge: The Secret War Between the FBI and CIA* (New York: Alfred A. Knopf, 1994), p. 61.

11. A copy of the Park Report is in Folder 44, OSS-Park's Report, March 1945, Troy Papers, RG 263, NA.

12. Troy, *Donovan and the CIA*, pp. 280–282; Theoharis and Cox, *The Boss*, pp. 190–191; Gentry, *J. Edgar Hoover*, pp. 325–326.

13. The wartime propaganda issue and the controversies that it generated are well examined in Clayton B. Laurie, *The Propaganda Warriors: America's Crusade Against Nazi Germany* (Lawrence: University Press of Kansas, 1996).

14. Smith to Truman, 20 April 1945, Series 39.27 (Intelligence), General Records of the Director, Record Group 51, Records of the Bureau of the Budget/Office of Management and Budget, NA; Smith to Roosevelt, 2 March 1945, ibid.

15. A copy of Roosevelt's directive to Smith is in Folder 41, Donovan's Plan, Sept.–Nov. '44, Troy Papers, RG 263, NA.

16. Copies of these memos in ibid.

17. Donovan to Smith, 25 August 1945, "Strategic Services Unit as of 1 October 1945," 004.7 SSU, Office of the Assistant Secretary of War, RG 107, Records of the Secretary of War, NA.

18. Harry S. Truman, *Memoirs: Year of Decisions* (Garden City, N.Y.: Doubleday, 1955), pp. 58–59. Papers of Harold Smith: Diaries—Conferences with the President, entry for 18 April 1945, FDRL.

19. Bureau of the Budget, *The United States at War: Development and Administration of the War Program by the Federal Government* (Washington, D.C.: USGPO, 1947), pp. 499–500.

20. Smith to Truman, 20 April 1945, Series 39.27 (Intelligence), General Records of the Office of the Director, RG 51, NA.

21. Papers of Harold Smith: Diaries—Correspondence with the President, entry for 26 April 1945, FDRL.

22. Truman, *Memoirs: Year of Decisions*, p. 99.

23. Jeffreys-Jones, *The CIA and American Democracy*, p. 30.

24. Papers of Harold Smith: Diaries—Conferences with the President, entry for 4 May 1945, FDRL; Truman, *Memoirs: Year of Decisions*, p. 226.

25. Donald Stone to Smith, 27 August 1945, Series 39.19 (OSS Organization and Functions), General Records of the Office of the Director, RG 51, NA.

26. Smith to Truman, 18 September 1945, Official File, 892-C (Central Intelligence Group), Papers of Harry S. Truman, HSTL.

27. Tom Braden, "The Birth of the CIA," *American Heritage*, February 1977, p. 7.

28. In addition to the previously cited Braden essay, this account of Donovan's secret publicity campaign is based on Ranelagh, *The Agency*, p. 99; Smith, *The Shadow Warriors*, pp. 405–407; Troy, *Donovan and the CIA*, pp. 278, 280, 291; and Colby, *Honorable Men*, pp. 56, 59–60. A compilation of the press articles can be found in Folder 47, End of OSS—Part I, Troy Papers, RG 263, NA.

29. Donovan to Rosenman, 4 September 1945, Department of State, *Foreign Relations of the United States, 1945–1950: Emergence of the Intelligence Establishment* (Washington, D.C.: USGPO, 1996), p. 26. Hereafter cited as FRUS.

30. Donovan to Truman, 13 September 1945, Rose Conway File, Office of Strategic Services: Donovan—Intelligence Services, Papers of Harry S. Truman, HSTL.

31. Papers of Harold Smith: Diaries—Conferences with the President, entry for 13 September 1945, FDRL.

32. Donovan to the JCS, 13 September 1945, 004.7 Office of Strategic Services, Office of the Secretary of War, RG 107, NA.

33. CCS 385 (2-8-42), Section 1, pt. 10, JCS Central Decimal File, 1946–1947, RG 218, NA; JPS 754/1, 21 Sept. 1945, P & O Division, ABC Decimal File, 1942–1948, 334.3 (5-1-42), Sec. 3, ibid.

34. This exchange of correspondence is in Pentagon Office Correspondence, 1938–1951, Papers of George C. Marshall, George C. Marshall Research Foundation, Lexington, Virginia.

35. Papers of Harold Smith: Diaries—Conferences with the President, entry for 20 September 1945, FDRL.

36. Dunlop, *Donovan: America's Master Spy*, pp. 472–473.

37. EO 9621, 3 CFR 431 (1943–1948 Compilation).

38. Office of the Federal Register, National Archives and Records Administration, *Public Papers of the Presidents of the United States: Harry S. Truman . . . 1945* (Washington, D.C.: USGPO, 1961), p. 330. Hereafter cited as HST/PP.

39. Ibid., p. 331.

40. G. E. Ramsey to Leo Martin, "Disposition of OSS," 24 September 1945, Series 39.27 (Intelligence), General Records of the Office of the Director, RG 51, NA.

41. Dunlop, *Donovan: America's Master Spy*, pp. 473–475.

42. A copy of the 30 September 1945 cable is in 334.3 (5-1-42) Sec. 3, Plans and Operations Division, ABC Decimal File, 1942–1948, RG 319, NA.

43. "Global Gumshoeing," *Time*, 1 October 1945, p. 23.

44. Magruder to Bissell, Inglis, and McCormack on 1 October 1945 and responses on 4 October are in Folder 73, Post-OSS Oct 1945, Troy Papers, RG 263, NA.

45. Correspondence relating to this episode is in CCS 200.6 (9-13-44), Combined Chiefs of Staff Decimal File, RG 218, NA.

46. Dunlop, *Donovan: America's Master Spy*, pp. 482–483. Donovan was far too much an activist to submit to a quiet retirement. Despite his return to law practice and involvement in international business, he maintained his interest in intelligence matters and his ties with former OSS officers, coveted a Senate seat, and was involved on the fringes of cold war politics and policy making. With the return of the Republicans to power in 1953, he energetically but futilely lobbied to become director of Central Intelligence and even grasped at rumors that he might be appointed chief justice of the Supreme Court. In late 1956 he was diagnosed as suffering from a progressively debilitating brain disease. After a series of strokes, he declined rapidly and died on February 8, 1959, at the age of seventy-six. For information about Donovan's post-OSS years, see Dunlop, *Donovan: America's Master Spy*, pp. 485–507; Smith, *The Shadow Warriors*, p. 410; and Peter Grose, *Gentleman Spy: The Life of Allen Dulles* (Boston: Houghton Mifflin, 1994), pp. 336, 338.

47. Robert Patterson to Magruder, 27 September 1945, ABC 334.3 OSS Sec 4 (5-1-42), Plans and Operations Division, ABC Decimal File, 1942–1948, RG 319, NA. Also Troy, *Donovan and the CIA*, p. 303; and Colby, *Honorable Men*, pp. 60–62.

48. Magruder to Major General S. Leroy Irwin, 15 January 1946, Folder 78, SSU 1945–1946, Troy Papers, RG 263, NA. When illness forced Magruder to retire in April 1946, he was replaced by General William Quinn, who had worked closely with the OSS during the war as chief of the U.S. Seventh Army's G-2 during the invasion of southern France. Quinn continued Magruder's policies and was able to establish good relations with FBI director Hoover by allowing the FBI to conduct background investigations on SSU employees. In coping with bureaucratic disputes, Quinn was usually able to enlist the unofficial assistance of Donovan and other former OSS officers (Braden, "The Birth of the CIA," pp. 8–9; Dunlop, *Donovan: America's Master Spy*, pp. 483–484).

49. Texts of the directives are in *Department of State Bulletin*, vol. 13, no. 332 (4 November 1945): 739–740. Hereafter cited as DSB.

50. McCormack to Leahy, 31 October 1945, Folder 73, Post-OSS Oct 45, Troy Papers, RG 263, NA.

4. *The State Department and Central Intelligence*

1. Acheson, *Present at the Creation*, p. 16.

2. NYT, 27 November 1945.

3. Memo to Stettinius, 21 August 1944, "Intelligence" folder, Papers of Edward R. Stettinius, Jr., Alderman Library, University of Virginia, Charlottesville, Virginia.

4. Stettinius to Roosevelt, 16 November 1944, ibid.

5. Russell to Taft, 24 May 1944, Folder 75, State Department Intelligence—1944, Troy Papers, RG 263, NA.

6. Russell to Taft, 7 June 1944, ibid.

7. Russell memorandum, 10 October 1944, with attached draft departmental order, "Foreign Intelligence" folder, Papers of Edward R. Stettinius, Jr.; emphasis added.

8. Russell to Stettinius, 18 December 1944, ibid. Numerous memos by Russell on this topic can be found in the previously cited Folder 75 of the Troy Papers.

9. Roosevelt to Stettinius, 17 January 1945, "Memos for the Sec.: Oct 44–Feb 45" folder, Papers of Edward R. Stettinius, Jr.

10. Memos "Need for an Office of Research and Analysis," 21 February 1945, and "The Proposed Office of Intelligence," 25 April 1945, Folder 76, State Department Intelligence — 1945, Troy Papers, RG 263, NA.

11. Rowena Rommel to John Ross, 27 January 1945, and draft memo "Project O-27, Office of Intelligence," 19 May 1945, ibid.

12. NYT, 4 July 1945; David Robertson, *Sly and Able: A Political Biography of James F. Byrnes* (New York: W. W. Norton, 1994), pp. 414, 483. In his various autobiographical writings, Byrnes is largely silent on this issue.

13. Sherman Kent, *Reminiscences of a Varied Life* (n.p.: privately printed, 1991), p. 225; Acheson, *Present at the Creation*, pp. 119–211, passim. In all, Byrnes spent 330 of his 560 days in office away from the State Department.

14. Robertson, *Sly and Able*, passim. DSB, passim, for various announcements of appointments and reorganizations.

15. McCarthy to Acheson, 5 September 1945, FRUS, pp. 187–188.

16. Acheson to Byrnes, 12 September 1945, Decimal File 1945–1949, 111.111/9-1245, RG 59, General Records of the Department of State, NA.

17. DSB, vol. 13, no. 327 (30 September 1945): 499.

18. Ronald Lewin, *Ultra Goes to War* (New York: McGraw-Hill, 1978), pp. 245–248.

19. Kent, *Reminiscences of a Varied Life*, p. 226.

20. Ibid.

21. Acheson to McCormack, 1 October 1945, FRUS, pp. 191–193.

22. Byrnes to McCormack, 23 October 1945, ibid., p. 196.

23. State Department Circular Telegram, 22 October 1945, Decimal File 1945–1949, 103.918/10-2245, RG 59, NA.

24. Kent, *Reminiscences of a Varied Life*, pp. 227–230.

25. Ibid., p. 225.

26. Ibid., p. 227.

27. Ibid., p. 229.

28. Ibid., p. 231.

29. J. Anthony Panuch testimony in U.S. Senate, Committee on the Judiciary, *Interlocking Subversion in Government Departments: Hearings . . .* , 83d Cong., 1st sess., pt. 13 (Washington, D.C.: USGPO, 1953–1954), pp. 904–906. Hereafter cited as *Interlocking Subversion*.

30. *Washington Times-Herald*, 30 September 1945.

31. *Washington Star*, 20 January 1946.

32. Theoharis and Cox, *The Boss*, pp. 199–200.

33. Acheson, *Present at the Creation*, p. 160. In his memoirs and other writings, Braden made clear that he had no better an opinion of Acheson.

34. This account is based on *Interlocking Subversion*, pt. 13, pp. 861–863, and pt. 19, pp. 1373–1375; Spruille Braden, *Diplomats and Demagogues: The Memoirs of Spruille Braden* (New Rochelle, N.Y.: Arlington House, 1971), pp. 346–349; and Acheson, *Present at the Creation*, pp. 159–160. There appears to have been no official record of the meeting.

35. U.S. Senate, Committee on Appropriations, *First Supplemental Appropriation Recission Bill: Hearings . . .* , 79th Cong., 1st sess. (Washington, D.C.: USGPO, 1945), pp. 227–235.

36. NYT, 19 April 1945.

37. Text in DSB, vol. 14, no. 355 (21 April 1946): 687.

38. NYT, 15–16 and 26–27 March 1946.

39. Russell to Byrnes, 3 November 1945, Decimal File 1945–1949, 101.5/11-345, RG 59, NA; emphasis in the original.

40. Basic chronology is found in *Interlocking Subversion*, pt. 13, pp. 861–863, and pt. 19, pp. 373–375. A copy of the 12 December 1945 document outlining the ORI proposals is in Folder 77, State's IRIS-ORI, 1945–1946, Troy Papers, RG 263, NA.

41. Russell to Byrnes and Acheson, 29 December 1945, Folder 77, State's IRIS-ORI, 1945–1946, Troy Papers, RG 263, NA.

42. Braden to Acheson, 31 December 1945, and Dunn to Acheson, 31 December 1945, ibid.

43. McCormack to Acheson, 31 December 1945, ibid.

44. Byrnes to Russell, 5 January 1946, ibid.

45. A copy of this "Russell Plan," 25 February 1946, is in ibid.

46. For example, McCormack's memo to Russell on 12 February 1946 and Russell's response of 23 February, reprinted in *Interlocking Subversion*, pt. 13, pp. 856–860, and pp. 865–870, respectively.

47. Panuch to Russell, 16 April 1946, FRUS, pp. 217–220.

48. Russell to Byrnes, 18 April 1946, ibid., p. 221.

49. Russell to Byrnes, 20 April 1946, ibid., pp. 221–222.

50. DSB, vol. 14, no. 357 (5 May 1946): 778–779; ibid., no. 358 (12 May 1946): 826–828; ibid., no. 361 (2 June 1946): 928–931, 945.

51. Langer, *In and Out of the Ivory Tower*, p. 200.

52. Quoted in *Interlocking Subversion*, pt. 19, p. 1375. In his memoirs, Braden later commented: "At the time I thought we had won a good fight on a good sound basis—proper organization, economical administration, and the elimination of some Communists and socialists. It was quite a time before I realized how really important it had been. . . . The merger was intended to get the Communist agents in; the intelligence scheme to put them in control" (Braden, *Diplomats and Demagogues*, p. 350).

53. Panuch memo, 20 May 1946, Folder 77, State's IRIS-ORI, 1946, Troy Papers, RG 263, NA.

54. Kent, *Reminiscences of a Varied Life*, p. 228.

55. Ibid., pp. 228–229.

56. Extract from the minutes of the eighth meeting of the Advisory Committee on Intelligence, 3 December 1946, FRUS, pp. 224–225.

57. Eddy to Acheson, 30 January 1947, ibid., p. 227.

58. Peurifoy to Acheson and Marshall, with endorsements, 31 January 1947, ibid., p. 229.

59. DSB, vol. 16, no. 399 (23 February 1947): 366.

60. Acheson, *Present at the Creation*, pp. 190, 214.

61. Ibid., p. 214.

62. Ibid.

5. Designing a Postwar System

1. OSS Internal Memorandum, 31 August 1945, ASW 004.7, "WD Intelligence Study—1945," Office of the Assistant Secretary of War, Classified Decimal File, 1940–1947, RG 107, NA. In the best secret intelligence fashion, neither individual was identified by name on the memo.

2. Quoted in Ranelagh, *The Agency*, p. 100.

3. Smith to Rosenman, 10 January 1946, Subject File 1946—Intelligence, Papers of Samuel I. Rosenman, HSTL.

4. Clifford, *Counsel to the President*, pp. 165–166; Senate History, pp. 7–10.

5. Memos by Admiral Leahy to the President and the Secretaries of War and Navy and the Draft, "Directive Regarding the Coordination of Intelligence Activities," 19 September 1945, in Section I, OPD 350.05 TS (Cases 1–45), Top Secret General Correspondence, 1942–1945, Office of the Director of Plans and Operations, RG 165, NA; emphasis added.

6. Ammi Cutter to John McCloy, 11 October 1945, ASW 004.7, "WD Intelligence Study—1945," Office of the Assistant Secretary of War, Classified Decimal File, 1940–1947, RG 107, NA. General Henry Hodes to Robert Lovett, 22 October 1945, ibid. Robert Lovett circular memo to War Department, 23 October 1945, ibid.

7. Memorandum for the Secretary of War, "Preliminary Report of the Committee Appointed to Study War Department Intelligence Activities," RPP/Intelligence Matters—Safe File, Secretary of War Subject File (Safe File), Sept. 27, 1945–July 24, 1947, RG 107, NA.

8. Magruder to Lovett, 26 October 1945, ASW 004.7, "WD Intelligence Study—1945," Office of the Assistant Secretary of War, Classified Decimal File, 1940–1947, RG 107, NA.

9. Extract from Magruder's undated report "Intelligence Matters," FRUS, pp. 74–81.

10. OPD to Lovett, 28 October 1945, Section I, OPD 350.05 TS (Cases 1–45), Top Secret General Correspondence File, 1942–1945, Office of the Director of Plans and Operations, RG 165, NA.

11. Pearsons to Lovett, 31 October 1945, ASW 004.7, "WD Intelligence Study—1945," Office of the Assistant Secretary of War, Classified Decimal File, 1940–1947, RG 107, NA.

12. Text of the report, 3 November 1945, in ibid.

13. For an account of Forrestal's life, career, and tragic end, see Townsend Hoopes and Douglas Brinkley, *Driven Patriot: The Life and Times of James Forrestal* (New York: Alfred A. Knopf, 1992).

14. Correa to Forrestal, 19 September 1945, File 80-1-9, Records of Secretary James Forrestal, 1944–1947, RG 80, Central Records of the Department of the Navy, NA.

15. Robinson to Forrestal, 4 October 1945, ibid.

16. King to Forrestal, 9 October 1945, SecNav/CNO Top Secret Correspondence File, 1945, Folder A-8, RG 80, NA.

17. King to Forrestal, 12 October 1945, Folder 73, Post-OSS Oct. 1945, Troy Papers, RG 263, NA.

18. "Communications intelligence" (COMINT), a discipline closely related to code-breaking, is defined as "technical and intelligence information derived from foreign communications by other than the intended recipients" (Department of Defense, *Dictionary of Military and Associated Terms*, pp. 77). It is one of the most important and sensitive forms of intelligence in which governments engage.

19. Minutes of Top Policy Group Meetings, 36th Meeting, 15 October 1945, Records of Secretary James Forrestal, 1940–1947, RG 80, NA.

20. Forrestal to Patterson, 13 October 1945, FRUS, pp. 59–60.

21. Eisenhower to Nimitz, 29 December 1945, OPD 350.05 TS, Section II (Cases 46 through 64), Operations Division Decimal File 1945, RG 165, NA.

22. "Proposals for a Central Intelligence Service for the Federal Government together with the relationship of the Library of Congress thereto," by Ernest Griffith, 7 July 1941, Folder 3, OMB 1941, Troy Papers, RG 263, NA.

23. Undated memo from Schwarzwalder to Miles, Folder 39, BoB and Post-War Intell. Organization, ibid.

24. "Intelligence and Security Activities of the Government," 20 September 1945, and covering letter from Smith to Truman, 31 October 1945, Series 39.27 (Intelligence), General Records of the Director, RG 51, NA.

25. Hoelscher to Smith, 28 November 1945, Smith to Truman, 28 November 1945, ibid.

26. Copy of the study in Folder 63, FBI Docs.: Troy Papers, RG 263, NA.

27. Biddle to Truman, 20 April 1945, Rose Conway File, Office of Strategic Services: Donovan-Intelligence Services, Papers of Harry S. Truman, HSTL.

28. Hoover to Clark, 29 August 1945, Folder 63, FBI Docs., Troy Papers, RG 263, NA.

29. Clark to Smith and Paul Appleby, 21 September 1945, Series 39.27 (Intelligence), General Records of the Director, RG 51, NA.

30. Hoover to Clark, 27 September 1945, Folder 63, FBI Docs., Troy Papers, RG 263, NA.

31. Edwin Tamm to Hoover, 17 September 1945; Morton Chiles to Hoover, 22 September and 2 October 1945; ibid.

32. Stone to Appleby, 26 October 1945; Series 39.27 (Intelligence), General Records of the Director, RG 51, NA.

33. Appleby to Clark, 31 October 1945, ibid.

34. Extract of Committee of Three Meeting Minutes, 16 October 1945, FRUS, pp. 63–65.

35. Memorandum of conversation by Inglis, 2 November 1945, ibid., pp. 97–98.

36. "Development of a National Intelligence Program," 15 November 1945, ibid., pp. 111–116.

37. Memorandum of conversation by Souers, 19 November 1945, ibid., pp. 116–117.

38. Memorandum from Byrnes to Patterson and Forrestal, 3 December 1945, "National Intelligence Authority," Subject File—National Intelligence Authority, Papers of Clark Clifford, HSTL.

39. Memorandum by McCormack to the Secretaries of War and Navy, 15 December 1945, RPP/Intelligence Matters—Safe File, Secretary of War Subject File (Safe File), September 27, 1945–July 24, 1947, RG 107, NA.

40. Patterson to Eisenhower, 20 December 1945, ibid.

41. Undated memorandum from Nimitz to Forrestal, FRUS, pp. 145–146.

42. Correa to Forrestal, 27 December 1945, File 80-1-9, Records of Secretary James Forrestal, 1944–1947, RG 80, NA.

43. Souers to Clifford, 27 December 1945, Subject File: National Military Establishment—Central Intelligence Agency, Papers of Clark Clifford, HSTL.

44. Memorandum of meeting, 6 January 1946, 101.5/1-646, Central Decimal File, 1945–1949, RG 59, NA.

45. McCormack to Byrnes, 7 January 1946, 101.5/1-746, Central Decimal File, 1945–1949, ibid.

46. McCormack to Smith, 10 January 1946, Subject File, 1946—Intelligence, Papers of Samuel I. Rosenman, HSTL. McCormack had written this paper earlier and postdated it before leaving the city.

47. For example, see the memo by Arnold Miles to L. H. Hoelscher, 3 January 1946, Series 39.19 (OSS Organization and Functions), General Records of the Director, RG 51, NA, and Memorandum for the Record by "HAC," 27 October 1945, FRUS, pp. 154–155.

48. Unsigned memo to Truman, 7 November 1945, Official File: 892, Papers of Harry S. Truman, HSTL.

49. Committee of Three Meeting Minutes, 14 November 1945, ASW 334.8, Office of the Assistant Secretary of War, Classified Decimal File, 1940–1947, RG 107, NA.

50. Papers of Harold Smith: Diaries—Conferences with the President, entry for 28 November 1945, FDRL.

51. Memoranda by Forrestal, Royall, and Byrnes to Truman, 7 January 1946, Official File: 892, Papers of Harry S. Truman, HSTL.

52. Papers of Harold Smith: Diaries—Conferences with the President, entry for 9 January 1946, FDRL.

53. Truman, Memoirs: Years of Trial and Hope, p. 57.

54. Copies of various drafts can be found in Subject File: National Intelligence Authority, Papers of Clark Clifford, HSTL.

55. Clark to Truman, 19 January 1946, Official File: 892, Papers of Harry S. Truman, HSTL.

56. Text in HST/PP:1946, p. 88.

57. Truman to Leahy, 23 January 1946, Official File: 892, Papers of Harry S. Truman, HSTL.

58. Bruce to Forrestal, 18 January 1946, File 80-1-9, Records of Secretary James Forrestal, 1944–1947, RG 80, NA.

59. Truman to Souers, 23 January 1946, Official File: 892, Papers of Harry S. Truman, HSTL.

60. Truman to Byrnes, Patterson, and Forrestal, 23 January 1946, ibid.

61. Robert H. Ferrell, ed., *Truman in the White House: The Diary of Eben A. Ayers* (Columbia: University of Missouri Press, 1991), pp. 123–124.

62. Press conference of 24 January 1946, HST/PP:1946, pp. 93–94.

63. "Intelligence," *Time,* 4 February 1946, p. 24.

64. NYT, 23 January 1946.

65. Ibid., 6 February 1946.

6. The Central Intelligence Debate

1. General Henry Arnold, *Third Report of the Commanding General of the Army Air Forces to the Secretary of War* (n.p., 1945), pp. 59–60.

2. "The 36-Hour War," *Life,* 19 November 1945, pp. 27–35.

3. U.S. House of Representatives, Select Committee on Post-war Military Policy, *Proposal to Establish a Single Department of Armed Forces: Hearings . . .* , 78th Cong., 2d sess. (Washington, D.C.: USGPO, 1944), pp. 303–304.

4. James F. Byrnes, "Why We Must Give the President a Clear Road," *American Magazine,* August 1945, p. 102.

5. U.S. Senate, Committee on Military Affairs, *Department of the Armed Forces, Department of Military Security: Hearings . . .* , 79th Cong., 1st sess. (Washington, D.C.: USGPO, 1945), p. 61. Hereafter cited as 1945 Hearings.

6. Ibid., p. 28.

7. Arnold, *Third Report,* pp. 65, 67.

8. One indication of the Navy Department's concrete views appeared in a press release of November 28, 1945, that summarized its position in the unfolding military "unification" controversy. The release called for a "central intelligence agency" subordinate to a "National Security Council" and serving "all departments of the Government." A similar press release for the War Department on November 5 was silent on the intelligence issue. Texts of both releases are in the 1945 Hearings, pp. 469–470 and 473–474, respectively.

9. U.S. Senate, Committee on Naval Affairs, *Unification of the War and Navy Departments and Postwar Organization for National Security,* 79th Cong., 1st sess. (Washington, D.C.: USGPO, 1945), pp. iii–vi; Hoopes and Brinkley, *Driven Patriot,* p. 321.

10. U.S. Senate, Committee on Naval Affairs, *Unification of the War and Navy Departments*, pp. 159–163.

11. Ibid., pp. 12–13, 173.

12. 1945 Hearings, p. 99. Forrestal's position was endorsed by Admiral Leahy in a brief appearance on December 4; ibid., p. 519.

13. Ibid., pp. 599–600. In his testimony, Forrestal was of the opinion that it had been a "terrible tragedy" to have made known the facts behind the breaking of the Japanese codes.

14. Now called the Foreign Broadcast Information Service, this organization is the part of the CIA responsible for collecting, translating, analyzing, and disseminating material originated by foreign public media. How it became part of the CIA is described in chapter 7.

15. Text of the broadcast is in DSB, vol. 13, no. 339 (23 December 1945), pp. 987–993, 1006.

16. NYT, 5 September and 21 September 1945.

17. Text in 1945 Hearings, pp. 62–63.

18. NYT, 17 September 1946.

19. William J. Donovan, "Intelligence: Key to Defense," *Life*, 30 September 1946, pp. 108–120.

20. David K. E. Bruce, "The National Intelligence Authority," *Virginia Quarterly Review* 22 (Summer 1946): 355–369.

21. Sherman Kent, "Prospects for the National Intelligence Service," *Yale Review* 36 (Autumn 1946): 116–130.

22. Jeffreys-Jones, *The CIA and American Democracy*, p. 25.

23. George S. Pettee, *The Future of American Secret Intelligence* (Washington, D.C.: Infantry Journal Press, 1946), passim.

24. Zacharias, *Secret Missions*, passim. There is an interesting footnote to the publication of this book. Secretary Forrestal, ever the rigid national security manager, was so outraged by the revelations of security classified information that he thought the book contained that he considered pressing criminal charges against Zacharias. There is a file on this episode in RG 80, NA.

25. John Chamberlain, "OSS," *Life*, 19 November 1945, pp. 119–130; emphasis in the original.

26. WP, 29 April 1946.

27. NYT, 26 May 1946. Phillips's correspondence with Donovan can be found in the latter's papers at the Army Military History Institute, Carlisle Barracks, Pennsylvania.

28. Hanson W. Baldwin, *The Price of Power* (New York: Harper and Brothers, 1947), pp. ix–xii.

29. Ibid., pp. 204–205.

30. Ibid., pp. 211, 215–216.

31. Gallup poll reported in WP, 22 March 1946.

32. U.S. Congress, Joint Committee on the Investigation of the Pearl Harbor Attack, *Investigation of the Pearl Harbor Attack: Report*, 79th Cong., 2d sess. (Washington, D.C.: USGPO, 1946), pp. 257–258; emphasis in the original.

33. U.S. House of Representatives, Committee on Military Affairs, *A Report on the System Currently Employed in the Collection, Evaluation, and Dissemination of Intelligence Affecting the War Potential of the United States*, 79th Cong., 2d sess. (Washington, D.C.: USGPO, 1946), pp. 1–10, passim.

34. Ibid.

35. A copy of the report is located in File 80-1-9, Records of Secretary James Forrestal, 1944–1947, RG 80, NA. The navy regarded the various proposals in the report with disapproval for a number of reasons. See John V. Connerton to Capt. William Smedberg, 18 December 1946, ibid.; Admiral Thomas Inglis to Smedberg, 18 December 1946, ibid.; and Connerton to Forrestal, 14 December 1947, ibid. The memo from Inglis to Smedberg gives details on how the report came to be released. White's articles appear in the NYT on 18 and 19 December 1946, and Alsop's column is in the *New York Herald Tribune* on 12 January 1947. See also Fletcher Pratt, "How Not to Run a Spy System," *Harper's Magazine*, September 1947, pp. 241–246.

36. The postwar debate relating to military unification and national security "reform" is detailed in Caraley, *The Politics of Military Unification*, pp. 125–289.

37. Truman's message is in HST:PP/1945 (Washington, D.C.: USGPO, 1961), pp. 543–547. Summaries of the Senate drafting efforts are in Truman, *Memoirs: Years of Trial and Hope*, p. 50; and U.S. Senate, Committee on Military Affairs, *Department of Common Defense*, Senate Report 1328, 79th Cong., 2d sess. (Washington, D.C.: USGPO, 1946), pp. 1, 7.

38. Text of the draft legislation creating the CIA in 1946 is in U.S. Senate, Committee on Naval Affairs, *Unification of the Armed Forces: Hearings . . .* , 79th Cong., 2d sess. (Washington, D.C.: USGPO, 1946), pp. 7–8.

39. Transcripts of the hearings are in ibid.

7. *Establishing a Structure*

1. This story is related in Braden, "The Birth of the CIA," p. 10.

2. Souers to Allen Dulles, 6 February 1964, Papers of Sidney W. Souers: General Correspondence, HSTL.

3. For the official account of Souers's tenure as DCI, see Arthur Darling, *The Central Intelligence Agency: An Instrument of Government to 1950* (University Park: Pennsylvania State University Press, 1990), pp. 75–105.

4. Memorandum from Souers to the NIA, 2 February 1946, FRUS, pp. 320–321.

5. Minutes of the First NIA Meeting, 5 February 1946, Decimal File 1945–1949, 811.022/1-2446, RG 59, NA.

6. Text of the directive in Folder 132: NIA Papers, Chairman's File: Admiral Leahy, 1942–1948, RG 218, NA.

7. NIA Directive No. 2, "Organization and Functions of the Central Intelligence Group (Tentative)," 8 February 1946, FRUS, pp. 331–333.

8. This overview of Souers's actions as DCI is based on his memo "Progress Report on the Central Intelligence Group," 7 June 1946, reproduced in Michael Warner, ed., *The CIA Under Harry Truman* (Washington, D.C.: CIA History Staff, 1994), pp. 41–51. CIG Administrative Order No. 3, "Activation of the Central Reports Staff," 19 April 1946, FRUS, pp. 343–345.

9. "Progress Report . . . ," passim, in Warner, *The CIA Under Harry Truman*, pp. 41–51.

10. This assessment of General Vandenberg is based on Meilinger, *Hoyt S. Vandenberg*, passim.

11. Eisenhower to Truman, 27 April 1946, Memoranda, 1945–1946, President's Secretary's File—Intelligence File, Papers of Harry S. Truman, HSTL.

12. Souers to Leahy, 7 May 1946, ibid.

13. Leahy to Truman, 9 May 1946, Folder 131: National Intelligence Authority, Chairman's File: Admiral Leahy, 1942–1948, RG 218, NA.

14. Truman to Patterson, 16 May 1946, Official File, 892-C, Central Intelligence Group, Papers of Harry S. Truman, HSTL.

15. Truman to Vandenberg, Byrnes, Patterson, and Forrestal, 7 June 1946; ibid.

16. Vandenberg's tenure is described in Meilinger, *Hoyt S. Vandenberg*, pp. 66–78. His account is relatively thin, however, since the relevant documentation was removed from Vandenberg's papers prior to their retirement. The official account of Vandenberg's service as DCI is Darling, *The Central Intelligence Agency*, pp. 106–165. Vandenberg sets forth his goals and accomplishments as DCI in "Objectives and Operations of the CIG: Lecture at the Air War College, Maxwell Field, Alabama, 11 December 1946," obtained by the author under the Freedom of Information Act.

17. Memorandum from Vandenberg to the IAC; "Functions of the Director of Central Intelligence," 20 June 1946, FRUS, pp. 373–379.

18. NIA Directive No. 5, "Functions of the Director of Central Intelligence," 8 July 1946, Folder 132: NIA Papers, Chairman's File: Admiral Leahy, 1942–1948, RG 218, NA.

19. Irwin to McCloy, 28 January 1946, FRUS, pp. 250–251.

20. Memorandum by Magruder, 14 February 1946, ibid., pp. 253–254.

21. CIG Directive No. 1, 19 February 1946, Folder 130: CIG Papers, Chairman's File: Admiral Leahy, 1942–1948, RG 218, NA.

22. Text of the Fortier Committee report, 14 March 1946, FRUS, pp. 256–271.

23. Minutes of the Second Meeting of the IAB, 26 March 1946, ibid., pp. 334–336.

24. Souers to Leahy, 28 March 1946, and NIA Directive No. 4, 2 April 1946, Folder 132: NIA Papers, Chairman's File: Admiral Leahy, 1942–1948, RG 218, NA.

25. Peterson to Quinn, 3 April 1946, and Souers to Quinn, 4 April 1946, are enclosures

to CIG Directive No. 6, "Liquidation of the SSU," 8 April 1946, Folder 130: CIG Papers, Chairman's File: Admiral Leahy, 1942–1948, RG 218, NA.

26. Memorandum by the Director of Central Intelligence's Executive, 11 July 1946, FRUS, pp. 282–283.

27. Vandenberg to Leahy, 12 September 1946, Folder 131: National Intelligence Authority, Chairman's File: Admiral Leahy, 1942–1948, RG 218, NA.

28. General Order No. 16, "Termination of SSU Operations," 19 October 1946, FRUS, pp. 304–305.

29. Vandenberg to Galloway, 25 October 1946, reproduced in Warner, The CIA Under Harry Truman, pp. 87–89.

30. Vandenberg to Truman, 25 February 1947, Memoranda: 1945–1948, President's Secretary's File—Intelligence File, Papers of Harry S. Truman, HSTL.

31. C. H. Carson to Milton Ladd, 21 June 1946, FRUS, pp. 379–383.

32. Addendum by Tolson and Tamm, as well as Hoover's comment, ibid., p. 384.

33. Minutes of the Sixth Meeting of the IAB, 28 June 1946, ibid., pp. 387–390.

34. Vandenberg to Hoover, 3 July 1946, ibid., pp. 280–281.

35. Vandenberg to Hoover, 19 July 1946, ibid., pp. 283–284.

36. Acheson to the NIA, 5 August 1946, ibid., pp. 286–287.

37. Minutes of the Fifth Meeting of the NIA; 7 August 1946, Folder 132: NIA Papers, Chairman's File: Admiral Leahy, 1942–1948, RG 218, NA.

38. NIA to Clark, 8 August 1946, FRUS, pp. 290–291.

39. Hoover to Clark, 8 August 1946, Folder 63: FBI Docs., Troy Papers, RG 263, NA. Tamm to Hoover, 10 August 1946, ibid.; Tamm to Hoover, 12 August 1946, ibid.; Hoover to Clark, 12 August 1946, ibid.; Memorandum for the Record by James S. Lay Jr., 19 August 1946, FRUS, p. 301; Hoover to Vandenberg, 19 August 1946, ibid., pp. 301–302.

40. Leahy to Vandenberg, 12 August 1946, Folder 131: National Intelligence Authority, Chairman's File: Admiral Leahy, 1942–1948, RG 218, NA.

41. Vandenberg to Hoover, 31 December 1946, Folder 63: FBI Docs., Troy Papers, RG 263, NA.

42. Quoted in Reibling, Wedge, p. 74.

43. Vandenberg, "Objectives and Operations of the CIG," pp. 19–20.

44. Vandenberg to the NIA, 13 August 1946, Decimal File 1945–1949, 101.5/8-1546, RG 59, NA.

45. Minutes of the Sixth Meeting of the NIA, 21 August 1946, Folder 132: NIA Papers, Chairman's File: Admiral Leahy, 1942–1948, RG 218, NA.

46. Telegram from Leahy to Truman, 21 August 1946, Folder 131: National Intelligence Authority, ibid. Leahy outlined Truman's view in the Minutes of the Seventh Meeting of the NIA, 25 September 1946, Folder 132: NIA Papers, ibid.

47. Groves to the Atomic Energy Commission, 21 November 1946, FRUS, pp. 458–460.

48. NIA Directive No. 9, "Coordination of Intelligence Activities Related to Foreign

Atomic Energy Developments and Potentialities," 18 April 1947, Folder 132: NIA Papers, Chairman's File: Admiral Leahy, 1942–1948, RG 218, NA.

49. FRUS, p. 511 n. 1.

50. CIG Directive No. 2, 5 March 1946, "Survey of the Function of Monitoring Press and Propaganda Broadcasts of Foreign Powers," Folder 130: CIG Papers, Chairman's File: Admiral Leahy, 1942–1948, RG 218, NA.

51. Minutes of the Fourth Meeting of the Intelligence Advisory Board, 9 May 1946, FRUS, pp. 350–354.

52. Minutes of the Fifth Meeting of the Intelligence Advisory Board, 10 June 1946, ibid., pp. 369–372.

53. FBIS also is unique among CIA components in that it is entirely overt and its publications are unclassified and available to the general public.

54. Vandenberg, "Objectives and Operations of the CIG," pp. 13–15.

55. Harrison Salisbury, *Without Fear or Favor: The New York Times and Its Times* (New York: Times Books, 1980), pp. 576–579. Vandenberg also made reference to this special relationship in his 1946 speech, but that portion was expurgated from the copy made available to the author under FOIA. Phillip Meilinger's references to this document in his biography of Vandenberg (*Hoyt S. Vandenberg*, p. 74, p. 228 n. 57) suggest that, as an air force officer, he obtained special access to an unredacted copy, although the Air Force Historical Research Agency (the document's repository) claims to have no record of his presence at that facility (personal communication, Acting Director Warren Trest to author, 6 April 1992). In any event, the *Times* became disenchanted with the relationship over the years as the CIA exploited and manipulated it for its own operational purposes. Finally, after years of difficulty, it was formally terminated in May 1976 by DCI George Bush, who promised that American journalists would not be used for intelligence purposes. Wrote James Reston: "Whether this promise was kept by other intelligence agencies . . . or by ensuing administrations, I have no way of knowing, but I have my suspicions." See James Reston, *Deadline: A Memoir* (New York: Random House, 1991), pp. 209, 327.

56. Hoover to Leahy, with attached letter to Vandenberg, 23 August 1946, Folder 132: NIA Papers, Chairman's File: Admiral Leahy, 1942–1948, RG 218, NA.

57. Minutes of the Seventh Meeting of the Intelligence Advisory Board, 26 August 1946, FRUS, pp. 405–409.

58. Leahy to Hoover, 4 September 1946, Folder 63: FBI Docs., Troy Papers, RG 263, NA.

59. Hoover to Leahy, 6 September 1946, ibid.

60. Minutes of the Eighth Meeting of the Intelligence Advisory Board, 1 October 1946, FRUS, pp. 416–426, passim. Almost all of the information pertaining to this subject was deleted from the text of the minutes prior to publication.

61. A heavily expurgated copy of this directive is in Folder 130: CIG Papers, Chairman's File: Admiral Leahy, 1942–1948, RG 218, NA.

62. CIG Directive No. 14, "Reorganization of the Central Intelligence Group," 19 July

1946, FRUS, p. 393; Vandenberg, "Objectives and Operations of the CIG," pp. 9–13. A directive of 28 March 1947 established a Nuclear Energy Group within the Office of Reports and Estimates (memorandum by Executive Director Col. Edwin Wright, FRUS, pp. 503–505).

63. Leahy to Chief, Bureau of Naval Personnel, 17 February 1947, Folder 131: National Intelligence Authority, Chairman's File: Admiral Leahy, 1942–1948, RG 218, NA; Truman to Vandenberg and Hillenkoetter, 30 April 1947, Folder 128: Correspondence Signed by the President, ibid.; NYT, 26 February 1947; W. J. Holmes, *Double-Edged Secrets: U.S. Naval Intelligence Operations in the Pacific During World War II* (Annapolis, Md.: Naval Institute Press, 1979), p. 113. A favorable profile of Hillenkoetter appears in the WP on 4 May 1947.

64. NYT, 2 May 1947.

65. Senate History, p. 15.

8. Legislating a New Order

1. Souers to Allen Dulles, 25 February 1964, Souers to L. L. Montague, 13 August 1970, Papers of Sidney W. Souers: General Correspondence, HSTL.

2. Colby, *Honorable Men*, pp. 69–70.

3. Cline, *Secrets, Spies, and Scholars*, pp. 91–92.

4. Vandenberg, "Objectives and Operations of the CIG," p. 17; Ranelagh, *The Agency*, p. 106.

5. Houston to Vandenberg, 13 June 1946, FRUS, pp. 523–524.

6. Meilinger, *Hoyt S. Vandenberg*, p. 75; Ranelagh, *The Agency*, p. 106; Cline, *Secrets, Spies, and Scholars*, p. 93. Pforzheimer to Vandenberg, 23 January 1947, FRUS, pp. 550–553; Pforzheimer undated memo of record, ibid., pp. 553–557; Edwin Wright to Clifford, 28 January 1947, ibid., pp. 559–561; Pforzheimer to Wright, 5 March 1947, ibid., pp. 561–564.

7. Minutes of the Fourth Meeting of the NIA, 17 July 1946, Folder 132: NIA Papers, Chairman's File: Admiral Leahy, 1942–1948, RG 218, NA.

8. Minutes of the Ninth Meeting of the NIA, 12 February 1947, ibid.

9. Clark Clifford interview with Thomas Troy, 6 November 1975, Folder 56, Interviews and Letters . . . , Troy Papers, RG 263, NA.

10. Truman to the Secretaries of State, War, and Navy and the DCI, 3 May 1946, Official File: 50-B, Aides to the President (1945–1946), Papers of Harry S. Truman, HSTL; Clifford, *Counsel to the President*, pp. 64–68, 75–77.

11. Quoted in Meilinger, *Hoyt S. Vandenberg*, p. 75, based on an interview with Walter Pforzheimer.

12. Testimony of Admiral Forest Sherman, 2 May 1947, U.S. House of Representatives, Committee on Expenditures in the Executive Departments, *National Security Act of 1947: Hearings . . .* , 80th Cong., 1st sess. (Washington, D.C.: USGPO, 1947), p. 166. Hereafter cited as 1947 House Hearings.

13. Troy, *Donovan and the CIA*, p. 373.

14. Copy of the draft bill in Subject File: National Military Establishment—Central Intelligence Agency, Papers of Clark Clifford, HSTL.

15. Clifford to Vandenberg, 12 July 1946, ibid.

16. Memorandum of Conversation by George Elsey, 17 July 1946, ibid.

17. Pforzheimer to Vandenberg, 26 November 1946, ibid.; Col. Edwin K. Wright to Clifford, 2 December 1946, ibid.

18. Draft text in ibid.

19. Clifford, *Counsel to the President*, p. 169.

20. An account of this meeting is found in ibid., pp. 168–169, and memorandum of conversation by George Elsey, 9 January 1947, Subject File: Central Intelligence, Papers of George M. Elsey, HSTL. Although Elsey's contemporary account lacks the color of Clifford's retrospection, it clearly reflects the testiness of the meeting.

21. Note for files by George Elsey, 9 January 1947; ibid.

22. Eddy to Acheson, 6 February 1947, Decimal File 1945–1949, 811.20/2-647, RG 59, NA.

23. Marshall to Truman, 7 February 1947, Subject File: Unification—Congressional Hearings (1946–1947), Papers of Clark Clifford, HSTL.

24. Eddy to Marshall, 15 February 1947, Decimal File 1945–1949, 101.61/2-1547, RG 59, NA.

25. HST/PP, p. 153, for text.

26. Caraley, *The Politics of Military Unification*, pp. 156–157.

27. Text of the section establishing the CIA is in U.S. Senate, Committee on Armed Services, *National Defense Establishment: Hearings . . .* , 80th Cong., 1st sess., pt. 1 (Washington, D.C.: USGPO, 1947), p. 18. Hereafter cited as 1947 Senate Hearings. The House version was identical.

28. A useful contemporary analysis on the section by Hanson Baldwin appears in NYT, 4 April 1947.

29. Steven L. Rearden; *The Formative Years: 1947–1950*, vol. 1 of the History of the Office of the Secretary of Defense (Washington, D.C.: Office of the Secretary of Defense, 1984), p. 142; Jeffreys-Jones, *The CIA and American Democracy*, p. 41.

30. Senator Thomas's statement appears in the *Congressional Record* 93, no. 49 (14 March 1947), p. 2139.

31. Meilinger, *Hoyt S. Vandenberg*, pp. 76–77.

32. The official text of Vandenberg's statement is in 1947 Senate Hearings, pp. 491–501.

33. Vandenberg to Leahy, Marshall, Patterson, and Forrestal, 29 April 1947, Folder 131: National Intelligence Authority, Chairman's File: Admiral Leahy, 1942–1948, RG 218, NA. The missing text can be found in a copy in Folder 91, Senate, Troy Papers, RG 263, NA.

34. For example, Ferdinand Eberstadt to Donovan, 6 March 1946, forwarding a draft of initial legislative efforts, Papers of William J. Donovan, "Central Intelligence, 1941–1950, Volume I," U.S. Army Military History Institute, Carlisle Barracks.

35. Donovan to Gurney, with enclosures, 7 May 1947, ibid.; emphasis in the original.

36. Donovan to Gurney, 19 May 1947, ibid.

37. Memorandum of conversation by Walter Pforzheimer, 26 May 1947, FRUS, pp. 571–572.

38. Text of Dulles letter in 1947 Senate Hearings, pp. 525–528.

39. Text of Cheston memorandum in ibid., pp. 667–669.

40. Text of Libby statement in ibid., pp. 649–651.

41. U.S. Senate, Committee on Armed Services, *National Security Act of 1947*, 80th Cong., 1st sess., Senate Report 239 to Accompany S. 758 (Washington, D.C.: USGPO, 1947), p. 10; Caraley, *The Politics of Military Unification*, p. 170.

42. Caraley, *The Politics of Military Unification*, pp. 189, 209.

43. Forrestal's testimony, 25 April 1947, 1947 House Hearings, pp. 113–117.

44. Ibid., pp. 125–129.

45. Ibid., p. 438.

46. Memorandum for the record by Walter Pforzheimer, 12 June 1947, Folder 90, House, Troy Papers, RG 263, NA.

47. Memorandum for the record by Walter Pforzheimer, 19 June 1947, FRUS, p. 576.

48. Patterson's testimony on 2, 24, and 29 April 1947 in 1947 House Hearings, pp. 26, 149–150; Eisenhower's testimony, 8 May 1947 in ibid., p. 301; Bush's testimony, 24 June 1947 in ibid., pp. 555, 559. As head of the wartime OSRD, Bush had played an important role in U.S. wartime intelligence activities through the development of arcane weaponry and espionage equipment for the OSS. His relations with that organization usually had been troubled, however. He found the OSS "a highly undisciplined outfit" and "a strange and somewhat poorly organized agency." He was always annoyed when "OSS wild men were running all over my shop and butting into things that didn't concern them, interfering with my contractors and generally making quite a nuisance of themselves." The regular practice of OSS officers to bypass him when seeking OSRD technical assistance ultimately provoked a confrontation with Donovan. Although the OSS chief promised that all requests for such OSRD support would come only through his office, the two men, both self-promoters with massive egos, never established a harmonious working relationship. By 1947, Bush, thanks to his ability to slip into the limelight, was something of a media celebrity. He endorsed the national security management system envisioned by the 1947 legislation in the belief that policy making in this area was the province of "experts" like himself. Highly ambitious, he also coveted the newly created post of secretary of defense (G. Pascal Zachary, *Endless Frontier: Vannevar Bush, Engineer of the American Century* [New York: Free Press, 1997], pp. 153–157, 322).

49. Zacharias's testimony in 1947 House Hearings, p. 489.

50. Edson's testimony in ibid., pp. 454, 471–472.

51. U.S. House of Representatives, Committee on Expenditures in the Executive Departments, *National Security Act of 1947*, 80th Cong., 1st sess., House Report 961 to Accompany HR 4214 (Washington, D.C.: USGPO, 1947), pp. 1–4; U.S. House of Representatives, Com-

mittee of Conference, *National Security Act of 1947*, 80th Cong., 1st sess., Conference Report 1051 to Accompany S. 758 (Washington, D.C.: USGPO, 1947), pp. 1, 3–5, 18–19; Caraley, *The Politics of Military Unification*, pp. 178–179, 181.

52. 61 Stat 497.

53. These events are recounted in NYT, 27 July 1947. The text of Executive Order 9877 is in HST/PP: 1947, pp. 359–361.

54. NYT, 30 August and 27 September 1947.

55. Quoted in Braden, "The Birth of the CIA," p. 11.

56. NYT, 3 August 1947.

9. The Emergence of Central Intelligence

1. *What's News at CIA*, CIA 50 Edition, no. 2, March 1997, p. 8. The CIA shares this birthday with the National Security Council and the U.S. Air Force.

2. Truman, *Memoirs: Years of Trial and Hope*, p. 58.

3. This report is reproduced in Warner, *The CIA Under Harry Truman*, pp. 139–148.

4. Hillenkoetter to the Secretaries of State, War, and Navy, 11 September 1947, Folder 129: Central Intelligence Group, Chairman's File: Admiral Leahy, 1942–1948, RG 218, NA. Leahy routinely noted an endorsement of Hillenkoetter's proposal on September 20.

5. Hillenkoetter to the NSC, 19 September 1947, Records of the National Security Council: CIA File, Papers of Harry S. Truman, HSTL.

6. Minutes of the First Meeting of the NSC, 26 September 1947, FRUS, pp. 588–590.

7. The FBI was added in 1949.

8. National Security Intelligence Directive No. 1: "Duties and Responsibilities," 12 December 1947, is reproduced in Warner, *The CIA Under Harry Truman*, pp. 169–171.

9. For the texts or extracts of these NSC directives, see FRUS, pp. 1105–1117.

10. The records needed to do such a topic justice are not yet in the public domain. An adequate—if discursive, colorless, and outdated—account of the CIA during the years 1947–1950 is Darling, *The Central Intelligence Agency*, pp. 193–421.

11. The literature concerning the onset of the cold war is vast, growing, and controversial. Since this topic is not the subject of the present study, extended discussion and lengthy bibliographic citations are unnecessary. For those interested in exploring the issue, probably the best place to start is John L. Gaddis, *Now We Know: Rethinking Cold War History* (New York: Oxford University Press, 1997).

12. Jeffreys-Jones, *The CIA and American Democracy*, p. 42.

13. Memo for the files by John H. Ohley, 24 October 1947; Department of Defense File—Subject File, 1947–1949: Central Intelligence Agency, Papers of John H. Ohly, HSTL. Unfortunately, Ohly does not elaborate on this statement.

14. Eddy to Acheson, 28 February 1947, Decimal File 1945–1949, 101.61/2-2847, RG 59, NA.

15. Blum to Ohly, 30 October 1947, CD 2-1-5, Office of the Administrative Secretary,

Correspondence Control Section, Numerical File: Sep 1947–Jun 1950, Record Group 330, Records of the Secretary of Defense, NA. This file would have been the mother lode of documentation for the early years of the CIA had it not been so heavily expurgated in the course of declassification review.

16. Ohly to Blum, 8 December 1947, Records of the National Security Council: CIA File, Papers of Harry S. Truman, HSTL.

17. Beckler to Clark, 2 December 1947, ibid.

18. Clark to Bush, 3 December 1947, ibid.

19. Ohly to Blum, 28 March 1948, CD 2-1-45, Office of the Administrative Secretary, Correspondence Control Section, Numerical File: Sep 1947–Jun 1950, RG 330, NA.

20. Memorandum by Stephen Penrose, 2 January 1948, attachment to memo from W. J. McNeil to Mathias Correa, 2 February 1948, FRUS, pp. 829–834.

21. Ohly to Johnson, 23 February 1949, Department of Defense File—Subject File, 1947–1949: Central Intelligence Agency, Papers of John H. Ohly, HSTL.

22. NYT, 20, 22–25 July 1948.

23. Baldwin, *The Price of Power,* p. 208.

24. Frank Gervasi, "What's Wrong with Our Spy System?" *Collier's,* 6 November 1948, pp. 13ff.

25. These letters, some barely literate, can be found in the President's Secretary's File and the Records of the National Security Council, Papers of Harry S. Truman, HSTL.

26. Souers to Eberstadt, 31 May 1948, Records of the National Security Council: Chronological File, 1947–1950, Papers of Harry S. Truman, HSTL.

27. Hillenkoetter undated statement, apparently made in September 1948, FRUS, pp. 871–875.

28. Committee on National Security Organization, *National Security Organization: A Report with Recommendations Prepared for the Commission on Organization of the Executive Branch of Government* (Washington, D.C.: USGPO, 1949), pp. 4, 76–77.

29. "Report to the Commission on the National Security Organization," vol. 2, chap. 2, "The Central Intelligence Agency," pp. 25–60, passim, Records of the Commission on Organization of the Executive Branch of Government, Herbert Hoover Library. Copy provided to the author upon request. The official CIA account of the Eberstadt commission's work is Darling, *The Central Intelligence Agency,* pp. 282–298.

30. For an overview, see Darling, *The Central Intelligence Agency,* pp. 298–380.

31. Ohly to Forrestal, 1 January 1948; CD 4-1-14, Office of the Administrative Secretary, Correspondence Control Section, Numerical File: Sep 1947–Jun 1950, RG 330, NA.

32. Souers to Ludwell Montague, 30 October 1969, Papers of Sidney W. Souers: General Correspondence, HSTL.

33. Quoted in Rearden, *The Formative Years: 1947–1950,* p. 144.

34. National Security Council Resolution, 13 January 1948, FRUS, p. 827.

35. Grose, *Gentleman Spy,* pp. 283–284.

36. Confirmation letters by James Lay Jr. to Dulles and Correa, 27 January 1948, and

by Souers to Jackson, 3 February 1948; Records of the National Security Council: Chronological File, 1947–1950; Papers of Harry S. Truman, HSTL.

37. Souers to Dulles, Jackson, and Correa, 13 February 1948, FRUS, p. 841.

38. Souers to Montague, 30 October 1969, Papers of Sidney W. Souers: General Correspondence, HSTL.

39. Souers to Dulles, Jackson, and Correa, 13 February 1948, Records of the National Security Council: Chronological File, 1947–1950, Papers of Harry S. Truman, HSTL.

40. Souers to Dulles, Jackson, and Correa, 17 March 1948; ibid.

41. Grose, *Gentleman Spy*, pp. 290–291; Darling, *The Central Intelligence Agency*, p. 346.

42. Despite the assertion of Peter Grose and the indications given by Stephen Rearden, the report, at the time of this writing, is not yet in the public domain. The copy cited by Rearden in RG 330 at the National Archives has been removed from the appropriate file in the course of national security review on the grounds of national security sensitivity; the copy referenced to RG 59 on page 903 of FRUS is in records that had not yet been released to the National Archives for public use by the State Department (telephone conversation with archivist Milton Gustafson, 6 January 1998). As far as the Harry S. Truman Library is concerned, the archivists at that institution were unaware that there was a copy in their holdings until I discovered a reference to it in the papers of John Ohly during my visit there in September 1996. In response to a request to examine it, the staff determined that it remained unavailable while in the process of a protracted declassification review. The custodians of the Allen Dulles Papers at the Seeley Mudd Library at Princeton University have stated that no copy has been located in those records (personal communication from curator Carl Esche to author, 20 September 1996).

43. Text of the executive summary of the report is in FRUS, pp. 903–911.

44. For example, memorandum by the Office of Reports and Estimates, 14 February 1949, FRUS, pp. 922–924; memorandum by Frank Wisner to Hillenkoetter, 14 February 1949, ibid., pp. 924–927.

45. Grose, *Gentleman Spy*, p. 290.

46. NSC 50, "Report by Secretary of State Acheson and Secretary of Defense Johnson to the National Security Council," 1 July 1949, FRUS, pp. 974–984. See also Rearden, *The Formative Years: 1947–1950*, pp. 143–145; and Darling, *The Central Intelligence Agency*, pp. 346–380 passim.

47. Hillenkoetter's circular memo of 12 July 1949 is reproduced in Warner, *The CIA Under Harry Truman*, pp. 315–318.

48. Hillenkoetter to Souers, 27 December 1949, FRUS, pp. 1045–1049.

49. Elsey to Clifford, 17 March 1947, Subject File: Central Intelligence, Papers of George M. Elsey, HSTL.

50. Memorandum from the NIA to Hillenkoetter, 14 May 1947, Decimal File 1945–1949, 101.5/5-1947, RG 59, NA.

51. Minutes of the Tenth Meeting of the NIA, 26 June 1947, Folder 132: NIA Papers, Chairman's File: Admiral Leahy, 1942–1948, RG 218, NA.

52. Hillenkoetter to Webb, 15 December 1948, Records of the National Security Council: CIA File, Papers of Harry S. Truman, HSTL; Hillenkoetter to House Speaker Sam Rayburn and Senate Armed Services Committee Chairman Millard Tydings, 11 February 1949, in U.S. House of Representatives, *Providing for the Administration of the Central Intelligence Agency: Report*, 81st Cong., 1st sess., Report 160, 24 February 1949 (Washington, D.C.: USGPO, 1949), p. 2. Hereafter cited as 1949 House CIA Report.

53. 1949 House CIA Report, pp. 2–6 passim.

54. NYT, 5 March 1949.

55. NYT, 7 March 1949.

56. NYT, 8 March 1949.

57. U.S. Senate, Report No. 106, *Providing for the Administration of the Central Intelligence Agency . . . : Report*, 81st Cong., 1st sess., 10 March 1949 (Washington, D.C.: USGPO, 1949), pp. 1–5 passim.

58. NYT, 28 May 1949.

59. U.S. House of Representatives, *Administration of the Central Intelligence Agency: Conference Report*, 81st Cong., 1st sess., Report No. 725, 6 June 1949 (Washington, D.C.: USGPO, 1949), p. 1.

60. Hillenkoetter to White House, 9 June 1949; Ernest Gross to Frank Pace, 10 June 1949; Roger Jones to William Hopkins, 16 June 1949, in White House Bill File, Papers of Harry S. Truman, HSTL; NYT, 21 June 1949.

61. *Statutes at Large*, 63 Stat 208.

62. Central Intelligence Agency, *A Consumer's Guide to Intelligence*, p. 38. A great deal has been written about the nature and purpose of covert action. An early, and generally poor, study is Paul Blackstock, *The Strategy of Subversion: Manipulating the Politics of Other Nations* (Chicago: Quadrangle Books, 1964). An informative but now outdated discussion is Roy Godson, ed., *Intelligence Requirements for the 1980s: Covert Action* (Washington, D.C.: National Strategy Information Center, 1981). A valuable, evenhanded assessment is Gregory Treverton, *Covert Action: The Limits of Intervention in the Postwar World* (New York: Basic Books, 1987). Considering covert action from a legal point of view is W. Michael Reisman and James E. Baker, *Regulating Covert Action: Practices, Contexts, and Policies of Covert Coercion Abroad in International and American Law* (New Haven, Conn.: Yale University Press, 1992).

63. Senate History, p. 26.

64. Clifford, *Counsel to the President*, pp. 169–170.

65. Stephen F. Knott, *Secret and Sanctioned: Covert Operations and the American Presidency* (New York: Oxford University Press, 1996).

66. Smith, *The Shadow Warriors*, p. 417.

67. Ibid., p. 418.

68. ORE 47/1, "The Current Situation in Italy," reproduced in Warner, *The CIA Under Harry Truman*, pp. 181–189.

69. Smith, *The Shadow Warriors*, p. 410.

70. There is no adequate history of the origins and development of covert action as

an instrument of policy. Two excellent pathbreaking studies on this topic, however, are Sallie Pisani, *The CIA and the Marshall Plan* (Lawrence: University Press of Kansas, 1991); and Evan Thomas, *The Very Best Men: Four Who Dared—The Early Years of the CIA* (New York: Simon and Schuster, 1995). The official account is in Darling, *The Central Intelligence Agency*, pp. 245–281.

71. Department of Defense, *Dictionary of Military and Associated Terms*, p. 264.

72. SWNCC 304/1, "Psychological Warfare," 12 December 1946, Folder 132: NIA Papers, Chairman's File: Admiral Leahy, 1942–1948, RG 218, NA.

73. Souers to Forrestal, 24 October 1947, FRUS, pp. 627–628.

74. Souers to the NSC, 9 December 1947, ibid., pp. 639–642; emphasis in the original.

75. NSC Memorandum to the DCI and attached directive, 17 December 1947, ibid., pp. 649–651.

76. Hillenkoetter to Galloway, 22 December 1947, ibid., pp. 651–652.

77. OSO Directive No. 18/5 (Interim), 24 February 1948, ibid., p. 653.

78. Hillenkoetter to Galloway, 22 March 1948, reproduced in Warner, *The CIA Under Harry Truman*, pp. 191–192.

79. OSO Directive No. 18/5, 29 March 1948, FRUS, pp. 655–661.

80. It is interesting to note that Kennan, in two volumes of memoirs, chooses to completely ignore this aspect of his career.

81. Policy Planning Staff Memorandum, 4 May 1948, FRUS, pp. 668–672.

82. NSC 10/2, 18 June 1948, ibid., pp. 713–715.

83. Houston to Hillenkoetter, 25 September 1947, ibid., pp. 622–623.

84. Kennan to Lovett, 30 June 1948, FRUS, p. 716; Memorandum of Conversation and Understanding, 6 August 1948, ibid., pp. 719–722; Memorandum for the President of Discussion at the Eighteenth Meeting of the National Security Council (extract), 19 August 1948, ibid., p. 723; Central Intelligence Agency General Order No. 10, 27 August 1948, ibid., p. 724; Lovett to Forrestal, 1 October 1948, ibid., pp. 724–725; Forrestal to Lovett, 13 October 1948, ibid., p. 728.

85. Houston to Hillenkoetter, 19 October 1948, reproduced in Warner, *The CIA Under Harry Truman*, pp. 235–239; emphasis in the original.

86. Rearden, *The Formative Years: 1947–1950*, pp. 169–175, passim; Hoopes and Brinkley, *Driven Patriot*, pp. 315–316; Pisani, *The CIA and the Marshall Plan*, pp. 108–120.

87. Colby, *Honorable Men*, p. 73.

88. The mind-set of the "secret warrior" is well described in Pisani, *The CIA and the Marshall Plan*, pp. 3–4, 9–23, passim, and 53–57. Pisani interviewed several of these individuals. When one of them used the term "determined interventionists," she applied it to the others, who accepted the designation with relish. Also illuminating for the mind-set of these individuals is Thomas, *The Very Best Men*, passim. A third useful volume is Burton Hersh, *The Old Boys: The American Elite and the Origins of the CIA* (New York: Scribner's, 1992).

89. Pisani, *The CIA and the Marshall Plan*, p. 68.

90. Between 1949 and 1952—abetted by the fall of China and the outbreak of the

Korean War—OPC grew from 302 to 2,812 persons (plus 3,142 overseas contract employees), its budget from $4.7 million to $82 million, and its presence in overseas stations from 7 to 47 (Senate History, p. 43). NSC 10/5 of 23 October 1951 mandated the "immediate expansion" of the covert organization established in NSC 10/2 in order to "[p]lace the maximum strain on the Soviet structure of power . . . ; and . . . contribute to the retraction and reduction of Soviet power and influence to limits which no longer constitute a threat to U.S. security," as well as to "strengthen the orientation toward the United States of the peoples and the nations of the free world, and to increase their capacity and will to resist Soviet domination" and to develop underground resistance and facilitate covert guerrilla operations in strategic areas." The document also reaffirmed the DCI's responsibility and authority for the covert operations and requested that the secretary of defense "provide adequate means whereby the Director of Central Intelligence may be assured of the continuing advice and collaboration of the Joint Chiefs of Staff in the formulation of plans for paramilitary operations during the period of the cold war" (NSC 10/5, 23 October 1951, reproduced with deletions in Warner, The CIA Under Harry Truman, pp. 437–439). As it happened, at a staff meeting on the previous day, DCI Walter Bedell Smith remarked with more prescience than he realized that "operations have assumed such a very large size in comparison to our intelligence function that we have almost arrived at a stage where it is necessary to decide whether CIA will remain an intelligence agency or become a 'cold war department' " (Extract from the Minutes of the DCI's Staff Conference of 22 October 1951, reproduced in Warner, The CIA Under Harry Truman, pp. 435–436).

91. Quoted in Meilinger, Hoyt S. Vandenberg, pp. 228–229 n. 22.

92. Quoted in Thomas, The Very Best Men, p. 42.

93. In addition to the quoted portions, this paragraph is based on the Senate History, p. 11; and Ludwell L. Montague, General Walter Bedell Smith as Director of Central Intelligence: October 1950–February 1953 (University Park: Pennsylvania State University Press, 1992), pp. 53–54.

94. Montague, General Walter Bedell Smith, p. 55.

95. This profile of Smith is based on ibid., pp. 5–6, 55–56; and Cline, Secrets, Spies, and Scholars, pp. 107–118, passim.

96. Lyman Kirkpatrick Jr., The Real CIA (New York: Macmillan, 1968), p. 121.

97. Montague, General Walter Bedell Smith, p. 56.

98. "Soldier for Sailor," Time, 28 August 1950, p. 14.

99. W. J. Hopkins to Truman, 2 October 1950, Official File: 1290-B, Central Intelligence Agency, Papers of Harry S. Truman, HSTL.

100. Hillenkoetter to Truman and Truman to Hillenkoetter, 6 October 1950, ibid.

101. Cline, Secrets, Spies, and Scholars, pp. 108–109.

102. Houston to Smith, 29 August 1950, reproduced in Warner, The CIA Under Harry Truman, pp. 341–346.

103. Quoted in Montague, General Walter Bedell Smith, p. 56.

104. Grose, Gentleman Spy, pp. 306, 309.

105. Ibid., p. 309.

106. Montague, *General Walter Bedell Smith*, pp. 88–89, 92–95, 111–183 passim; Langer, *In and Out of the Ivory Tower*, p. 185.

107. Langer, *In and Out of the Ivory Tower*, pp. 218–221.

108. Unless otherwise cited, this account is based on the Senate History, pp. 36–38. A more detailed account originally appeared in Montague, *General Walter Bedell Smith*, pp. 217–227, but heavy-handed redacting prior to public release has seriously disrupted the coherence of the narrative.

109. Wisner to Smith, 12 October 1950, reproduced in Warner, *The CIA Under Harry Truman*, p. 347.

110. Smith to Senior Staff, 15 July 1952, reproduced in ibid., pp. 465–467.

111. Quoted in Thomas, *The Very Best Men*, p. 48.

112. Montague, *General Walter Bedell Smith*, p. 92; Grose, *Gentleman Spy*, p. 327.

113. A concise description of the creation of this important program is in Montague, *General Walter Bedell Smith*, pp. 96–100.

114. "Report by the Director of Central Intelligence," 23 April 1952, reproduced in Warner, *The CIA Under Harry Truman*, p. 458.

10. *Ends and Beginnings*

1. Senate History, p. 12. The Directorate of Plans was renamed the Directorate of Operations in 1973. A fourth directorate (Research) was established in 1962 and reorganized the following year as the Directorate of Science and Technology.

2. Reston, *Deadline*, p. 194. For accounts of Eisenhower's foreign intelligence policy, see Stephen Ambrose, *Ike's Spies: Eisenhower and the Espionage Establishment* (Garden City, N.Y.: Doubleday, 1981), pp. 181–322; Cline, *Secrets, Spies, and Scholars*, pp. 119–183; and Grose, *Gentleman Spy*, pp. 330–506. Noted one scholar of U.S. cold war diplomacy: "In Eisenhower's use of covert operations to wage the cold war, ideology and pragmatism met. Ideology demanded that the United States carry on the struggle against communism; pragmatism required that the struggle be conducted by means other than direct confrontation with the Soviet Union. Covert operations seemed ideally suited for the task. Never has the Central Intelligence Agency been more influential than during Eisenhower's administration. . . . In part, the free rein Eisenhower gave the CIA reflected the administration's ideological assurance. So morally self-confident were Eisenhower and his advisors that they willingly countenanced, with little apparent soul-searching, activities that under circumstances other than those of the cold war they would have found repellant" (W. J. Brands Jr., *Cold Warriors: Eisenhower's Generation and American Foreign Policy* [New York: Columbia University Press, 1988], p. 48).

3. The two best overall histories of the CIA remain John Ranelagh's *The Agency* and Rhodri Jeffreys-Jones, *The CIA and American Democracy*. Interestingly, both authors are British nationals.

4. For a concise "official" statement of how well (or badly) the CIA performed its cold war "mission," see Robert Gates, "CIA and the Cold War" (address to the International Programs Center, University of Oklahoma, 12 September 1997; copy in possession of the author).

5. Clifford, *Counsel to the President*, p. 170.

6. Quoted in Senate History, p. 31.

7. Souers to Truman, 27 December 1963, Papers of Sidney Souers: Correspondence With the President, HSTL.

8. WP, 22 December 1963. Truman's broadside caused Dulles to complain to Souers: "I fear he may have forgotten his own very important part in providing certain new and classified functions for the CIA in 1948 after experiences with Czechoslovakia, the threat of Communist takeover in Italy, the Berlin blockade, etc." (Dulles to Souers, 10 February 1964, Papers of Sidney W. Souers: General Correspondence, HSTL). Dulles himself may have had a change of heart, however. Shortly before his death in 1969, he was approached by an enthusiastic new CIA operations officer who sought some inspiration at the beginning of his career. After reflecting for a bit, the old spymaster observed that "perhaps we have already intervened too much in the affairs of other people" (Grose, *Gentleman Spy*, p. 562).

9. Reston, *Deadline*, p. 210. In fairness, however, it must be recognized that the CIA was never a "rogue elephant," as it has sometimes been called, but one driven by "rogue mahouts" — the presidents of the United States, who, during the course of the cold war considered the CIA their chosen instrument for waging "secret war" against the "evil empire."

10. Commission on the Organization of the Executive Branch of Government, *Intelligence Activities: A Report to the Congress* (Washington, D.C.: USGPO, 1955), pp. 14–15, 59–60.

11. On the issue of congressional oversight, see Frank Smist Jr., *Congress Oversees the Intelligence Community, 1947–1993* (Knoxville: University of Tennessee Press, 1994). A balanced study of the CIA as part of a democratic polity is Loch K. Johnson, *America's Secret Power: The CIA in a Democratic Society* (New York: Oxford University Press, 1989). Other important books are Pat Holt, *Secret Intelligence and Public Policy: A Dilemma of Democracy* (Washington, D.C.: Congressional Quarterly Books, 1994); and Kathryn Olmsted, *Challenging the Secret Government: The Post-Watergate Investigations of the CIA and FBI* (Chapel Hill: University of North Carolina Press, 1996).

12. The unanticipated collapse of the Soviet empire is rapidly becoming encrusted with myth. Reliable accounts of this historic event include Adam B. Ulam, *The Communists: The Story of Power and Lost Illusions, 1948–1991* (New York: Scribner's, 1992); Hedrick Smith, *The New Russians* (New York: Random House, 1993); and David Remnick, *Lenin's Tomb: The Last Days of the Soviet Empire* (New York: Random House, 1993). The best account of the man who — quite inadvertently — set the process in motion is Archie Brown, *The Gorbachev Factor* (New York: Oxford University Press, 1996).

Until the diplomatic archives are opened, the best studies of relations between the

United States and the dying Soviet Union are Raymond Gartoff, *The Great Transition: American-Soviet Relations at the End of the Cold War* (Washington, D.C.: Brookings Institution, 1994); Don Oberdorfer, *The Turn: From the Cold War to a New Era — The United States and the Soviet Union, 1983–1990* (New York: Poseidon Press, 1991); Michael Beshloss and Strobe Talbott, *At the Highest Levels: The Inside Story of the End of the Cold War* (Boston: Little, Brown, 1993); and Jack F. Matlock Jr., *Autopsy of an Empire: The American Ambassador's Account of the Collapse of the Soviet Union* (New York: Random House, 1996). An important, albeit meretricious, "insider" account of these years is Robert Gates, *From the Shadows: The Ultimate Insider's Story of Five Presidents and How They Won the Cold War* (New York: Simon and Schuster, 1996).

13. James Adams, *The New Spies: Exploring the Frontiers of Espionage* (London: Hutchinson, 1994), p. 316.

14. For statements of official CIA views of the post–cold war world order, see John Deutch, "The Future of U.S. Intelligence: Charting a Course for Change" (address to the National Press Club, Washington, D.C., 12 September 1995); George Tenet, "Statement . . . Before the Senate Select Committee on Intelligence Hearing on Current and Projected National Security Threats," 28 January 1998; and John Gannon, "Intelligence Challenges for the Next Generation: Remarks to the World Affairs Council," Washington, D.C., 4 June 1998 (copies in possession of the author).

15. The CIA's painful entrance into the post–cold war world is described in Mark Perry, *Eclipse: The Last Days of the CIA* (New York: William Morrow, 1992).

16. The official U.S. government statement on the nature and shape of the post–cold war intelligence system is the *Report of the Commission on the Roles and Capabilities of the U.S. Intelligence Community* (Washington, D.C.: USGPO, 1996). The primary congressional statement on the topic is U.S. House of Representatives, Permanent Select Committee on Intelligence, *IC 21: The Intelligence Community in the 21st Century* (Washington, D.C.: USGPO, 1996). Other important quasi-official proposals for intelligence "reform" are *Making Intelligence Smarter: The Future of U.S. Intelligence,* prepared by a task force of the Council on Foreign Relations (New York: CFR, 1996); *In from the Cold: The Report of the Twentieth Century Fund Task Force on the Future of U.S. Intelligence* (New York: TCF, 1996); and John H. Hedley, *Checklist for the Future of Intelligence,* Occasional Paper 1 of the Institute for the Study of Diplomacy, Edmund J. Walsh School of Foreign Service, Georgetown University, Washington, D.C., 1995.

Bibliography

Archival Sources

National Archives
    Record Group 51, Records of the Bureau of the Budget/Office of Management and
        Budget
    Record Group 59, General Records of the Department of State
    Record Group 80, General Records of the Department of the Navy
    Record Group 107, Records of the Office of the Secretary of War
    Record Group 165, Records of the War Department General and Special Staffs
    Record Group 218, Records of the U.S. Joint Chiefs of Staff
    Record Group 263, Records of the Central Intelligence Agency
    Record Group 319, Records of the Army Staff
    Record Group 330, Records of the Secretary of Defense
Franklin D. Roosevelt Library
    Papers of Franklin D. Roosevelt: President's Secretary's File
    Papers of Harold Smith: Diaries—Conferences with the President
Harry S. Truman Library
    Papers of Clark Clifford: Subject File
    Papers of George M. Elsey: Subject File
    Papers of John H. Ohly: Department of Defense File
    Papers of Samuel I. Rosenman
        Alphabetical File (C–T)
        Subject File, 1946
    Papers of Sidney W. Souers
        General Correspondence, 1953–1972
        Correspondence with the President
    Papers of Harry S. Truman
        Official File
        President's Secretary's File: Intelligence
        President's Secretary's File: Daily Sheets
        Rose Conway File

Records of the National Security Council
  White House Bill File, 1949
Herbert C. Hoover Library
  Records of the Commission on Organization of the Executive Branch of Government
Alderman Library, University of Virginia
  Papers of Edward R. Stettinius, Jr.
George C. Marshall Research Foundation
  Papers of George C. Marshall
U.S. Army Military History Institute, Carlisle Barracks
  Papers of William J. Donovan
Air Force Historical Research Agency, Maxwell Air Force Base
  "Objectives and Operations of the CIG: Lecture at the Air War College, Maxwell Field,
    Alabama, 11 December 1946," by Hoyt Vandenberg. Copy obtained under the
    Freedom of Information Act.

Published Primary Sources

Complete Press Conferences of Franklin D. Roosevelt: Vol. 25, 1944–1945. New York: Da Capo Press,
  1972.
Department of State. *Foreign Relations of the United States, 1945–1950: Emergence of the Intelligence
  Establishment.* Washington, D.C.: USGPO, 1996.
Nicholas, H. G., ed. *Washington Despatches, 1941–1945: Weekly Political Reports from the British Em-
  bassy.* London: Weidenfeld and Nicholson, 1981.
Office of the Federal Register, National Archives and Records Administration. *Public Papers of
  the Presidents of the United States: Harry S. Truman . . . 1945–1947.* Washington, D.C.: USGPO,
  1961–1963.
Warner, Michael, ed. *The CIA Under Harry Truman.* Washington, D.C.: CIA History Staff, 1994.

Official Publications

Arnold, General Henry. *Third Report of the Commanding General of the Army Air Forces to the Secretary
  of War.* N.p., 1945.
Central Intelligence Agency. *A Consumer's Guide to Intelligence.* Washington, D.C.: CIA Office
  of Public and Agency Information, 1995.
Commission on the Organization of the Executive Branch of Government. *Intelligence Activities: A Report to the Congress.* Washington, D.C.: USGPO, 1955.
Committee on National Security Organization. *National Security Organization: A Report with Recommendations Prepared for the Commission on Organization of the Executive Branch of Government.*
  Washington, D.C.: USGPO, 1949.

Department of Defense. *Dictionary of Military and Associated Terms*. Washington, D.C.: Joint Chiefs of Staff, 1974.

Department of State Bulletin. 1945–1947.

Executive Order 9621. *3 Code of Federal Regulations* 431 (1943–1948 Compilation).

Statutes at Large. 61 Stat 497, National Security Act of 1947.

Statutes at Large. 63 Stat 208, CIA Act of 1949.

U.S. House of Representatives, Committee on Military Affairs. *A Report on the System Currently Employed in the Collection, Evaluation, and Dissemination of Intelligence Affecting the War Potential of the United States*, 79th Cong., 2d sess. Washington, D.C.: USGPO, 1946.

U.S. Senate, Committee on Naval Affairs, *Unification of the War and Navy Departments and Postwar Organization for National Security*, 79th Cong., 1st sess. Washington, D.C.: USGPO, 1945.

U.S. Senate, Select Committee to Study Government Operations with Respect to Intelligence Activities. *Final Report: Supplementary Detailed Staff Reports on Foreign and Military Intelligence*, 94th Cong., 2d sess. Book IV. Washington, D.C.: USGPO, 1976.

Congressional Documentation

Congressional Record 93, no. 49 (14 March 1947).

U.S. Congress, Joint Committee on the Investigation of the Pearl Harbor Attack. *Investigation of the Pearl Harbor Attack: Report*, 79th Cong., 2d sess. Washington, D.C.: USGPO, 1946.

U.S. House of Representatives, Select Committee on Post-war Military Policy. *Proposal to Establish a Single Department of Armed Forces: Hearings . . .* , 78th Cong., 2d sess. Washington, D.C.: USGPO, 1944.

U.S. House of Representatives, Committee on Expenditures in the Executive Departments. *National Security Act of 1947: Hearings . . .* , 80th Cong., 1st sess. Washington, D.C.: USGPO, 1947.

U.S. House of Representatives, Committee on Expenditures in the Executive Departments. *National Security Act of 1947*, 80th Cong., 1st sess. House Report 961 to Accompany HR 4214. Washington, D.C.: USGPO, 1947.

U.S. House of Representatives, Committee of Conference. *National Security Act of 1947*, 80th Cong., 1st sess. Conference Report 1051 to Accompany S. 758. Washington, D.C.: USGPO, 1947.

U.S. House of Representatives, Report 160. *Providing for the Administration of the Central Intelligence Agency: Report*, 81st Cong., 1st sess. 24 February 1949. Washington, D.C.: USGPO, 1949.

U.S. House of Representatives, Report 725. *Administration of the Central Intelligence Agency: Conference Report*, 81st Cong., 1st sess. 6 June 1949. Washington, D.C.: USGPO, 1949.

U.S. Senate, Committee on Appropriations. *First Supplemental Appropriation Rescission Bill: Hearings . . .* , 79th Cong., 1st sess. Washington, D.C.: USGPO, 1945.

U.S. Senate, Committee on Armed Services. *National Defense Establishment: Hearings* . . . , 80th
Cong., 1st sess. Washington, D.C.: USGPO, 1947.

U.S. Senate, Committee on Armed Services. *National Security Act of 1947*, 80th Cong., 1st sess.
Senate Report 239 to Accompany S. 758. Washington, D.C.: USGPO, 1947.

U.S. Senate, Committee on the Judiciary. *Interlocking Subversion in Government Departments: Hearings* . . . , 83rd Cong., 1st sess. Pts. 13, 19. Washington, D.C.: USGPO, 1953–1954.

U.S. Senate, Committee on Military Affairs. *Department of the Armed Forces, Department of Military
Security: Hearings* . . . , 79th Cong., 1st sess. Washington, D.C.: USGPO, 1945.

U.S. Senate, Committee on Military Affairs. *Department of Common Defense*, 79th Cong., 2d sess.
Senate Report 1328. Washington, D.C.: USGPO, 1946.

U.S. Senate, Committee on Naval Affairs. *Unification of the Armed Forces: Hearings* . . . , 79th Cong.,
2d sess. Washington, D.C.: USGPO, 1946.

U.S. Senate, *Providing for the Administration of the Central Intelligence Agency* . . . : *Report*, 81st Cong.,
1st sess. Report No. 106. Washington, D.C.: USGPO, 1949.

First-Person Accounts

Acheson, Dean. *Present at the Creation: My Years in the State Department*. New York: W. W. Norton,
1969.

Biddle, Francis. *In Brief Authority*. Garden City, N.Y.: Doubleday, 1962.

Braden, Spruille. *Diplomats and Demagogues: The Memoirs of Spruille Braden*. New Rochelle, N.Y.:
Arlington House, 1971.

Clifford, Clark, with Richard Holbrooke. *Counsel to the President: A Memoir*. New York: Random
House, 1991.

Cline, Ray S. *Secrets, Spies, and Scholars: Blueprint of the Essential CIA*. Washington, D.C.: Acropolis
Books, 1976.

Colby, William, with Peter Forbath. *Honorable Men: My Life in the CIA*. New York: Simon and
Schuster, 1978.

Ferrell, Robert H., ed. *Truman in the White House: The Diaries of Eben A. Ayers*. Columbia: University of Missouri Press, 1991.

Hoover, Calvin. *Memoirs of Capitalism, Communism, and Nazism*. Durham, N.C.: Duke University
Press, 1965.

Kent, Sherman. *Reminiscences of a Varied Life*. N.p.: privately printed, 1991.

Kirkpatrick, Lyman, Jr. *The Real CIA*. New York: Macmillan, 1968.

Langer, William L. *In and Out of the Ivory Tower: The Autobiography of William L. Langer*. New York:
Neale Watson Academic Publications, 1977.

Millis, Walter, ed. *The Forrestal Diaries*. New York: Viking Press, 1951.

Reston, James. *Deadline: A Memoir*. New York: Random House, 1991.

Trohan, Walter. *Political Animals*. Garden City, N.Y.: Doubleday, 1975.

Truman, Harry S. *Memoirs: Year of Decisions*. Garden City, N.Y.: Doubleday, 1955.

————. *Memoirs: Years of Trial and Hope.* Garden City, N.Y.: Doubleday, 1956.

Zacharias, Ellis M. *Secret Missions: The Story of an Intelligence Officer.* New York: G. P. Putnam's Sons, 1946.

Secondary Sources

Adams, James. *The New Spies: Exploring the Frontiers of Espionage.* London: Hutchinson, 1994.

Baldwin, Hanson. *The Price of Power.* New York: Harper and Brothers, 1947.

Bureau of the Budget. *The United States at War: Development and Administration of the War Program of the Federal Government.* Washington, D.C.: USGPO, 1946.

Caraley, Demetrios. *The Politics of Military Unification.* New York: Columbia University Press, 1966.

Darling, Arthur. *The Central Intelligence Agency: An Instrument of Government to 1950.* University Park: Pennsylvania State University Press, 1990.

Dunlop, Richard. *Donovan: America's Master Spy.* Chicago: Rand McNally, 1982.

Gentry, Curt. *J. Edgar Hoover: The Man and His Secrets.* New York: W. W. Norton, 1991.

Grose, Peter. *Gentleman Spy: The Life of Allen Dulles.* Boston: Houghton Mifflin, 1994.

Haynes, Richard F. *The Awesome Power: Harry S. Truman as Commander-in-Chief.* Baton Rouge: Louisiana State University Press, 1973.

Hoopes, Townsend, and Douglas Brinkley. *Driven Patriot: The Life and Times of James Forrestal.* New York: Alfred A. Knopf, 1992.

Jeffreys-Jones, Rhodri. *The CIA and American Democracy.* New Haven, Conn.: Yale University Press, 1989.

Lewin, Ronald. *Ultra Goes to War.* New York: McGraw-Hill, 1978.

Meilinger, Phillip. *Hoyt S. Vandenberg: The Life of a General.* Bloomington: Indiana University Press, 1989.

Montague, Ludwell Lee. *General Walter Bedell Smith as Director of Central Intelligence: October 1950–February 1953.* University Park: Pennsylvania State University Press, 1992.

Petee, George S. *The Future of American Secret Intelligence.* Washington, D.C.: Infantry Journal Press, 1946.

Pisani, Sallie. *The CIA and the Marshall Plan.* Lawrence: University Press of Kansas, 1991.

Ranelagh, John. *The Agency: The Rise and Decline of the CIA.* New York: Simon and Schuster, 1986.

Rearden, Steven L. *The Formative Years: 1947–1950.* Vol. 1 of the History of the Office of the Secretary of Defense. Washington, D.C.: Office of the Secretary of Defense, 1984.

Riebling, Mark. *Wedge: The Secret War Between the FBI and CIA.* New York: Alfred A. Knopf, 1994.

Robertson, David. *Sly and Able: A Political Biography of James F. Byrnes.* New York: W. W. Norton, 1994.

Salisbury, Harrison. *Without Fear or Favor: The New York Times and Its Times.* New York: Times Books, 1980.

Smith, Bradley F. *The Shadow Warriors: OSS and the Origins of the CIA.* New York: Basic Books, 1983.

Theoharis, Athan G., and John Stuart Cox. *The Boss: J. Edgar Hoover and the Great American Inquisition.* London: Harrap, 1988.

Thomas, Evan. *The Very Best Men: Four Who Dared — The Early Years of the CIA.* New York: Simon and Schuster, 1995.

Troy, Thomas F. *Donovan and the CIA: A History of the Establishment of the Central Intelligence Agency.* N.p.: CIA Center for the Study of Intelligence, 1981.

Ungar, Sanford. *FBI.* Boston: Little, Brown, 1975.

Articles

Braden, Tom. "The Birth of the CIA." *American Heritage,* February 1977, pp. 7ff.

Bruce, David K. E. "The National Intelligence Authority." *Virginia Quarterly Review* 22 (Summer 1946), pp. 355–369.

Byrnes, James F. "Why We Must Give the President a Clear Road." *American Magazine,* August 1945, p. 30ff.

Chamberlain, John. "OSS." *Life,* 19 November 1945, pp. 119–130.

Donovan, William J. "Intelligence: Key to Defense." *Life,* 30 September 1946, pp. 108–120.

Gervasi, Frank. "What's Wrong with Our Spy System?" *Collier's,* 6 November 1948, pp. 13ff.

"Global Gumshoeing." *Time,* 1 October 1945, p. 23.

"Intelligence." *Time,* 4 February 1946, pp. 24–25.

Kent, Sherman. "Prospects for the National Intelligence Service." *Yale Review* 36 (Autumn 1946), pp. 116–130.

"Personality Parade." *Parade,* 30 April 1978, p. 2.

Pratt, Fletcher. "How Not to Run a Spy System." *Harper's Magazine,* September 1947, pp. 241–246.

"Soldier for Sailor." *Time,* 28 August 1950, p. 14.

"The 36-Hour War." *Life,* 19 November 1945, pp. 27–35.

Newspapers

New York Herald Tribune
New York Times
Washington Evening Star
Washington Post
Washington Times-Herald

Index